LEAVENWORTH
BOULDERING

Central Washington Bouldering
by Kelly Sheridan

©2015 Sharp End Publishing, LLC

ISBN: 978-1-892540-95-9

Library of Congress Control Number: 2015938670

Cover photo credit
Cortney Cusack on *Fridge Center* (V4).

Unlabeled photo credits by the author

Read This Before Using This Guide

Rock climbing, including bouldering, is extremely dangerous. A small and incomplete list of possible dangers include: loose rock, bad landings (eg. landing on uneven or rocky terrain, landing on a spotter.) Unlike roped climbing, every bouldering fall is a ground fall. As a result, the boulderer risks serious injury or death with every attempt. Falls are common while bouldering.

The symbols used in this guide describe boulders with almost certain injury potential. It is, however, highly probable that you could seriously injure yourself on a problem that doesn't receive a highball or bad landing designation.

It is your responsibility to take care of yourself while bouldering. Seek a professional instructor or guide if you are unsure of your ability to handle any circumstances that may arise. This guide is not intended as an instructional manual.

THE AUTHOR AND PUBLISHER EXPRESSLY DISCLAIM ALL REPRESENTATIONS AND WARRANTIES REGARDING THIS GUIDE, THE ACCURACY OF THE INFORMATION CONTAINED HEREIN, AND THE RESULTS OF YOUR USE HEREOF, INCLUDING WITHOUT LIMITATION, IMPLIED WARRANTIES OR MERCHANTABILITY AND FITNESS FOR A PARTICULAR PURPOSE. THE USER ASSUMES ALL RISK ASSOCIATED WITH THE USE OF THIS GUIDE.

I began the 2007 *Central Washington Bouldering* with an anecdote about a trip I had recently taken to Hueco Tanks, Texas, during which I became concerned about the prospect that Leavenworth would one day become as popular – and as heavily regulated – as El Paso's improbable bouldering mecca. I wrote about the crowds, the bureaucracy, the litter and tick marks (and the hair gel) I had seen in Hueco, and weighed the risk that these same things would "happen" to Leavenworth and Gold Bar as a result of a new guidebook. As I re-read this piece now, I'm struck by both the naiveté and the earnestness of what I wrote; the simultaneous irony and prescience of my words:

> *It took me a few worried weeks to believe it, but the truth is, it won't happen. Both of these gorgeous areas are extremely spread-out, and can totally handle the small amount of people who'll even believe that boulders this good could possibly be found in central Washington. Sure, Squamish is just a few hours away, but that's the kicker: nobody's going to believe that these areas are even better. Furthermore, with Leavenworth's areas so scattered and diverse, a 'real' guide will help get people on the good stuff and freed from overused areas like Forestland and Swiftwater.*

Eight years after I wrote this, many of the things that "worried" me have materialized. Leavenworth has received national attention in print, video, and online media, and visitors have flocked to the area from far and wide, both as a pit stop on the way to Squamish and as a destination in its own right: people most certainly "believe" the area is as good as it is. And while *Central Washington Bouldering* has guided people to some of Leavenworth's more obscure areas, Forestland, Mad Meadows, and Swiftwater still receive the vast majority of attention, especially from first-time visitors and beginners, and it is not uncommon to see three or four dozen cars in the Forestland parking lot on a spring or fall weekend, a sight that would have been inconceivable when I first came to the area in 2005. Bouldering's popularity is growing at an ever-increasing rate, and as I wrote in long post on this issue on my blog, nwgranite.blotspot.com, in the spring of 2014: Climbing is not just for "climbers" anymore – it's also for strangers who just happen to rock climb (I used an uglier term). It is a brave new world.

But while many of my "worries" were borne out in fact, they no longer worry me as much. Leavenworth continues to absorb boulderers with grace, and many positive results have accompanied the growth in the practice's popularity. New areas and problems continue to be developed at a remarkable pace, the Forest Service has begun to give resources and attention to bouldering in a positive manner, and groups like the Washington Climbers Coalition and Leavenworth Mountain Association have devoted significant energy to fostering sustainable and rewarding bouldering in the area. And at the risk of sounding trite, it is truly a good thing that more people are getting outside, interacting with the natural environment, and enjoying themselves. I am proud to share these areas rather than shutting the gate behind me. These sentiments recall another passage from the introduction to *Central Washington Bouldering*, which is as true today as when I first wrote it:

> *In a way, Washington has come to embody this spirit of sharing for me. There have been so many moments when I've found myself just glowing about a problem, ripe with the desire to show it to others and share in their joy. And if it weren't for the altruistic friends who coaxed me to the area to begin with, showed me the fantastic boulders, and encouraged me as I thrutched my way up some of them, I would never have seen Washington for the bouldering paradise it is.*

So welcome to Leavenworth Bouldering, and the bounty of raw granite contained herein. I hope you appreciate the area's beauty and magic, on scales both grand and miniscule, and that you find adventure, challenge, and joy in your climbing here. But I also hope you respect the area and the efforts of those who have come before you, and leave the place better than you found it. Develop a deep respect for what you see, and pass it on to those who come after you. Happy Climbing!

Kelly H. Sheridan
March, 2015

I'D LIKE TO THANK:

My family, R. Kelly, Connie, Kara, and David. Nothing in my life would have been possible without your love and support. Though I live across the country from you, our relationship has never been stronger, and you hold a special place in my heart.

My friends, for accepting me, bringing me along, and putting up with my endless questions about this problem or that area ever since I invited myself into this community almost ten years ago. You know who you are. This book would not be what it is without your efforts or your willingness to share the fruits of your labor.

And most of all, Cortney, for showing me with a love that never wavers, committing to a life with me despite all my flaws, and putting up with three years of neglect as I spent every spare moment working to finish this book. You are my mate. I love you.

INTRODUCTION

ICICLE CANYON

TUMWATER CANYON

MOUNTAIN HOME ROAD

OTHER AREAS

APPENDICES

Leavenworth is located at the eastern edge of the Cascades, near the geographical center of Washington State, roughly two hours east of Seattle.

FROM THE WEST

There are two options for getting to Leavenworth from Seattle and other points west:

SOUTHERN ROUTE

From I-5, take Exit 164A for I-90 east. Follow I-90 over Snoqualmie Pass and take Exit 85 for WA-970 N near the town of Cle Elum. Stay on Route 970 for 10 miles until it become US-97 N. Follow Route 97 for roughly 35 miles up and over Blewett Pass until it intersects US-2. Turn west onto Highway 2 and follow it four miles to the eastern edge of Leavenworth. This route is best when coming from downtown Seattle, Sea-Tac, Olympia, and other places along Puget Sound.

NORTHERN ROUTE

From I-5, take either Exit 171 for Lake City Way / WA-522 or Exit 175 for NE 145th St. / WA-523. Follow either until they join Route 522 at the northern end of Lake City, following 522 east through Bothell and a few other suburbs until it crosses under I-405 and becomes a two-lane road. Reach the town of Monroe roughly 22 miles from Lake City. Follow the exit for Highway 2 east and follow it 85 miles over Stevens Pass to Leavenworth. On the way, you'll pass climbing/bouldering destinations in Gold Bar, Index, Skykomish, Stevens Pass, Smithbrook, and Nason Ridge. This route is best when coming from points north or east of Seattle.

BELLEVUE ETC.: When coming from the east side of Lake Washington, this route is best accessed via I-405 N. Take Exit 23 onto Route 522 and proceed as above.

BELLINGHAM/CANADA: When coming from Bellingham or the Canadian border, it's best to take Highway 2 directly from I-5 in the city of Everett. Take Exit 194 off I-5 (about 25 miles north of Seattle) and follow Highway 2 100 miles through Monroe and over the pass to Leavenworth.

FROM THE EAST

When approaching from the east, you also have two options:

SOUTHERN ROUTE

The easiest way to get to Leavenworth from the east is to take I-90 west to Exit 106 in Ellensburg for US-97 N. Follow Route 97 north for 51 miles over Blewett Pass to the intersection with Highway 2, turn left, and follow it four miles west to Leavenworth.

NORTHERN ROUTE

When coming from Spokane and other points directly east of Leavenworth, it's sometimes nice to take Exit 277 off I-90 and follow Highway 2 west all the way through Coulee City and Wenatchee to Leavenworth. While scenic, this route is two lanes for most of the way and generally isn't faster unless you're willing to push the speed limit – but watch out, as there are plenty of speedtraps along the way!

Johnny Goicoechea on a project at The Locksmith.

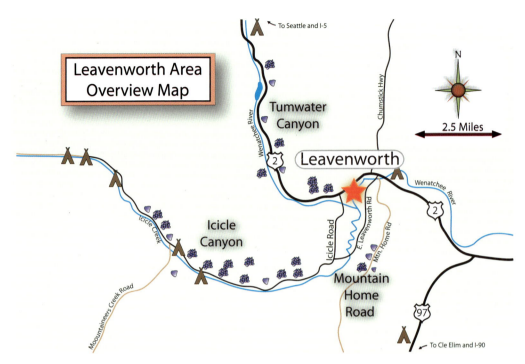

The small tourist village of Leavenworth is nestled at the edge of the granitic Wenatchee Mountains, on the eastern edge of Wenatchee National Forest. Bizarre festival weekends, a cornucopia of kitschy gift shops, and an abundance of overpriced hotels make this faux Bavarian village in the middle of the state Washington's second-biggest tourist destination. Visitors to Leavenworth who don't appear horribly out of shape are probably there to sample many of the outdoor recreational activities available in and around the town. Each weekend brings groups of helmet-heads to Leavenworth to climb moderate trad climbs in the Icicle and Tumwater Canyons, and in recent years, hordes of boulderers eager to sample the area's bounty. Leavenworth's bouldering had been locally well-known but underappreciated for many years before the publication of *Central Washington Bouldering*, with most people seeming to equate it to much of the area's roped climbing: off-vertical, sandy, and not especially exciting. Even John Sherman wrote in *Stone Crusade* that "Swiftwater Picnic Area is one of the few spots with enough problems to constitute a circuit, and even then one must hunt around in the woods for some of the boulders." The venerable Verm must have donned an awfully thick pair of beer-goggles for his visit, as Leavenworth's canyons are literally lined with a diverse array of pristine bouldering areas! In addition to Little Bavaria's well-traveled classics, the area is home to many newer problems that are steep, high, or hard – or all three. For a good sampling of the bouldering here in Leavenworth, make an attempt to check out all three major areas in this guide: Icicle Canyon, Tumwater Canyon, and Mountain-Home Road. Each individual area within these chapters sports a unique blend of stone, a pleasant setting, and at least one problem guaranteed to make your day. So go and explore for yourself – who knows what you might find?

LA SPORTIVA ATHLETE NALLE HUKKATAIVAL

A Wenatchi tribesman uses a weir to slow – and spear – salmon near the mouth of the Tumwater Canyon. Photo courtesy of the Upper Valley Museum at Leavenworth.

FIRST PEOPLES OF THE WENATCHEE VALLEY

Before the first arrival of white settlers, the Wenatchee Valley, and the confluence of the Wenatchee and Icicle Rivers in particular, were long inhabited and visited by several Native American tribes. Early humans in the Americas are generally thought to have reached the continent through the Beringian land bridge over the current-day Bering Strait between Alaska and Russia, created by extreme glaciation and a lower sea level. Though the earliest date of these migrations is not known with certainty, specimens dating as old as roughly 13,500 years have been found, and the land bridge is believed to have existed until approximately 12,000 years ago. Very little is known about these earliest peoples; the best evidence we have regarding Washington's specific populations and cultures comes from oral history as it existed at the time Europeans began settling the area in the early- to mid-1800s.

The Leavenworth area was visited and fished annually by the Wenatchi, Chinook, and Yakima tribes, with the former living a semi-nomadic life centered around the Wenatchee Valley. The word Wenatchi (likely a bastardization of the traditional pronunciation "Winatsa") means "water rushing out," and is thought to be a reference to the gushing waters at the foot of the Tumwater Canyon, the modern kayaker's class V Exit Drop. Interestingly, the word "Wenatchee" comes from the Sahaptin (a language group used by Yakima bands) term for the tribe; the Wenatchi went by the name "P'squosa" or "Pisquouse" in their own Interior Salish language. The tribe is referenced herein as the "Wenatchi" based on modern-day tribal members' preferred usage.

During the spring months, the Wenatchi would travel to "Cottonwood Place" near Ephrata, 30 miles east of the modern-day city of Wenatchee, to dig for camas, a.k.a. Indian Hyacinth, a root vegetable that is pit-roasted or boiled and tastes more or less like sweet potato, as well as other edible roots. The Wenatchi mixed camas root, dried berries, and sugar with deer or bear fat to make pemmican, a dense, highly nutritional, and, most important of all, highly portable food source for the hot summer months. At the beginning of the summer, the tribe would travel most of the way up the valley to Lake Wenatchee, and in the late summer would head back down the valley to spend the fall in the Leavenworth area, living in portable teepee-like homes. The tribe would winter in modern-day Cashmere or Wenatchee, hunkering down in slightly excavated pit houses supported by a wood frame. These pit houses have even been found in remote locations at higher elevations near Mount Stuart, suggesting that the tribe's ranks included mountain-going types as well as lowland dwellers. The Wenatchi were also known to travel as far south as Celilo Falls (a spectacular fishing mecca now tragically submerged by the backwaters of The Dalles dam on the southern Columbia) and as far west as the Puget Sound coast. Does the Wenatchi's annual migration sound anything like the Leavenworth local's calendar, revolving around winters spent climbing in the desert, summers in the mountains, and fall in the Icicle and Tumwater Canyons?

The flat, open groves around the confluence of the Wenatchee River and Icicle Creek were a well-known fall gathering place

A young Wenatchi man spearfishing in Nasikelt, called "Icicle Creek" today. Photo: Albert Simmer Collection courtesy of the Upper Valley Museum at Leavenworth.

for the Wenatchi, Chinook, Yakima, and even Spokane tribes, who would fish the rivers' annual salmon runs, hunt deer, elk, and even bear, and preserve a supply of protein for the long, snowy winters. The Wenatchi called the area "Wenatshapam" in their native Salish, a term that referred not to the land, but the various places, plants, and animals that comprised their experience of the area. Many members of the Wenatchi also spoke the Yakima's Shapatin, even though the languages are mutually unintelligible and the tribes did not regularly interact during most of the year. The Icicle Canyon, termed "Nasikelt," meaning "narrow bottom canyon," was a favorite fishing spot for First Peoples in the fall. Tribesman would fish the legendary salmon runs using 15-30 foot fishing poles with a barbed spike on the end, assisted by naturally-constructed weirs that would slow the salmon in their arduous upstream journey. Salmon was the central focus of the tribes' experience in Leavenworth, and Wenatchi legend taught that Coyote fashioned the Peshastin Pinnacles as a sacred memorial to the Salmon People, a mythological group of ancestors; Coyote told the people that they should thank the spirits for the annual salmon runs and should have a big feast every spring that would bring the salmon back that fall.

The fall gatherings in Leavenworth did not revolve solely around work, however, and the tribes enjoyed a friendly competitiveness in horse racing and "salmon races," which involved testing how far a young tribal member could run with a live and squirming salmon clutched in their arms! The fall gatherings in Leavenworth were also an important time for socialization among and between the tribes, with as many as 2,000 First Peoples congregating for the fall season.

Members of the Wenatchi tribe were present when Merriwether Lewis and William Clark passed through Celilo Falls in 1805, and reportedly traveled down the Wenatchee River several years later to meet northwest explorer David Thompson in modern-day Wenatchee, then dubbed "Wenatchee Flats" in 1811. The first recorded references to the Wenatchi were made by William Clark in October 1805, as "Wah na a cha" when an envoy from the tribe travelled down river to greet the strange visitors. Between the reports of these early explorers and the United States' unrepentant fever for expansion, the region was mapped and its bounties advertised. Fort Vancouver was built on the Columbia in 1825 as the southern headquarters of the Hudson's Bay Company, an outfit from British Columbia, permitting fur trappers and government employees to traverse the Columbia and explore the many Cascade valleys that feed it. Word spread. Two years after the Oregon Trail was opened in 1841, a 1,000-person wagon train left Independence, Missouri for the Willamette Valley but, encountering difficulties, fanned throughout the northwest region. Present-day Washington, Oregon, and Idaho were annexed into the United States as the Oregon Territory in 1848, and the floodgates opened.

The invasion of European settlers in the Wenatchee Valley during the mid-1800s was devastating to the Wenatchi tribe. As with many other bands throughout the west, smallpox and measles plagued the Wenatchi, and the tribe's numbers plunged from an estimated 1,400 in 1780 to an estimated 550 in 1853. Moreover, the United States' aggressive homesteading and prospecting policies imposed ownership on land that had never been owned, threatening the Wenatchi's very way of life. In the 1847 Whitman Massacre, tribal members angered by disease and displacement of traditional territory killed 14 European settlers. In 1853, Captain George B. McClellan visited the Wenatchi tribe, noting in his reports that the Wenashtapam area contained traces of gold. Thus the most tragic event of the Wenatchi's modern history: the signing of the Walla Walla Treaty of 1855 by Wenatchi Chief Owhi, for whom the Icicle Canyon had special family significance. The treaty, which was was pushed through by territorial Governor Isaac Stevens, deeded Wenatchi land to the Yakima Nation and purported to preserve a 36-square-mile area at the confluence of rivers in modern-day Leavenworth as the "Wenatshapam Fishery Reservation." The treaty was not intended to take effect until March of 1859, but prospectors and settlers immediately encroached on all lands not actually occupied by the tribe.

By the time 1859 rolled around, an internal report of the Bureau of Indian Affairs noted that "landed interests have already become uneasy" about the prospect of a reservation; by the railroad's construction in 1892, the idea had flatlined, and the reservation was "sold" by the Yakima tribe in 1893. In one of many disgraceful ex post 'revisions' of agreements with the continent's First Peoples, the United States government has never honored its treaty obligation to establish the Wenatshapam Reservation. The issue was "settled" in 1963, when the tribe was given a four million dollar settlement based on the 1859 value of the land: $0.50 an acre. Despite the adversity the tribe has faced due to the United States' reprehensible abdication of its treaty obligations, the Wenatchi remain vibrant today, federally-recognized as one of the Confederated Tribes of the Colville Reservation and having recently obtained recognition of their natural right to fish what's left of the Wenatchee/Icicle fishery in *United States v. Confederated Tribes of the Colville Indian Reservation* (9th Cir. 2010).

Professor Richard Scheurman tells the story of Gustav Sohon, an early northwest immigrant whose exceptional linguistic abilities permitted him to befriend and converse with many Native American leaders during his five-year enlistment in the United States army in 1857, and who was present at the signing of the Walla Walla Treaty:

Like many others who came to the Pacific Northwest from Germany or other distant lands, Gustavus Sohon was changed forever when he met the native peoples of the Columbia Plateau. In his last years of retirement in Washington, D.C., he was visited by a delegation of Northwest chiefs led by the Salish leader Charlot. Sohon's daughter later recalled that the only time she ever saw her father smoke was when the pipe was passed to commemorate the presence of esteemed old friends. Perhaps it reminded him of a moment in 1855 when he partook of the solemn rite in the presence of the Wenatchi Chief Tecolekum and his companions Owhi and Kamiakin in unfulfilled promise to safeguard a sacred place known in the time of the Animal People for its beauty and welcome.

BOOM AND BUST: TRAINS, TREES, AND TUNNELS

After the mouth of the Columbia River was discovered by Captain Robert Gray in 1792, the United States laid claim to modern-day Washington, Oregon, and Idaho, later formally adopted as the Oregon Territory. Gold fever struck northern Washington in 1858-59, and tiny outposts popped up all over the north central Cascades like rainblossoms after a drought. Leavenworth began as an offshoot of the Blewett mining town, established 1869, which earned the distinction, apparently noteworthy, of being "one of the most violent towns in Chelan County." In perhaps the state's greatest gold legend, Captain Ben Ingalls is reported to have discovered a massive lode of gold high in the mountains above the Wenatchee Valley. When Ingalls returned with a party of 50 to look for the gold in 1861, he was mysteriously killed when a branch whipped back and struck his friend John Hansell's gun, causing it to fire – into Ingalls' back. Ingalls survived for two nights and a day, and shared the secret location of his discovery, but the party found no gold. When gold was discovered in the Ingalls Creek drainage in 1873, a massive influx of prospectors, miners, and homesteaders flooded the area, but Ingalls' legendary trove was never discovered. The lode, if it existed, is thought to have been buried by the earthquake of 1872, which was so violent it caused the collapse of Ribbon Cliffs, just upstream of the town of Wenatchee, damming the Columbia River entirely for several hours and causing a 30-foot geyser to appear for several days at Chelan Falls.

Other stories of gold abounded. In the late 1800s, a German man appeared at the pioneer general store in Wenatchee with gold, reporting that his partner had been killed by a grizzly bear when returning from the mine, and that he was returning to Europe. The prospector brought others to the Entiat Mountains to show them the site of his find, but fell to his death along the way, taking the location of the claim with him.

The first white men to explore the Icicle were prospectors, and a small settlement called "Icicle Flats" gradually grew at the site of modern-day Leavenworth, with the first two homesteads appearing in 1885, four years after the first homestead in Cashmere in 1881. In 1891, the town's first store and post office opened in a ten-by-ten-foot shack on the south bank of the Wenatchee River. Other homesteads developed in the Chumstick Valley and Plain (then called Beaver Valley), eventually creeping up the valley to Lake Wenatchee. In addition to deer, elk, and black bears, early settlers encountered foxes, cougars, wolves, marten, fishers, and even grizzly bears. The early winters were significantly tougher than they are now, with formidable snowfalls and huge spring floods. Leavenworth was also plagued by violent forest fires in its early days, with destructive fires raging in and around town in 1894, 1896, and 1902, '04, and '14.

Downtown Leavenworth in 1890. Photo courtesy of the Upper Valley Museum at Leavenworth.

In 1892, the Great Northern Railroad bought a one-mile-long, 400-foot-wide strip of forest through the center of current-day Leavenworth to serve as a divisional hub for the ever-westward-stretching railroad, and the town of Icicle Flats moved to the north side of the Wenatchee. An enterprising man named Charles Leavenworth of the Oakanogan Investment Co. platted a town next to the railroad's facilities, which included offices, a depot at the present-day site of Gustav's, a "roundhouse" for turning locomotives, and seven sets of tracks over what is now Highway 2. With the railroad's construction came workers, their homesteading families, and merchants, and by the time the railroad was completed in 1893, Icicle Flats had a population of roughly 300. There was no bridge across the Wenatchee River, and residents headed to Wenatchee or Ellensburg from Leavenworth had to travel the northern side of the river to the closest ferry, four miles away in Peshastin. Such was the reality of life in Leavenworth before Washington became the forty-second State in 1889.

Lafayette Lamb, the son of a prominent Idaho lumber family, came to Leavenworth in the late 1800s and built a sawmill. Lamb invested a tremendous amount of capital in timber stands up the Wenatchee River valley and around Lake Wenatchee and built a dam on the Wenatchee River in Leavenworth to serve as a lumber pond. After loggers felled the massive old-growth fir and pine with two-man hand saws, so-called "river rats" ferried the logs downriver, using dynamite to loose large stacks of logs built the previous fall and to free stuck logs. Pilings from the mill's lumber pond dam are still visible in the Wenatchee just downstream of Blackbird Island, which is said to have formed by sediment backed up behind the dam. The Lamb-Davis sawmill became a huge operation, and employed 250 men by the time Icicle Flats was incorporated as Leavenworth in 1906 – a full quarter of the town's population of 1,000.

In addition to the railroad and mill workers, Leavenworth was a watering hole for miners from the Trinity copper mine on Red Mountain, and for ordinary prospectors. An Idaho prospector named John Sadoske claimed to have found a vein of quartz worth $20,000 a ton on Hog Back Mountain in Tumwater Canyon, just two miles from Leavenworth, and claims were filed over the entire mountain by the next spring. The Wenatchee Valley also came to be well known for its apple and pear growing, with orchards planted along the banks of the Wenatchee and the lower Icicle.

Leavenworth's first sheriff was a legendary horseman named Dude Brown. Stories of Brown's toughness and bravery abound. Brown had first gained notoriety in the Valley for riding an ornery bronco named "Kicking Duck," thought to be unridable, in 1913. Before becoming sheriff, Brown had made his living buying cattle in the Tonasket and the Okanagan and driving them south to Wenatchee; when the notorious cattle rustler Johnny McLean tried to take his herd, Brown traded fire with McLean and lived to tell the tail, a privilege few others enjoyed. Brown was the type of man needed for the job: Leavenworth in the early twentieth century was a classic rough-and-tumble frontier town where whorehouses and saloons were said to outnumber churches. As the inimitable JoAnn Roe wrote in *Stevens Pass: Gateway to Seattle*:

> *As a mill town and headquarters of the Cascade Division of the Great Northern Railroad (in 1905 renamed the Great Northern Railway), Leavenworth could not be called quiet. Every weekend it was the target of workers bent on assaulting their weekday loneliness by drinking, fighting, and womanizing. The buildings were crude, the streets virtual cattle tracks. Household water was carried in barrels from the river.*

In 1907, a drunken logger named W.L. Davis shot his friend and drinking buddy John McGee point-blank in a saloon in Leavenworth because McGee slapped him on the back one too many times. In the same decade, police in Leavenworth raided a gambling house for Japanese railroad workers that featured poker, blackjack, moonshine, and imported sake. In 1907, Methodist reverend Melvin Rumohr organized a petition to "either abolish from the town a certain class known as 'sporting women,' or restrict them to a section of the town out of the business portion and off the main street." The city council declined to approve the measure.

In 1908, Leavenworth was chosen as the site of the Wenatchee National Forest's first headquarters. As Roe writes, the forest's first supervisor, Hal Sylvester, "established a headquarters at Leavenworth and set out to patrol the forest with twenty underpaid, underequipped men." The Forest Service's primary focus in its early days was verifying homestead claims, which came to include fire detection and fighting, which in turn came to include trail building. During his time as supervisor, Sylvester named more than 1,000 of the mountains, lakes, and other geologic features in the central Cascades, supposedly more than any other white man. Some names were utilitarian, so that he could direct his rangers to fires and other work assignments; others were more fanciful. Lake Alice is named for Sylvester's wife, and Lake Augusta is named for his mother. "Timber cruisers" managed timber cutting permits by hiking and making rough visual estimates of board-feet, and rangers also regulated the estimated 150,000 sheep grazing throughout the Wenatchee National Forest. Beginning in 1911, the Forest Service began stringing wires linking the numerous fire lookouts to Leavenworth in a crude telephone system that allowed a ranger anywhere along the line to hook his phone to the wire and connect; by 1927, more than 430 miles of line had been hung, and the remnants of this old knob and tube system are still visible in many places around Leavenworth today. A fire camp (with no structure) established at the top of Tumwater Mountain in 1920-22, near modern-day Punk Rock, was one of the first fire lookouts in the country to be staffed by a female. The Fourth of July fire lookout on top of Icicle Ridge was built in 1929, and though it was abandoned in 1964 and burned in 1969, its platform and debris can still be found at the top of the Fourth of July trail. Sylvester died in 1944, at the age of 73, from injuries he suffered when his horse lost its footing and fell on a steep mountain trail.

More than anything else, central Washington's early history was shaped by the promise of, search for, and execution of a viable east-west route over the Cascades: The wagon road over Snoqualmie Pass was completed in the late 1850s, while the Stevens Pass highway did not open until 1925, and was not paved until 1951. Even more important than roads, however, were railroads. The Northern Pacific railroad route over Stampede Pass, just south of Snoqualmie, was completed in 1888, but business interests in the eastern part of the state called for a more direct route over the mountains from Wenatchee. In 1890, Stevens Pass was "discovered" by John Frank Stevens, the Great Northern's legendary engineer who went on to be the chief engineer of the Panama Canal in 1905-07.

The rail route over Stevens Pass was finished in January of 1893. Signs of the railroad's construction can still be seen in the Tumwater Canyon, including domelike structures called "beehive ovens" that were constructed by Greek and Italian workers at construction camps. At the pass, the route followed a series of switchbacks back and forth across the steep mountainside; trains would pull to the end of one section, then reverse direction and "switch back" to the next, lower section of track in a delicate series of maneuvers resembling the arc of a falling leaf. The early pass also included a "horseshoe tunnel" at the bottom of the pass where the train entered the mountain, performed a constant 10-degree turn, then exited parallel to the rear of the train entering the tunnel. Portions of the former railroad route that were not paved over during construction of the Stevens Pass Highway now form part of the Pacific Crest Trail over the pass.

Early winter travel over Stevens Pass was plagued by terrible avalanches sloughing off the recently-denuded slopes above, and the railroad began to scout locations for a tunnel through the pass almost as soon as the first rail route was completed. Work on the first Stevens Pass tunnel commenced in August of 1897, and 400-600 young men were employed to conduct the repetitive work of blasting, loading the rubble and debris to cars to be carried to the surface, lining each section with several feet of concrete, and repeating. Progress continued at the rate of 350 feet per month – not too shabby for having no mechanized equipment! Numerous construction camp settlements appeared on either side of the pass that today range from small Highway 2 pit stops to all-but-forgotten ghost towns: Chiwaukum (present-day Tumwater Campground), Winton (present-day Longview Fibre mill), Merritt, Berne, Cascade Tunnel, Mill Creek Camp, Wellington, Martin City (present-day Deception Falls), Scenic, Nippon, Berlin, Grotto, and Baring. The 2.6-mile-long tunnel was completed in 1900, providing a temporary lifeblood to many of these communities. In Scenic, which now sits at the top of an unmarked, gated dirt road off of Highway 2 on the west side of the pass, developers built a 100-bed hotel in 1904 that featured lavish details like oak paneling, electric lights, and steam heat. Water from nearby sulfurous hot springs was piped to pools at the hotel, and business was booming – until the hotel burned down four years later, in 1908.

The original Great Northern Railway tracks traveled through the Tumwater Canyon over the site of present-day Highway 2, through five snowsheds that protected the tracks from huge avalanches. Because the coal-powered locomotives could not safely travel through the tunnel at the pass, state-of-the-art electric engines were hooked to the trains on either side of the tunnel and the trains were dragged, locomotives and all, through the heart of the mountain. To power the electric engines, the Great Northern Dam was constructed in Tumwater Canyon just upstream from the present-day site of the Lake Jolanda dam, near The Alps Candy Store. A huge wooden penstock pipe was used to transport the water thus collected 11,654 feet down canyon to a huge power plant where the Beach Parking lot is today. Believe it or not, this parking lot formerly housed a 210-foot-tall water tower and a 76-by-117-foot, three story high powerhouse that provided 6,600 volts of power to the pass. Because the east side of the canyon was too narrow to accommodate both the railroad tracks and the pipeline, the pipe was laid on the west side of the Wenatchee, and the Beach Bridge was constructed to carry the pipe over

The Great Northern Power Plant in the Tumwater Canyon, at the site of today's Beach Parking Area. Photo courtesy of the Upper Valley Museum at Leavenworth.

the river; a small, now-collapsed tunnel was also drilled through a cliff a few hundred yards past the Beach Boulders proper. The electric engines were used until cleaner diesel locomotives appeared in 1956.

With the opening of the pass, Leavenworth's railroad industry started to boom. Huge coal bunkers were built on either side of the tracks, and the hub's switchyard handled more than 1,000 cars a day. In 1906, an overpass was built over the tracks in town to facilitate schoolchildren's crossing. Even with the 1900 tunnel, however, winter travel over the Cascades was highly unreliable and dangerous. On March 1, 1910, one of the worst train disasters in United States history occurred at Wellington, near the site of the Iron Goat Interpretive Site at the foot of the Stevens Pass. Two passenger trains were stalled outside on the western side of the tunnel, unable to enter the tunnel because avalanche slides had blocked the eastern exit. After seven days of blizzard, it began to rain, and a massive avalanche swept both passenger trains and three rotary snowplows nearly 1,000 feet down the hillside, burying them under 40 feet of thick, wet snow. Ninety-six people perished. Three years later, an avalanche struck and killed a party of 50-60 people shoveling out a stalled train. Though more than four miles of snowsheds were built to protect the entrances to the tunnel (the walls of many of which are still visible today), the railroad began an enormous project: the construction of an eight-mile-long tunnel that would avoid the dangerous avalanche-prone slopes above the 1900 tunnel.

The work of surveying the site of the new tunnel began in 1925, and ground was broken later that year. If the construction of the 1900 tunnel provided a bolus of jobs and development to either side of the pass, the construction of the eight-mile tunnel more than doubled it. Up to 1,700 men were employed on the new tunnel at a time. Because the Great Northern Railway only gave contractor A.B. Guthrie and Co. three years to complete the tunnel, special methods were devised so that as many "fronts" as possible could be worked at the same time. Work was done from both ends of the tunnel as well as through an eight-by-twenty-four-foot, 622-foot-deep shaft and a "pioneer tunnel" running parallel to the main shaft that allowed workers to burrow ahead of the work being done at the tunnel's main openings. Workers were given footage bonuses, and intense rivalries developed between the up to 11 teams working different fronts; workers set a world record at the time by drilling 1,157 feet in a single month. Workers kept the tunnel on line using a primitive but effective technique called "transiting" that involved sighting a distant marker placed directly in line with the planned tunnel prior to construction; incredibly, when the 7.79-mile-long tunnel was completed after almost three years of work, the opposing tunnels were only off by 0.64 feet on line and 0.78 feet on grade. The final "bore through," on May 1, 1928 was done by President Calvin Coolidge via a remote control button in the White House, and the tunnel was officially completed on December 24, 1928. On January 12, 1929, the Great Northern Railroad's first "Oriental Limited" passenger train crossed through the tunnel filled with dignitaries.

With so much activity in town and in the Tumwater Canyon, the Icicle Canyon's pristine feel today is due in large part to the fact that it has played an ancillary role during the course of Leavenworth's history. Icicle Road was initially built to support an early pre-Stevens-Pass plan for an east-west highway through the Cascades, the Icicle-Kittitas Road, which would connect Leavenworth to Cle Elum via the west side of Mount Stuart. A state bill authorizing funding for the road was passed and signed in 1907, but the plan was discarded in favor of the Stevens Pass route over the Cascades – many now-popular bouldering areas likely dodged a bullet with this decision! The Icicle Irrigation canal was completed in 1910, diverting water from the Snow Creek drainage, at the junction of the creek's intersection with the Icicle (now the site of the off-limits Government Boulders), to a canal feeding water to the thirsty agricultural land down the Wenatchee Valley; irrigation water from the Icicle is in large part responsible for the region's fame as a fruit and wine region.

Despite the promise of the eight-mile tunnel, the 1920s brought desertion and despair to Leavenworth. The Forest Service headquarters relocated to Wenatchee in 1921, leaving only a small outpost behind. In 1925, the Great Northern Railway was rerouted through the Chumstick Valley to avoid the terrible avalanches in Tumwater Canyon, and the railroad's divisional hub was pushed east to Wenatchee. The Lamb-Davis sawmill closed in 1926, devastating a local economy that had had millworkers at its core. In 1928, the railroad workers who had been working at a feverish pace to complete the eight-mile tunnel realized they had worked themselves out of jobs, and many left the central Cascades to find work in the booming industrial cities along Puget Sound. Black Tuesday hit one year later in 1929, and the nation plunged into recession.

BORN-AGAIN BAVARIA

With large-scale industry gone from Leavenworth by the late 1920s, what economy there was in town was driven primarily by tourism. Tourism had first come to the Wenatchee Valley in the early 1900s, with a hunting and fishing lodge established for wagon-going visitors to Lake Wenatchee in 1906, but the logistics of travel and the reality of early-twentieth-century life did not foster a recreational industry in town. There was one notable exception: Leavenworth's Ski Hill was built in the 1920s, featuring numerous toboggan runs and two ski jumps, and was home to huge ski-jumping tournaments from the 1930s to the 1970s. The 1937 tournament brought 1,800 visitors by train alone, and a total of 10,000 spectators descended on the town. The United States national championships were held in Leavenworth five times between 1941 and 1978. Ski Hill remains open and vibrant today, though you are much more likely to see youngsters from town doing tricks on their snowboards than the traditional distance ski jumping of yesteryear!

Leavenworth received an injection of federal funds in 1933 when one of four major Civilian Conservation Corps camps in central Washington was established near the junction of the Icicle and Wenatchee, where the Sleeping Lady resort is today. "Camp Icicle" housed up to 226 young men for six-month enlistments that could be extended for up to two years at the men's election. CCC workers are responsible for the construction of Ski Hill Lodge, the Snow Lakes trail, and numerous fire lookouts throughout the area, as well as the Washington section of the Pacific Crest Trail, built between 1935 and 1941; the entire PCT was not completed, and its land fully preserved, until 1980. Camp Icicle operated until 1946, then after a decade as the Icicle River Ranch dude ranch, the area was operated as a Catholic summer camp named Camp Field for several decades. In 1992, the camp was purchased by Harriet Bullitt, daughter of pioneering female media mogul Dorothy Bullitt, and the Sleeping Lady Resort was opened.

Salmon also played an important role in Leavenworth's burgeoning revival, though not to the extent they had played a role in the lives of the area's First Peoples. The land adjacent to Camp Icicle was home to a modest state-run salmon hatchery, opened in 1919. In the late 1930s, in an effort to counter the impact on salmon migrations from the Grand Coulee Dam further up the Columbia, the federal government began to plan hatcheries to bolster the downstream salmon runs, including the "world's largest salmon hatchery" in Leavenworth. Huge spawning pools were built on the 170-acre site of the Leavenworth National Fish Hatchery, and to provide cold water during the hot summer months, a 2,500-foot-long, seven-foot-diameter tunnel was bored from Upper Snow Lake, one tier down from the Enchantments, to Nada Lake, the lowest of the Snow Creek lakes. When the flow valve on this tunnel is open in the mid-to-late summer, a gushing torrent of water can be observed 100 yards from the Snow Lakes trail, roughly six miles from the trailhead; during construction, a huge camp was built at Nada Lake replete with dormitories, a mess hall, a blacksmith shop, etc. Though the hatchery is billed as a success by the federal government, environmental groups criticize the hatchery's mission as outdated and its techniques – whereby water draining from hundreds of miles of pristine spawning ground is partially (and at some times completely) diverted through an industrial-scale complex so that farmed fish can be air-dropped into alpine lakes for fishermen – as counterproductive and foolish. Go check the hatchery out and form your own opinions; admission is free.

Despite these advances, Leavenworth's economy was very slow to recover from the blows it was dealt in the 1920s. The slow pace of development of a vehicular route over the central Cascades did not help matters. The first trip over Stevens Pass by car was accomplished on November 1, 1924; it took more than 32 hours and involved winches and horse teams (think about that next time you're sitting in traffic on a Sunday evening!). The Stevens Pass highway was officially "opened" in July of 1925, but it remained a boggy and adventurous route until the state took responsibility over it in the late 1940s. After considering and rejecting the idea of widening the 1928 tunnel through the pass to accommodate a road, the state paved the Stevens Pass Highway in 1951. Present-day Highway 2 largely follows the route of the old highway, but separate sections can be driven on the west side of the pass for an interesting detour. Despite the town's fame as a ski jumping destination, main-stream tourism did not catch on in the first part of the twentieth century, and Leavenworth was dubbed a "welfare town" by 1960.

In the early 1960s, the Leavenworth Chamber of Commerce contacted the University of Washington Bureau of Community Development for assistance in conducting a redevelopment process, and Project LIFE (a hokey acronym for the even-hokier "Leavenworth Improvement for Everyone") was born. In 1960, two businessmen and "bachelor friends" from the Seattle area, Ted Price and Bob Rodgers, opened the Squirrel Tree Restaurant at modern-day Cole's Corner, using a Swiss Bavarian theme, and Price and Rodgers convinced the Chamber to adopt a similar theme for the entire town. After a heated debate, the Chamber adopted the Bavarian theme in 1964, and despite the acrimony surrounding the decision, nearly every business owner in town complied by adding window-boxes, shutters, and Bavarian-themed trim and murals to the exterior of their buildings. The "Willkommen" sign was placed in the park downtown, and Leavenworth was re-born as a Bavarian-themed tourist village in a matter of a couple years. Leavenworth was rewarded for its efforts in 1968, when Look Magazine named it an All-American City, awarded to cities that had shown an ability to transform themselves for the better.

With the adoption of the Bavarian theme, the town slowly transformed from a decrepit lumber down with a facelift to a bona fide tourist trap, and many of the businesses operating today were born. What is today Gustav's restaurant was the Gateway Shell station, built in the 1930s; the building that is now home to the Leavenworth Pizza Co. and Sandy's Waffle House was formerly a Ford dealership. Nowadays, the city's retail economy is booming, and Leavenworth is frequently described as Washington's second-largest tourist destination after Seattle. In addition to the chotchkies-and-calories economy, Leavenworth's outdoor recreation industry has taken off, with a vibrant hiking scene, two river guiding outfits, mountain bike tours, and, of course, rock climbing and bouldering. In the winter, Leavenworth is a resort town by proxy for Steven's Pass, where skiers and snowboarders flock to play in the snow where so many toiled – and perished – over the years.

Leavenworth has also been the location for several Hollywood movies, though no blockbusters yet. The town and its surroundings were the site of the 1925 film *The Ancient Highway* featuring Jack Holt and Billie Dove, bringing what one can imagine was a significant "buzz" to the small town. Steven Segal's 1994 "environmental action film" *On Deadly Ground*, in which Segal takes on a murderous oil refinery owner played by Sir Michael Cane, includes action scenes shot in the vicinity of Nurse Rock and the Boudreaux Cellars Winery. In *Surviving the Game*, also released in 1994, a down-on-his-luck homeless man played by Ice T is hired by a group of wealthy businessmen to lead a hunting expedition – only to find out that *he* is the prey! More recently, Leavenworth's Christmas-lighting ceremony served as the setting for the 2011 B-movie *Switchmas*, in which a Christmas-obsessed Jewish boy swaps families with a friend to find laughter, love, and a bunch of other heartwarming crap in "Christmastown, WA." When you're hunkered down in the winter months, track down a DVD of these films and see how many locations you can recognize (the Ice T movie is actually pretty awesome; you may want to skip the Christmas movie).

To learn more about Leavenworth's early days and absorb a wealth of historical images and information, visit the Upper Valley Museum at Leavenworth, which was opened in 2002 in the former summer home of Lafayette Lamb, now at 347 Division Street near downtown. Admission is $3.00 per adult – money better spent than on that nutcracker or goofy hat you may be contemplating...

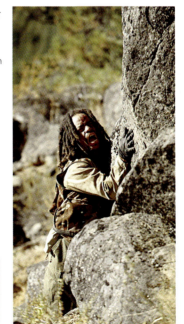

Rapper-turned-actor Ice T wishing he hadn't worn gloves to out-climb the group of armed businessmen hunting him for sport in the 1994 action flick *Surviving the Game*, filmed in the Leavenworth area.
[PHOTO] New Line Cinema

EARLY CLIMBING HISTORY

Most Washington-area climbing histories start with Fred Becky, Wes Grande, and Jack Schwabland's 1948 ascent of *Midway* (5.5) on Tumwater Canyon's Castle Rock. This landmark climb was the first technical rock climb in the Leavenworth area, and ushered in an era of exploration and development in both Tumwater Canyon and the "Cashmere Crags" of the Enchantments region. This initial buzz of development continued into the 1960s and resulted in the first white-man's ascents of most of the area's prominent towers and peaks by Beckey himself. Leavenworth's famous multi-pitch showpiece, *Outer Space* (5.9), was first climbed by Beckey and Ron Niccoli in 1960, and freed in 1963 by Beckey and Steve Marts, a year before Leavenworth's Project LIFE resulted in the adoption of the Bavarian theme. Imagine what the town must have looked like to visiting climbers back then, a drug store and a handful of old pubs and diners dressed up with fancy new Bavarian signs, trim, and window boxes!

The Peshastin Pinnacles and the now 'lost' Chumstick Snag also received attention during this time. In 1949, Pete Schoening climbed the Trigger Finger formation at the Pinnacles, an ascent that may have been the first in Washington to employ bolts for protection. This relic was unfortunately destroyed when the tower collapsed during a winter storm in 1979 – a testimony to the rock quality in Peshastin! In 1974, Peshastin saw another landmark climb with Don Harder's free ascent of *Bomb Shelter*, perhaps the state's first 5.11. Fred Beckey and Erik Bjornstead's 1965 *Guide to Leavenworth Rock Climbing Areas* became Leavenworth's first guidebook, as well as the State of Washington's.

The 1970s and 80s saw the development of most of Leavenworth's popular established crags, and is probably the only time there was anything of a climbing 'scene' in town. Leavenworth was a very different place then, as were the Tumwater and Icicle Canyons. Initially a Shell gas station, Gustavs used to be Das Berghaus, a casual burger joint where climbers would hang out. Rumor has it that you were once able to trade climbing pictures for food – check out your server's expression if you try that one today! The lower portion of Icicle Canyon also saw much change during the first part of the 1980s, when much of the land in the vicinity of Icicle Island became privatized. Before the extensive privatization of the lower Icicle, climbers could essentially go wherever they wanted, and climb on whichever rocks they wished. Many of the backyard boulders in the stretch of road following the Fridge Boulder are home to historic problems that have been off-limits since this time. This time of privatization also ushered in the era of "no trespassing" and "no camping" signs in the Icicle, and dramatically changed the feel of the canyon.

BOULDERING HISTORY

Some of the oldest established bouldering in the area can be found at Swiftwater in the Tumwater Canyon, and at the Fridge, Bolt Rock, The Pumphouse and Barney's Rubble in the Icicle. It's worth noting that two of the above areas are now off-limits, further victims of privatization. The 1990s saw the development of Leavenworth's major bouldering areas like The Beach, Mad Meadows, and Forestland. Early developers included the ubiquitous Dick Cilley, Greg Collum, and many others who have since retreated into the shadows… Clamshell Cave, the JY Boulders, Egg Rock, Fuzz Wall, and similar smaller areas also saw new problems during the 90s, though the actual timeline is a bit hazy. Some of the first boulderers to bring a new-school devotion to hard moves and problem development were Chris Kirschbaum, Dobrisa Jurkovic, Jason Mikos, Brian Doyle, Ben Shrope, Jason Duckowitz, and others, who established a bevy of problems that are still testpieces today, including *Premium Coffee* (V7), *Big Booty Bitch Slap* (V10), and *The Coffee Cup* (V10 pre-break). The devastating Rat Creek fire of 1994 left a good deal of Icicle Canyon charred and smoldering for months. Many climbing areas were affected, and the entire canyon was closed until the following spring for restoration efforts and salvage logging; the Forestland parking lot served as a staging area and helipad for the Forest Service's efforts.

The "golden age" of Leavenworth's bouldering development continued well into the late 1990s. Frequent visits by then-teenagers Cole Allen, Johnny Goicoechea, Ryan Paulsness, and Joel Campbell resulted in the establishment of many of the area's hardest lines, including *The Sail* (V9), *Goicoechea* (V9), *Musashi* (V9), *The Peephole* (V10), *The Ram* (V11/12), and many others. In the summer of 1999, Leavenworth locals Jeff Hashimoto and Damian Potts developed the bulk of the bouldering at Mountain Home Road, including such classics as *Darth Maul* (V5), *Emperor's Lightning* (V7), and *Punk Ass Kid* (V6). Campbell, Allen, and Goicoechea quickly added their own contributions to Mountain Home Road, including *Yoda* (V9), *Obi Wan* (sandbagged V9), *Darth Vader* (V9), and *The Cattleguard Arête* (V8). Another fire swept through the Icicle in 2001, but did significantly less damage than the 1994 fire.

The turn of the century also saw the self-publication of *Leavenworth Bouldering*, a.k.a. *A Cheesy Guide to Pleasing Rock*, by the late Damian Potts. Then-owners of Leavenworth Mountain Sports Alec Gibbons and Brian Behle carried the torch after Damian's passing, producing several subsequent editions of the guide, the fifth and final edition of which was printed in 2004. Most visitors to Little Bavaria's boulders during the early- to mid-2000s benefited greatly from the happy rantings of this storied pamphlet. Leavenworth's 'old' guide sports a ton of character, and without it, *Central Washington Bouldering* would not have been a reality, let alone this guide. Check it out someday if you can find a copy, and while you're at it, pick up Viktor Kramer's *Leavenworth Rock* if you don't already have it. It's the definitive guide to Leavenworth's roped climbing, and makes a valuable tool for the boulderer on the hunt for new areas.

While Leavenworth's golden age could be said to have come to an end by the mid-2000s, the pace of development has barely slowed since the largest areas were discovered and developed, with many smaller areas and isolated boulders discovered and rediscovered. Icicle Canyon areas like The Bond Boulders, The Sleeping Lady, The Pretty Boulders, and Tin Man were all developed in 2005-07, as were Tumwater areas like The Labyrinth, The Range Boulders, The Beach Parking Area, The Pitless Avocado, Jenny Craig, and That Demon. Climbers active in developing new areas during this time include Joel Campbell, Cole Allen, Kyle O'Mara, Dave Thompson, and Kelly Sheridan. Many of these 'new' areas may even have seen bouldering activity in the past but had been forgotten, the slow march of time returning them to a seemingly-untouched state.

Since the publication of *Central Washington Bouldering* in 2007, the area's popularity has steadily grown, leading to the discovery of many new areas as well as the establishment of many longstanding projects and previously-unnoticed problems in existing areas. This book includes 21 new areas/boulders in the Icicle, 8 in the Tumwater, and 4 along Mountain Home Road, all of which have been developed since 2007. Many of these areas have been developed a result of the efforts of long-time Leavenworth climbers like Johnny Goicoechea and Cole Allen, but this decade has also brought many new faces to Leavenworth's development, including Drew Schick, Joe Treftz, Ben Herrington, Andrew Deliduka, and many others. Drew Schick in particular has been especially active in seeking out, brushing, and climbing new problems in both canyons, and had a significant role in developing at least two-thirds of the new areas included in this guide.

The 2000-teens also saw Leavenworth's difficulty standards pushed, with Dave Thompson bringing V13 to the area with his impressive ascent of *The Teacup*, and the number of V11s and V12s in the area vastly increasing. In late 2013, pro climber Carlo Traversi established Leavenworth's first V14, the longstanding *Ladder Project*, now dubbed *The Penrose Step*. A month later, Jimmy Webb repeated the problem and established one of the best Leavenworth ticklists ever, with flash ascents of the *Teacup* (V13), *Turbulence* (V11/12), and a whopping *eight* other V11s in a matter of two weeks. The pace of development has continued unabated until this book went to print (and surely will thereafter), with three-star problems like *Watercolors* (V5), *Heartbreaker* (V7, V9 sit), *Daydream* (V8), and *Open Range* (V8) all established in the summer of 2014 – and those are just the problems that lie within 50 yards of a road or established trail! Every fall, it seems like the areas that popped up during the last year must be the "last great ones," but every spring, a new batch of boulders appears…

BIBLIOGRAPHY:

Laura Arksey, *Leavenworth – Thumbnail History* (available at http://www.historylink.org/index.cfm?DisplayPage=output.cfm&file_id=9475) (2010).

Mike Corrigan, *Lost Tribe,* Inlander.com (available at http://www.inlander.com/spokane/lost-tribe/Content?oid=2174482) (2002).

Joseph C. Dupris, Kathleen S. Hill, William H. Rodgers, Jr., *The Si'lailo Way*, Carolina Academic Press (2006).

Initiative for Rural Innovation & Stewardship, "Gathering our Voice" program, (available at http://gatheringourvoice.org) (2014).

Viktor Kramer, *Leavenworth Rock* (2010) (available for purchase at http://www.leavenworthrockclimbing.com).

Rose Kinney-Holck and the Upper Valley Museum at Leavenworth, *Images of America: Leavenworth*, Arcadia Publishing (2011).

Damian Potts, Alec Gibbons, Brian Behle, *Leavenworth Bouldering: A Cheesy Guide to Pleasing Rock* (5th ed. 2004).

Ted Price, *Leavenworth's Transformation in America's Bavarian Village* (available at http://www.leavenworthhistory.com) (2014).

JoAnn Roe, *Stevens Pass: Gateway to Seattle*, Caxton Press (2002).

Richard Scheuerman, *The Wenatchee Valley and Its First Peoples: Thrilling Grandeur, Unfulfilled Promise*, Washington State University Press (2007).

Sleeping Lady Resort, *Our Story* (available at http://www.sleepinglady.com/our-story.php) (2014).

Ira Spring and Byron Fish, *Lookouts: Firewatchers of the Cascades and Olympics*, Mountaineers Books (2nd Ed. 1996).

Vicky Spring, Ira Spring, and Harvey Manning, *100 Hikes in Washington's Alpine Lakes*, Mountaineers Books (2nd Ed. 1993).

Hill Williams, *The Restless Northwest: A Geological Story,* Washington State University Press (2002).

… and many, many generous and thoughtful boulderers!!

A late edition of Leavenworth's first bouldering guide, Leavenworth Bouldering: A Cheesy Guide to Pleasing Rock.

As soon as you hit Leavenworth's crowded Front street on a busy Saturday, you may ask your friends "So… just how far away is Squamish?" Fortunately, the same things that make Leavenworth a strange and busy little tourist trap make it quite hospitable to the traveling rock climber. If you can get over the traffic, the tourons waddling on your feet, and the hokey German music blaring nonstop during festival weekends, you will easily find everything you need (and so much more) in town.

LODGING

Leavenworth has more than its fair share of hotels, most of which are on Highway 2 or Commercial St. If you can afford it, The Sleeping Lady resort is located 2.5 miles up Icicle Canyon, where you can pamper your aching muscles in an outdoor granite hot tub minutes after sending. For the rest of us, there are a multitude of campgrounds in the area. The KOA behind Safeway on the east side of town is the closest to Little Bavaria, but at $22.00 a night and up, it isn't highly recommended unless you simply must have a cable TV hookup for your Winnebago. Coming from the west and want to crash quickly? The Tumwater Campground is 10 miles west of Leavenworth on Highway 2, with fancy flush toilets and a basketball court for $17.00 per night. If you're looking for a little peace and quiet, as well as some first-rate scenery, camp in the Icicle. There are six National Forest campgrounds in Icicle Canyon, excluding the Black Pine Horse Camp. The two closest to town, Bridge Creek and Eightmile campgrounds, open in mid-April when the upper spots are just beginning to thaw, and are fair game for free walk-in camping when officially "closed." Both are also within walking distance of bouldering, an obvious plus. All campgrounds have vault toilets and water (not always potable), and cost $14.00 per night per vehicle ($16.00 for Eightmile).

Icicle Canyon's "No Overnight Camping" signs can seem a bit unwelcoming to the dirtbag climber at first, but there are still a number of good free campsites to be found. Try the turnoffs on the left near the beginning of Mountaineers Creek Road or the various pullouts after the Icicle turns to dirt, especially on the right-hand side in the mile following Rock Island Campground. The Forest Service seems unable to make up its mind about Forestland and other areas on the right side of Icicle Road, at times stating that anything right of the road is fair game, only to turn around six months later and post "No Overnight Camping" or "Day Use Only" signs. At the time of writing, Forestland and other random spots in the lower- to mid-Icicle are closed to camping. **Please do not camp at any area in this guide.** Illegal camping, with its inevitable impact to vegetation, fire damage, and litter, is arguably the biggest threat to continued access in the Leavenworth area today. Do your part and demand that your fellow climbers do the same!

WATER

There are a number of reliable places to fill a water bottle in Leavenworth, including:
• All campgrounds in Icicle Canyon
• USFS Wenatchee Ranger Station, Icicle Road
• 76 Gas Station; Icicle Road & Highway 2
• O'Grady's Pantry, Sleeping Lady Resort, Icicle Road

If you need to clean up a bit, showers can be procured at the KOA for $5.00 plus tax. There are also two gyms / health clubs in Leavenworth that offer day rates: Club West Fitness Center off of Titus Road behind the school, and Balancepoint Health & Fitness, 0.3 miles up the Chumstick Highway. Swimming in the river is also a great way to fake some personal hygiene when it's warm enough. There are some great swimming holes in the Tumwater Canyon; try the parking for the Beach area and the sandy beach across from the Pitless Avocado for starters. If it's truly sweltering and you're feeling bold, try the unique 5.10 "deep river solo" Annie's Climax at Muscle Beach!

GROCERIES

Located just off Highway 2 on the east end of town, Leavenworth's Safeway chain is a generic modern supermarket, with the exception of the Bavarian-themed paintings on the exterior. For a bit more character, a great beer selection, and friendly local charm, check out Dan's market next to Der McDonald's on Highway 2. Dan's houses a small bakery, has a great sandwich counter, and even fries its own chicken!

LAUNDRY

Sadly, Leavenworth's sole Laundromat bit the dust some time ago, and the nearest place to do laundry is in neighboring Peshastin. Drive 4.0 miles east of town on Highway 2 and take the left turn for Peshastin at the first light. Turn left after passing under the train tracks and the laundromat will be on your right after four blocks. For a more scenic return route, continue straight on North Road until it ends. Turn left onto the Chumstick Highway, which soon intersects Highway 2 across from Dan's Market in Leavenworth.

GEAR

Leavenworth is home to two gear stores, Highway 2's Leavenworth Mountain Sports and Front Street's Der Sportsman. Der Sportsman is slightly more geared toward the tourist dollar, but both shops offer staples like shoes and chalk. Leavenworth Mountain Sports has a full selection of climbing gear and crashpads, and rents pads for $20/day, with multi-day and weekly rates.

INTERNET

Last but not least, access to the mighty Lethe of information: where to go for your email, weather, and slander fix. Leavenworth's public library is your only chance to use the internet without a handy laptop computer. There are four terminals with a maximum use of 30 minutes, and there is typically no wait during weekdays. The library also offers a wireless internet signal. If you're looking for free wireless internet on Highway 2, check out the 76 station at the corner of 9th, the Red Bird Café a.k.a. Good Mood Food, or the Icicle Coffee Roasters by the mini-golf on the west side of town. O'Grady's Pantry at the Sleeping Lady resort in the Icicle also has wireless internet in a relaxing setting.

Leavenworth's famous Willkommen sign at the west end of town, with Icicle Junction visible in the background.

CAMPGROUNDS
(BY DISTANCE FROM LEAVENWORTH)

KOA..0 (by Safeway)

Eightmile...7.1
Bridge Creek..................................... 8.5
Tumwater...........................10 (just outside Tumwater Canyon)
Johnny Creek.................................... 11.5
Ida Creek.. 13
Chatter Creek.................................... 15
Rock Island...................................... 16.5

THE BEST OF LEAVENWORTH

Best Last-Minute Coffee:
O'Grady's Pantry, 2.5 miles up Icicle Rd.
Best Lunch Deal:
$2.50 Subs @ Dan's Market, Highway 2
Best Pint:
Icicle Brewing Co., 935 Front St.
Best Summer Rest Day:
Osprey River Rafting, Icicle Junction
Best Fast Food:
Heidleburger, Highway 2 near Icicle Junction
Best Munchies:
The Gingerbread Factory, 828 Commercial St.
Best Mood Food:
Red Bird Café / Good Mood Food, Highway 2
Best Mexican Food:
South, 913 Front St.
Best Lazy Breakfast:
The Renaissance Café, 217 8th St.
Best Swords:
The Australian Store, 929 Front St.

CLIMATE

No doubt about it, the weather in the Northwest gets a bad rap. Non-residents enjoy citing statistics like "It rains 364 days a year in Seattle" and other such propaganda in justifying their reluctance to visit… I've even wondered if these rumors weren't started by the region's more selfish climbers, unwilling to share the Cascades' bounty with the rest of the country. All speculation aside, the truth of the matter is that the Northwest's notorious rain is really limited to the coast. East of the Cascade Mountains, one largely finds a desertous climate with dry, sunny weather throughout the spring, summer, and fall. As a rule of thumb, the internet's enigmatic "30% chance of precipitation" forecast typically means intermittent showers for Leavenworth, whereas it means a soggy, cloudy day when given for the west side.

Leavenworth is located in the 'rain shadow' at the very eastern edge of the Cascade Mountains, and is often sunny and dry when Seattle and the western slope are buffeted by Pacific rains. Related perks as minimal summer rain, four well-defined seasons, and a slightly higher average temperature all come as part of the package. Spring and fall are the ideal seasons to climb in Leavenworth, with average highs in the 50s to 70s and little precipitation. The summer months can be quite warm, with highs in the 80s, 90s, and even the triple digits. June through August are still good times to visit, but be prepared to take a break and go for a swim to escape the mid-day heat. Fortunately, these badass boulders never 'close,' and many enjoyable summer sessions have been had by headlamp and lantern. Winter conditions in Leavenworth can be pretty grim, but with the exception of a couple dire months around the turn of the year, intrepid boulderers can find dry rock during most of the snowy season. Some of my best climbing days in the Icicle have been sunny, 20 degree February afternoons. When you can find dry, south-facing rock, winter conditions are perfect in Leavenworth: the canyons empty, the friction immaculate, and the feel of rock under your fingertips a long-lost delight. For most climbers, however, Leavenworth is a two- or three-season area, the climbing season overlapping nicely (unfortunately?) with the town's busy festival schedule.

Two adult Osprey (*Pandion haliaetus*) prepare to mate on a treetop nest. Osprey nests, both natural and manmade, can be seen in several locations in the Tumwater and Icicle canyons. **[PHOTO]** Matt Edmonds

An adult north American river otter (*Lontra canadensis*) gliding through the water. River otters, which are most closely related to weasels, are prevalent throughout the western United States and Canada and are equally at home in water as on land, often making their underground burrows close to the water's edge near lakes, rivers, and other riparian habitats. The author had the magical experience a few years back of watching one of these *mustelidae*, which are increasingly threatened by habitat loss and pollution, playing in the rapids below the Sleeping Lady (V2) while he ran laps on the boulder problem over and over, each creature at play in their favored habitat. **[PHOTO]** Cacaphony

LEAVENWORTH FAUNA

Leavenworth is home to a great wealth of wild animals, many of which are never seen by the casual weekend visitor. Deer, elk, black bears, cougars, coyote, wolves, foxes, beavers, squirrels, chipmunks, rabbits, and even river otters are present, as well as a wide range of insects, rodents, birds, and reptiles including lizards and snakes. One of my favorite memories in Leavenworth is seeing a family of two adult foxes and four kits, moving silently through light snow cover in a tight line called a "skulk," on a sunny winter afternoon spent solo at the 420 Boulder. If you have the time and the will, spend a weekday off the beaten path in Icicle Canyon, moving minimally and maintaining a silence, and you might see a few of the species listed above!

While wildlife sightings are relatively infrequent during the bustle and noise of a bouldering session, let alone injuries relating to animal encounters, there are a number of potentially-dangerous animals to be aware of when climbing in the area.

First and foremost are snakes. There are two types of snakes prevalent in the bouldering areas around Leavenworth. First is the Bull Snake, which has no rattle, is not venomous, and is recognizable by its brown, squarish blocking pattern. Second is the Western Rattlesnake, which is functionally-speaking the most dangerous animal in Leavenworth. Western Rattlesnakes are recognizable by their white, brown and black, diamond-shaped pattern, their blunt nose, and by their visible facial "pits" used to sense prey – oh yeah, and the rattle. While rattlesnakes use their rattles primarily to warn potential predators, they are often reluctant to expend the energy to use them to warn oncoming hikers, especially during the sunnier parts of the day when boulderers are out and about. Snakes will often sense the vibrations of your footsteps and escape before you approach, so tread heavily, and never step where you cannot see. Carry a snakebite kit when bouldering in the summer; they are cheap and provide some triage if you are bitten far from the road. In the unlikely event you are bit, call ahead to the Cascade Medical Center (509-548-5815) on Commercial Street or Wenatchee's Central Washington Hospital (509-662-1511) and have them begin mixing the antivenom. Ninety-nine percent of rattlesnake bites that are treated within two hours do not caused serious injury; twenty percent of rattlesnake bites do not involve any envenomation (factors relevant to how much venom a rattlesnake releases include the degree of provocation, the snake's satiation, and whether the snake has been harassed). Rattlesnakes both hibernate and aestivate, and are typically only seen in Leavenworth during the beginning and end of summer.

Cougars. Virtually all of the "Dangerous Wildlife Incident Reports" on file for Chelan County on the Washington Department of Fish & Wildlife's web site involve cougars, though attacks are rare. Cougars, a.k.a. mountain lions, can reach seven to eight feet long, are active from dusk 'till dawn, and are relatively shy of humans. Mountain lions eat a diet of small mammals like raccoons and coyotes as well as deer and elk, and are generally extremely shy of people. If you do come in close proximity to a cougar, do not run, make yourself look large, yell in a low voice, throw things, and if you are attacked, fight back. In 10 years of bouldering in Leavenworth, I have only seen one cougar, and it became frightened and headed for the hills once I got within 100 yards of it – I was lucky to have even seen it.

Black bears (which can sometimes be brown) are prevalent throughout the Icicle, the Tumwater, and Mountain Home Road, and one will certainly encounter an ursine friend after enough time spent in the evening mountain air in Leavenworth… It's a good thing that black bears are much more docile than their roughneck cousin the Grizzly! Black bears typically don't pose a problem for hikers and campers in the area. Food is fine left in vehicles overnight, but should be hung if camping away from the car. If you see a black bear in the boulders, a good shout should send it lumbering off, but if bear cubs, dogs, or human food are present, calmly retreat to a safe distance. If charged, stand your ground and do not crouch, play dead, or run – you will not outrun the bear, and it is likely just asserting its dominance through a bluff charge. Grizzly bears are seen once every one or two years in the North Cascades, and have been sighted as far south as the Highway 20 town of Concrete in 2012, but do not pose a concern in the Leavenworth area.

Wolves, which were historically hunted to near-extirpation from the northwest and are only now making a gradual comeback, have been observed in recent years in the Leavenworth area; one was sighted in the Tumwater Canyon in February of 2012, and two wolf attacks on domestic animals were confirmed in Wenatchee in 2013. Though wolves conceivably present some danger to humans, many people (those who don't own livestock) are hopeful that these majestic and inspiring wild canids will someday return to the central Cascades.

An adult bull snake (*Pituophis catenifer sayi*) in a defensive posture. Note the lowered, as opposed to raised, tail and zig-zag, as opposed to coiled, body position. **[PHOTO]** Psyon

This western rattlesnake (*Crotalus oreganus*) is in a defensive position – rattle up, coiled, and ready to strike. Back off! **[PHOTO]** Bill Bouton

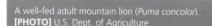

A well-fed adult mountain lion (*Puma concolor*). **[PHOTO]** U.S. Dept. of Agriculture

Black Bear (*Ursis americanus*). Black bears are omnivorous mammals that are ubiquitous throughout the northern and western United States, the most common species of bear on the planet. It is not at all uncommon to see a black bear when one finds themselves several miles from the road around dawn or dusk. This friendly specimen seems to be offering a spot… **[PHOTO]** U.S. Fish & Wildlife Service.

LEAVENWORTH FLORA

By Miles Berkey

The dry, leeward Cascade climate both determines and shapes the vegetative communities of Leavenworth. The Cascade Mountains act as a barrier to the moist air moving eastward from the Pacific Ocean. As moist air masses approach the western slope of the Cascades, precipitation significantly increases with the elevation; the air masses that move east of the pass are bereft of moisture. Stevens Pass, just 22 miles from Leavenworth, receives about 84 inches of precipitation each year, while Leavenworth receives 26. To the east of Leavenworth is the Columbia Plateau, the driest part of the state, in which some localities receive little more than 7 inches of rain a year! This phenomenon is called "orographic precipitation" and is the principal factor for Leavenworth's rich floristic diversity.

Leavenworth is located within the "East Cascade slope eco-region." Unlike the cool, damp moss-laden forest expanses west of the pass, the foothills and slopes around Leavenworth are a mosaic of open meadows and woodlands. The common patches and gaps of Ponderosa Pine, with Douglas Fir on the valley walls of the Tumwater Canyon and Icicle drainage reflect the strong influence of fire on forest stand formation in the area. The thick bark of both the Ponderosa Pine and Douglas Fir are keenly adapted to a short, low-intensity fire rotation interval (five to 15 years), making them co-dominant canopy formers. Frequent understory shrubs in these forests include Snowberry, Vine Maple, and Mock Orange. Snowbrush is the most common shrub in both the Tumwater and Icicle river valleys. It has glossy, aromatic leaves, and white flowers. The seeds of Snowbrush can lay dormant for nearly 200 years until they are stimulated and opened by an intense-enough blaze. Once Snowbrush colonizes, it tends to form dense, impenetrable thickets. Displays of Snowbrush's aggressive behavior are most conspicuous off Mountain Home Road near the Star Wars Boulder, Upper Forestland in the Icicle, and other open and exposed sites. Moving into more mesic sites, especially following the river margins, one will find populations of Western Red Cedar, Black Cottonwood, and Quaking Aspen. Very seldom encountered in the Tumwater Canyon, but with increasing frequency towards the Icicle, is Poison Ivy. Learn to identify Poison Ivy and avoid contact with this plant! Its sap contains a toxin called "urushiol," which can cause a blistering rash when it comes in contact with skin.

Due to the regularity of fire, the forest in Leavenworth is often interrupted by grassy meadows of Idaho Fescue, and throughout May the flowers of Arrowleaf Balsamroot and Broadleaf Lupine bring an illuminating contrast to the dark evergreens that surround. Springtime in Leavenworth is a flush of chromatic beauty. For every variation in land surface and exposure, there is an associated Aster, Lily, Phlox, and many other genera, whose flowers vividly express the diversity of the land. As the year proceeds towards fall nearly every deciduous shrub and tree casts the landscape into a procession of reds, yellows and oranges. Then, just prior to the passing of fall, take notice of the soft yellow glow of the sub-alpine larches growing high atop the surrounding ridgelines. If you have a rest day, drop into the bookstore at the Sleeping Lady and grab a plant identification book; become familiar with all the amazing plants of Leavenworth.

Snowbrush (*Ceanothus velutinus*). Snowbrush has oval shaped, alternate evergreen leaves. Its flowers as seen are aggregates of many small white flowers which from a distance look like hanging clumps of snow. Snowbrush occurs frequently on exposed sunny slopes, often times following a fire. **[PHOTO]** Walter Siegmund

Poison Ivy (*Toxicodendron radicans*). Poison Ivy can be found growing in numerous sites around Leavenworth, and in many forms: vines, bushes, trailing on the ground, or ascending trees. The leaves are broadly ovate in groups of three. Learn to identify this plant, and proceed warily in places like the Labyrinth and the Torture Chamber where this insidious ivy grows under boulders and in seepages. **[PHOTO]** Wikipedia Commons

RIGHT PAGE, RIGHT PHOTO Letharia (*Letharia sp.*). Several species of Letharia lichens can be found in many places around Leavenworth. These fluorescent yellow to chartreuse specimens can heavily populate the dead decorticate branches and stems of most local conifers in open, well ventilated forests and snags at timberline. *Letharia* contains vulpinic acid which is toxic. This lichen used to be hidden among bait to kill off wolves in Scandinavia. **[PHOTO]** Wikipedia Commons

RIGHT PAGE, LEFT PHOTO Arrowleaf Balsamroot (*Balsamorhiza sagitatta*). Arrowleaf Balsamroot can be found throughout Leavenworth and the surrounding canyons, especially the exposed slopes of Mountain Home Road. This abundantly sunny plant flowers in mid-spring and is one of the first signs that summer has arrived.

Ponderosa Pine (*Pinus ponderosa*). Ponderosa Pine is the most common coniferous tree in Leavenworth. Extreme examples of Ponderosa Pine are thought to be the tallest pine trees in the world. Key identifying features are needles in bundled groups of three, cinnamon colored bark, and a pleasant vanilla aroma that is best noticed on hot summer days. Ponderosa Pine is most frequently found on lower dry slopes in the Leavenworth area. Photo: Wikipedia Commons.

Douglas Fir (*Pseudotsuga menziesii*). Douglas Fir has needles like a fir, and cones like a hemlock, but it actually belongs to neither genus. Its genus *pseudotsuga* means "false hemlock." Douglas Fir's reddish-brown cones have large spreading scales that bear three-lobed bracts pointed towards the top of the cone. This tree attains heights greater than any northwest tree, and grows straight and fast, making it the preferred re-seeding tree of the timber industry. Keep an eye out for young Doug Firs in recently-burned areas, as they're usually the first conifer to succeed after a fire. Photo: Walter Siegmund.

LEAVENWORTH GEOLOGY
By Jon Stordahl

REGIONAL GEOLOGIC SETTING

The Cascade Range hosts one of the most exotic geological settings anywhere in the world. Nearly every major type of igneous, sedimentary and metamorphic rock exist somewhere in the range and, as a testament to its complexity, competing hypotheses about critical geological events throughout the range are still argued. Geology is still such a young science. Much of the earth has been understood through application of the scientific method, but little has been made into law. The geologist must observe something in nature, ask questions, find a way to test their ideas, then do their best to interpret what they find… Until someone else comes along with better research.

It is generally interpreted that the genesis of what is now the Cascades can be traced back to Jurassic time. 240 million years ago (Fig. 1), subduction zone tectonics began accreting exotic packages of continental material onto the western edge of North America. The emplacement of these terrains was made possible by the relatively light, silica rich continental material on the oceanic plate resisting the forces of subduction, enabling it to be scraped off of the dense down-going oceanic plate as it shunted under the continental plate.

By Cetaceous time, staggering quantities of foreign igneous, sedimentary and metamorphic rock had been emplaced along the west coast of North America. These collisions thickened the earth's crust and grew the edge of the continent all the way from Idaho and Nevada westward to where it is today. Continued subduction of the oceanic plate triggered magmatism, and large plutonic masses of igneous rock began to rise and force their way toward the surface. Orogenic processes intensified by the end of Cretaceous time, fueling the Tertiary formation of large andesite volcanoes across the Cascadian Arc – the predecessors of today's Mount Rainier, Mt. Baker, Mt. Adams, etc. Through time, the extinction of these giants allowed their magma chambers to slowly cool. Continued uplift and erosion brought large bodies of native igneous rock to the surface of the Cascades, riddling the exotic terrains with new stone. Much of the plutonic rock now visible once resided in the basement plumbing of these volcanos.

LOCAL GEOLOGY

Leavenworth resides along the eastern periphery of the Stuart batholith. The batholith covers roughly 20x40 km and is one of the largest bodies of granitic rock in the Cascades. The headwaters of the Icicle Canyon are some 30 miles up canyon, extending nearly to Stevens Pass and the Cascade crest. The Icicle hosts a staggering amount of exposed rock; large alpine towers guard the canyon rim, and the relief from the Icicle ridge and the Edwards plateau to the valley floor can exceed 5,000 feet.

The geomorphology of the Icicle has been greatly influenced by mountain uplift, erosion and multiple periods of glaciation beginning 70,000 years ago. Traces of the glaciers remain, and hanging valleys, polished slabs, terraces and glacial erratics can still be observed (and climbed on) in the canyon. Many of the groups of boulders described in this book, however, have likely come to rest through erosion of the canyon as the Icicle River incises downward through the canyon walls, triggering rock fall. In the spring of 2011, locals witnessed this process firsthand with the unearthing of a couple instant classics at what are now known as the Washout Boulders, when heavy rains triggered a debris flow that closed the canyon for weeks. Boulder problems created right before our eyes – the Icicle is geologically active indeed.

The Stuart batholith is believed to be 93 million years old and its intrusion is thought to have occurred in several phases, which may explain why such a wide variety of rock textures

FIGURE 1

GEOLOGIC AGE

			PRESENT
CENOZOIC	**QUATERNARY**	**HOLOCENE**	
			10,000 ya
		PLEISTOCENE	
			2 Mya
	TERTIARY	**PLIOCENE**	**5 Mya**
		MIOCENE	**24 Mya**
		OLIGOCENE	
			38 Mya
		EOCENE	**55 Mya**
		PALEOCENE	**63 Mya**
MESOZOIC		**CRETACEOUS**	
			132 Mya
		JURASSIC	**205 Mya**
		TRIASSIC	**240 Mya**
PALEOZOIC		**PERMIAN**	**290 Mya**
		PENNSYLVANIAN	
			330 Mya
		MISSISSIPPIAN	**360 Mya**
		DEVONIAN	**410 Mya**
		SILURIAN	**435 Mya**
		ORDOVICIAN	**500 Mya**
		CAMBRIAN	**570 Mya**
PRECAMBRIAN		**PROTEROZOIC**	**2500 Mya**
		ARCHEAN	**3800 Mya**
		HADEAN	**4550 Mya**

appear in the Leavenworth area. The differences between the fine-grained slopers at Swiftwater, the salt and pepper stone of Mountain Home Road, and the highly featured rock at Mad Meadows seem to support this idea, demonstrating finite differences in local chemical and cooling conditions within the batholith during its intrusion into the crust.

While Leavenworth's rock is invariably referred to as "granite" by climbers, the Stuart batholith generally lacks sufficient alkali feldspar content to be considered granite; instead, granodiorite and tonlite lithologies dominate throughout the batholith (Fig. 2). If the Stuart batholith is to be considered locally derived (which some believe it is not) the predominance of granodiorite can be attributed to the volcanic nature of the range and the realization that much of the rock is the plutonic equivalent of the andesite composite volcanoes that once resided above.

As hinted earlier, the actual emplacement of the Mount Stuart batholith is still contested and is generally broken down into two hypotheses. The first arose out of paleomagnetic research that studied the orientation of magnetite crystals (which are a trace component to the Stuart batholith). Prior to cooling, magnetite will orientate itself parallel to the flux lines of the earth's magnetic field and, upon crystallization, will be preserved in that position. This provides geologists with a record and a unique fingerprint that can be used to reconstruct the original latitude during crystallization of the batholith. The Baja-BC hypothesis postulates that the Stuart batholith intruded the crust near Baja Mexico 93 million years ago into the Nason terrane, then transform faulted some 3,000 miles from Mexico and heaved itself onto the North American margin as an exotic terrain. The second competing hypothesis is that the batholith was locally generated by subduction zone volcanism, forcing its its way into the crust and cooling in place, experiencing post-crystallization tilting from mountain-building activity that has displaced the batholith into its current position, leading to erroneous magnetite crystal orientation results. Sound wild? It is. Camps have been divided as to which hypothesis holds more water, and may continue to be for long into the future, but I believe one has to look no further than Occam's razor to be satisfied. I have to admit the imagining all of that rock travelling across the earth to be dumped at what is now *our* doorstep, creating one of the most beautiful places in the world, sounds pretty fantastic.

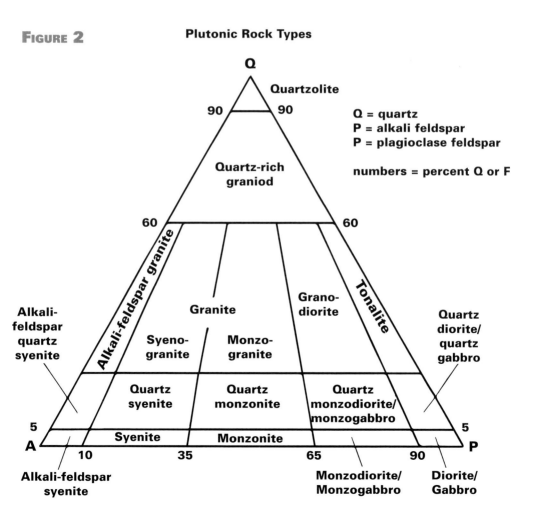

FIGURE 2

Plutonic Rock Types

ACCESS

The access situation for Leavenworth's bouldering areas is good but not perfect. Leavenworth's greatest blessing is that the neighboring Wenatchee Mountains are just within the edge of Wenatchee National Forest. But while much of the Tumwater Canyon is National Forest land, Icicle Canyon includes many small pockets of private land. Most of the bouldering areas in this guide are in the clear, but several are threatened and several have already been lost. Historic areas like the Pumphouse (a.k.a. The Government Boulders) and the wide boulder field below Careno Crag are posted against trespassing and cannot legally be accessed. Other spots on private property, like the Footbolt Dyno (across the river from Mountaineers Dome) and the Canal Boulders have been lost in recent years. Still other areas, like Bolt Rock, the Millennium Boulder, the Twisted Tree, and the Bridge Creek Boulders are on or directly adjacent to private property, but can still be accessed with discretion.

In May 2005, climbers won a sizeable access victory when the Trust for Public Land, the Washington Climbers' Coalition, and local climbers combined efforts to buy the 40-acre Sam Hill property in the lower Icicle, home to the Fridge, the Bond Boulders, and the Upper Bond Boulders. Access to other Leavenworth boulders areas has been fortunately stable in recent years, but the Washington Climbers' Coalition, in partnership with the Access Fund, continues to monitor the state of affairs. The Forest Service has also begun to give bouldering serious attention in the past several years, most recently evidenced by the cleanup of scrap metal, rental of a porta-potty, and placement of an informational kiosk in the Forestland parking lot, as well as the establishment of a pit toiled near Lower Forestland. This work, which was accomplished jointly by the Forest Service and the Leavenworth Mountain Association with support from a number of other access groups, is a sign of many good things to come.

What can you do to maintain a positive perception of boulderers and help preserve bouldering access in Leavenworth? Joining the WCC (*www.washingtonclimber.org*) is a good idea, for one. When you're out climbing, pay attention to how your presence will be perceived. Park well away from private property, driveways, etc., and always use established pullouts where you will be completely off the road. Stick to established trails. If you're exploring, take the time to avoid crossing private property even if it means going the long way. At sensitive areas bordering private property, take care to keep a low profile and minimize your impact. Access conditions may also have changed since the publication of this book. It is your obligation to be aware of current access status and to behave responsibly. Less is more; respect private property and avoid creating a nuisance, and let organized coalitions like the WCC and the Access Fund fight the battles.

Besides the dreadful threat of new "No Trespassing" signs appearing in the Icicle, Leavenworth offers little to worry about. The town is extremely safe and generally quite friendly toward its outdoor tourism industry. As with most climbing destinations, however, vehicle break-ins can and do occur at all three of the areas in this book. Keep all valuables at home or well out of sight, including all those shiny metal objects used to scale rocks. Even in the busy Tumwater Canyon, car windows have been smashed simply for climbing gear, so why give them a reason?

PENALTY FOR TRESPASSING ON PRIVATE LAND UP TO 90 DAYS IN JAIL AND $1,000 FINE

CHELAN CO. CODE 7.32.030
CRW 9A 52.080

Scary signs in the Icicle!

Cole Allen climbing at the now-off-limits Bolt Rock area in the early 2000's.

The brand-new informational kiosk in the Forestland parking lot.

TENAYA®

ethan pringle

Power Animal, V13

P: John Vallejo

ETHICS... A PLEA

Just as Leavenworth has been blessed with a relatively-stable access situation, it has remained largely free from the mistreatment and abuse that has plagued many other developing climbing areas around the county. However, the national recognition and attendant explosion in popularity Leavenworth has seen in recent years have put a significant amount of stress on the area, most notably at popular spots like Forestland and Mad Meadows. And while boulderers in the northwest generally follow sound ethical principles, the list of problems in Leavenworth that have been chipped or otherwise modified beyond normal wear-and-tear unfortunately continues to grow, including such problems as The Cotton Pony, The Lonely Fish, Resurrection Low, Caveman Cole, Immortal Techniques, and several others.

Observing the following recommendations is a good way to ensure that you're minimizing your impact as a boulderer and leaving the area the way you and others would want to find it. Be conscious of your actions, and demand the same of those around you. These boulders belong to all of us, and it is our privilege to visit them. Let's treat them well.

- Even though they relate largely to camping, familiarize yourself with the Seven Principles of Leave No Trace ethics and pay attention to how your bouldering practice measures up. The Seven Principles are: planning ahead and being prepared; traveling and camping on durable surfaces; disposing of waste properly; leaving what you find; minimizing campfire impacts; respecting wildlife, and being considerate of other visitors. Find more information at http://lnt.org.

- Stick to established trails, even if faint, and don't contribute to erosion by short-cutting switchbacks.

- Carry out ALL of your trash with you. Yes, that includes tape, cigarette butts, beer cans, chalk wrappers, pistachio shells - anything and everything (wtf is with the pistachio shells?!). Super-cool climbers keep an empty plastic bag in their pack and pick up trash even if it isn't theirs. It's an inexpensive way to feel good about yourself, and a very easy way to boost your good karma.

- If you feel the need to use tick marks, be discrete and please have the decency to brush them off before you leave. There's no better way to seem like a dumbass than to be seen flailing for the edge of a six-inch rookie-stripe you've ground into the face of a beautiful boulder. Be a better climber and use your eyes and brain – or stay in the gym.

- Don't camp or build campfires at *any* of the areas in this guide. This should go without saying, but in recent years, enough people have had the utter lack of judgment to build fires under boulders at high-traffic areas like Barney's Rubble, Lower Forestland, Mad Meadows, and Pimpsqueak that the obvious must be stated: fires are an extremely high-impact user activity that destroys an area's pristine feel, permanently damages stone, and endangers access for all climbers.

- Chipping, drilling, or gluing holds to the wall will not be tolerated. Reinforcing holds with glue definitely falls into this category. Broken holds, no matter how unfortunate, are part of the evolution of a climb. If a climb doesn't go, just climb on one of the thousands of other boulders around.

- The same ethic goes for cutting trees: just find another problem to climb. Playing lumberjack isn't a cardinal sin among the vast clear-cuts of the Washington's National Forests, but ugly stumps reflect poorly on climbers, and the tree in front of your proto-proj may already be useful for cleaning or descending from established problems.

- Blowtorches have become a trendy way for douchey gym climbers to appear gung-ho during a winter session, but the truth is they don't work very well and they absolutely do damage the stone. The Icicle is home to plenty of pink-hued, sandy boulders whose surface has been destroyed by the high heat of forest fires – think about it. If you've got to resort to pyrotechnics, stick to the slopers and please be gentle. For dry winter rock, why not just find a nice south-facing hillside like, say, almost all of the bouldering in Icicle Canyon?

- Last but not least, don't make poopy in the boulders. Take a walk at least 200 yards away from water and established trails and dig a minimum six-inch-deep hole (yes, six inches, and yes, *minimum*). Fill it in when you're done. Better yet, use one of the free, easy-access toilets at Eightmile and Bridge Creek Campgrounds in the Icicle, at Lower Forestland, or at The Beach and Swiftwater parking areas in the Tumwater.

Wandering around the quiet north side of Swiftwater one sunny afternoon, I was reflecting on this remarkable diversity in our array of bouldering spots... our 'bouldering gardens.' I'd always liked the way that phrase sounded, and the charmed quality it seemed to lay upon the stones. Absent-mindedly bending for a scrap of tape on the ground, I looked around at the worn dirt of the trail, the chalked handholds on the boulders beyond, and the piece of trash in my hand. Seeing evidence of our climbing everywhere, I came to realize a deeper meaning in the term. Just like gardens, bouldering areas are by no means examples of unchanging, frozen Nature, but are completely affected by human presence and human intention. From conscious actions like cleaning, climbing, and coating the stone in chalk to the inevitable effects of our pads, pets, and flip-flops, we determine every aspect of the appearance of our climbing areas. Even the lush vegetation surrounding me was only a result of logging and forest fires – more human impact. I was struck by the realization that to some degree, this is the one quality shared by every bouldering area in this guide. Each area is different, yes, but they have all been markedly saturated with the presence of boulderers.

As it relates to the 'ethics' of our bouldering, this is sort of a tricky realization. We are told to "leave no trace," yet it seems like traces are the least we can leave. Furthermore, looking around, all we can see are the traces of other climbers. But to write these areas off as lost, already 'unnatural' – the "it's screwed anyway" approach – is irresponsible and stupid. Precisely because these areas are so affected by us as boulderers, it's crucial for us to minimize our impact when visiting them. As conscious, intelligent beings, making good decisions about the nature of our impact is the very least we can do. These larger-than-life rock gardens literally become extensions of ourselves – why would we treat them as anything less?

PLEASE, PLEASE, PLEASE, *respect the local surroundings and the people around you. Locals generally like climbers and boulderers here, keep it going. You represent all climbers when you choose to be nice and mellow, or when you throw a screaming fit, burn this guide, smash your blaring boombox, and peel off for home leaving ugly tick marks behind, all because you can't send something. Remember how unimportant your problem is if it is environmentally unfriendly, pissing people off, or on someone's private land… enough soapbox!*

Brian Behle, *Leavenworth Bouldering*

"WHEN IN DOUBT, ERECT SCAFFOLDING."

-Warren Harding, *Downward Bound*

PROBLEM NAMES

When I wrote the *Central Washington Bouldering* guide, I was confronted with the awkward dilemma of cataloguing hundreds of undocumented problems while not wanting to publish a guide full of problems named, well, "unnamed." As a relative newcomer to Washington, I didn't want to overdraw my goodwill by unilaterally naming (or re-naming) half the problems in the area, but I also didn't want to reduce campfire banter to an uninspiring recitation of V grades for lack of proper nouns to identify climbs… Problem names can paint a boulder in shades epic, inspiring, intimidating, silly, or banal, and can imbue a boulder with the spirit of its founders, the story of its creation. There are hundreds of problems around the world that owe their legend not just to their beauty or difficulty, but also to their names and the stories and allusions they evoke; the metaphor and metonymy: Dreamtime, Power of Silence, Midnight Lightening, Stand and Deliver, Full Service (a.k.a. Serves you Right), Dark Horse, New Baseline, The Story of Two Worlds, Wheel of Life… the list goes on and on and on. Leavenworth has its own: The Sleeping Lady, Mad Max, The Pitless Avocado, Angelina Jolie, The Lonely Fish, Pimpsqueak, Jenny Craig, The Premonition, and more.

So back in 2006, I did my best to consult with first ascentionists when they were known, but many of the areas' problems were of such vintage or obscurity that it was impossible to find each and every route author. Eventually, I reached my own resolution of the problem by simply making up dozens of names in consultation with the locals I'd met and befriended. Some, like "*Tree Crack*," weren't very inspired, while others like "*Han Solo's Lightsaber Tournament*" and "*V13s Don't Have Kneebars*" involved a bit more of a creative process. I've received and noted corrections for a handful of these problems, but the vast majority have been slowly adopted by the community and are retained in this guide. Fortunately, I have not faced this dilemma with the myriad new areas included in this guide, as I've been lucky enough to either be present for their development or at least close enough with the developers that they were willing to share their secrets. But errors are unavoidable. If you feel you've established a problem incorrectly named/credited in this book, please drop me a line and let me know. A subsequent edition of this guide may include more accurate problem names. Please send an email to (*leavenworthbouldering@gmail.com*) or write to:

Kelly Sheridan
c/o Sharp End Publishing LLC
PO Box 1613
Boulder, CO 80306

PROBLEM GRADES

I don't care for grades. I believe V grades only create obstacles to the appreciation of a boulder problem's beauty, movement, and aura, and are the root of most of the problems in modern bouldering: competitiveness, negativity, chipping, and even littering and overcrowding; grades directly feed the ignorance and egotism that pose the primary threats to our beloved pursuit. John Sherman, the author of the Vermin grading scale, came to believe as much himself, describing V grades as a negative force he created but could not destroy in his classic essay "*To V or Not to V*":

> What started as a secret handshake in the cult of Hueco's hardcores turned into a monster. Every time I see a chiseled hold on a boulder, I know the demon has passed that way. The beast is a farce, possessing the trappings of bouldering, but none of the soul. Like Victor Frankenstein, I tried in vain to control and even to kill my unruly creation. Failing that, I disavowed it, and haven't rated a problem in years.

In a perfect world, I would have 'graded' the beautiful climbs in this book like ski trails: green circles, blue squares, and black and double-black diamonds. But grades have been popularized and integrated into mainstream bouldering, and it's readily apparent that any guide to utilize an easy/medium/hard grading scale would soon be superseded by a generic template-based Falcon guide that gave the *hoi polloi* the numerical satisfaction they supposedly demand. To this end, I've included a V-grade for almost every established problem in this guide. More than anything, I've strived to make the grades in this guide a consistent judge of difficulty within Leavenworth, but I've generally used Hueco Tanks, the birthplace of the Vermin grading scale, as a rough yardstick. A number of Leavenworth's grades have been modified since the publication of *Central Washington Bouldering*, hopefully with a general increase in both accuracy and precision. But I must beg a little understanding from each and every one of you: If a certain problem's grade doesn't seem quite right to you – please – don't sweat it. If it felt a little easy for the grade, pat yourself on the back. Great job! If it felt too tough, realize that it shouldn't detract from your experience or your self-worth as a climber. No biggie! Force yourself to imagine the area without any numbers – the goal is to have fun, right? Which climbs are the most inspiring? Which look like engaging challenges? The goal *is* to have fun, right???

Welcome to the smorgasboard that is bouldering. The boulderer picks a problem from the menu, tastes the moves, digests the sequence, then kicks back on the summit with a pleasant fullness. Shortly thereafter, out plops a V-grade, and not surprisingly, the bigger the grade, the more stink it causes. Strangely, at this buffet, most climbers act like flies, preferring to buzz around the grade, rather than the entrée.

— John Sherman, *"To V or Not to V"*

A big attraction of Leavenworth bouldering is the unexplored, adventurous side of the sport here. If you are willing to clean a little, there is a plethora of gems to be unearthed. Just don't be surprised if some old timer interrupts your spraying about your 'new route' to show you a picture of it being sent in EBs 20 years ago.

— Brian Behle, *Leavenworth Bouldering*

Suffice to say, this wouldn't be a very popular guide without John Sherman's Hueco Tanks grading scale. In fact, without it, the entire world of bouldering would be quite different these days. Many climbers began climbing with V-grades, have watched their progression through V-grades, and have come to take these 'objective' measurements very seriously. Unfortunately, bouldering is not an objective experience. It is a highly subjective, pointless, and fundamentally physical activity that continues to resist quantification. How can I help other climbers transcend the base pleasure of numbers and discover Gill's "kinesthetic soul of the art," while still providing the numbers we all love to bicker over? This is my dilemma.

— *Central Washington Bouldering*

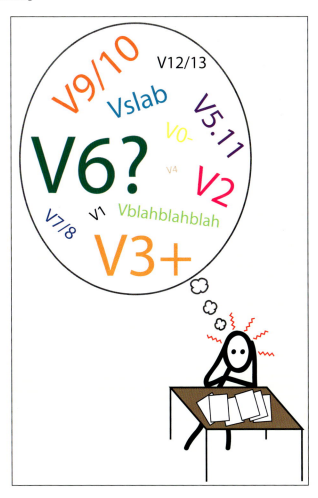

HOW TO USE THIS GUIDE

So you've got this book, you've traveled to Leavenworth, and you're psyched. But how do you get to the boulders?

For most areas covered in this guide, I've provided an overview map along with a verbal description of the approach. The maps are 'overviews' both in that they present a 'bird's eye view' of the area, and in the sense that they generally show other pertinent aspects of the area on the same map as the topos themselves. Parking areas are marked with mileage information, and approaches are noted in detail. Trees near boulders are precisely-placed, while those along trails or at the edges of areas are not. Long-distance photographs of an area or useful landmark are also sometimes included in the chapter introductions as a navigational aid. Be sure to check out both the map and the description before you start driving to an area. This guide also includes QR codes for each area covered, which should (hopefully) allow any user with a smartphone to access the Google map location for the area at issue.

Once you make it to the boulders themselves, you're in pretty good shape... Most areas include several topo photos of boulders with problem lines superimposed. A picture is worth a thousand words, yes, but many of the bouldering areas in this guide are constantly changing, especially in Leavenworth. Holds break, moss returns quickly, and seasonal change, fires, floods, and landslides all impact the landscape of Washington's bouldering areas. Some areas lack a map and/or topo photos, due to either a lack of necessity or a desire to keep them "off the beaten path" to some degree. So bring your sense of adventure, and don't be afraid to ask around if you get stumped trying to find a certain area or problem!

Johnny Goicoechea on a project at the Labyrinth area in Tumwater Canyon.

THE BEST OF LEAVENWORTH BOULDERING

V0

❐ The Rail (Barney's Rubble)
❐ Forget Your Rubbers (Straightaway Boulders)
❐ The Crack (The Sword)
❐ The Sloping Lady (Icicle Canyon)
❐ Brickwork (The Beach Forest)
❐ South Seas Arête (South Seas)

V1

❐ Fun House Stairway (V1+, Barney's Rubble)
❐ Shallow (Clamshell Cave)
❐ Breadline (Forestland)
❐ X1 (The Sword)
❐ Beach Slab (The Beach Beach)

V2

❐ The Sleeping Lady (Icicle Canyon)
❐ The Hesitator (Barney's Rubble)
❐ Sunny and Steep (Forestland)
❐ The Classic (The Sword)
❐ Beach Arête (The Beach Beach)
❐ Royal Flush (Swiftwater)

V3

❐ The Cube (Clamshell Cave)
❐ Yosemite Highball (JY Boulders)
❐ Pretty Girl (Icicle Canyon)
❐ The Sword (The Sword)
❐ U2 (The Beach Forest)

V4

❐ Fridge Center (The Fridge)
❐ Fridge Right (The Fridge)
❐ The Pocket (Made Meadows)
❐ Crimp, Crimp, Slap, Throw (Clamshell Cave)
❐ The Real Thing (Forestland)
❐ The Rib (Carnival Boulders)

V5

❐ Watercolors (Icicle Canyon)
❐ La Hacienda (Sleeping Lady)
❐ Alfalfa or Spanky (Barney's Rubble)
❐ The Ruminator (Upper Forestland)
❐ Shaniqua (420 Boulder)
❐ The Footless Traverse (Swiftwater)

V6

❐ Puxatawney Phil (The Airfield)
❐ Bootin' Dookie (Domestic Boulders)
❐ Taller (Straightaways)
❐ King Kong (JY Boulders)
❐ Reflection of Perfection (420 Boulders)
❐ Beckey's Problem (Labyrinth)

V7

❐ Premium Coffee (Swiftwater)
❐ Fridge Left (The Fridge)
❐ The Heartbreaker (Mad Meadows)
❐ The Shield (Forestland)
❐ The Hourglass (The Sword)
❐ Tin Man (Icicle Canyon)

V8

❐ Again the Grain (Bond Boulders)
❐ Pimpsqueak (V8/9, Mad Meadows)
❐ WAS (Straightaways)
❐ Ivy (Labyrinth)
❐ Geronimo (Mountain Home Road)
❐ Cattleguard Arête (The Pasture)
❐ The Coffee Cup (Forestland)

V9

❐ King Size (Tumwater Canyon)
❐ Kobra Kon (Forestland)
❐ Trickle of Silence (Forestland)
❐ Thunderdome (JY Boulders)
❐ Musashi (Egg Rock)
❐ Black Roses (Labyrinth)

V10

❐ The Peephole (Mad Meadows)
❐ The Shadow (Airfield)
❐ Cremation of Care (Forestland)
❐ The Cotton Pony (Straightaways)
❐ Nine Iron (Labyrinth)
❐ Swiftwater Cave Center (Swiftwater)

V11

❐ Cloaca (Mad Meadows)
❐ God is In the Details (Mad Meadows)
❐ The Practitioner (Forestland)
❐ Beautification (Straightaways)
❐ Thunderdome Low (JY Boulders)
❐ The Saber (Mountaineers Creek Road)

V12

❐ Turbulence (Straightaways)
❐ The Tornado Arête (Carnivals)

V13

❐ The Teacup (Forestland)

V14

❐ The Penrose Step (Straightaways)

"**WRITING ABOUT CLIMBING IS BORING. I WOULD RATHER GO CLIMBING.**" - Chuck Pratt

What are you planning on doing today?

Petzl / Photo: Kalice

PETZL® Access the inaccessible

ADAM HEALY

No matter what is going on in my life, whether it be joy or sadness, happiness or pain, I can always count on one constant: Leavenworth provides.

Some boulders exist with their stories and riddles laid out in chalked-up holds. Other boulders lay quiet and hidden, waiting for someone to stumble upon them and engage in a battle of will and skill. Memories stick with you forever, like epic sends on projects you have poured months or years into solving, or the simple things like a good beer or wine and conversation by the campfire with friends, howling at the moon, laughing and telling stories until the wee hours of the night. Leavenworth provides.

Lessons like patience are learned by getting shut down on projects yet staying positive, then unlocking that one key piece of beta to enable the send. Inspiration occurs when watching friends battle together on a sweet boulder problem, or when walking around a corner and getting stoked on the amazing climb staring you in the face. Leavenworth provides.

Sometimes it's the simple things like waking up to a gorgeous view of the Icicle Canyon, getting a fresh pastry at one of the local bakeries, or maybe feeling frisky enough to accept a La Hacienda challenge. I have had many amazing and incredible experiences in Leavenworth, and I know that many more are yet to come, because one thing never changes: Leavenworth provides!

[PHOTO] Max Hasson.

PART 1
ICICLE CANYON

Mountaineers Creek Road

Fourth of July Trailhead

Tin Man 9.3

Fuzz Wall 9.2

Egg Rock 9.0

The Sword 8.8

Machine Gun 8.7

Bridge Creek Free Site

Bridge Creek Cg.

Bridge Creek Free Site Boulders 0.4

8.5

Icicle Creek

Twisted Tree 8.2

420 Boulders 8.2

JCMB 7.5

Pretty Boulders 7.7

Carnival Boulders 7.4

Eightmile Cg.

The Washout 7.3

JY Boulders 7.1

Rat Creek Boulders

Bulge Boulders 6.8

Icicle Canyon Overview Map

N

1 Mile

Icicle Buttress Boulders 6.3

Icicle Butress

Straightaway Boulders 6.1

Hook Creek 6.0

The Lonely Fish 5.8

Domestic Boulders 5.7

Barney's Rubble 5.5

Forestland / Locksmith 5.7

Clamshell Cave / Mitchell Flats 5.2

Sleeping Lady 5.1

Mad Meadows / Airfield 5.1

Watercolors 4.8

The Moudra / Fern Gully 4.5

Snow Lakes Trailhead

Starfox 3.6

Icicle Creek

The Fridge 3.4

Bond Boulders

Wenatchee River

2

Sleeping Lady Resort

Icicle Road

0.0

E. Leavenworth Road

Leavenworth

ICICLE CREEK CANYON

Icicle Canyon is the true heart of Leavenworth bouldering. Beginning a few miles from town and stretching to the ten mile marker (and beyond!), the Icicle is lined with small roadside areas and larger hilltop clusters, each possessing a slightly different blend of granite. While more concentrated areas like Mad Meadows and Forestland have become extremely popular in recent years, the Icicle is rife with smaller spots where the boulderer can find solitude. Further up canyon, older areas like The Sword and Egg Rock are home to great medium-sized circuits as well as some difficult testpieces. Formerly-obscure areas like the Bond Boulders, the Domestic Boulders, the JY Boulders, and the Pretty Boulders are home to some new-school classics just waiting to be climbed on, as are recently-developed areas farther up the hill like Fern Gully, The Airfield, and The Locksmith – the further you hike, the more solitude you'll have. For folks willing to explore for new problems, the Icicle has the most potential of any area in this guide. The Icicle is a true boulderer's paradise, offering a lifetime's worth of climbing in a beautiful, accessible setting.

Icicle Road leaves Leavenworth from Icicle Junction, by the 76 gas station and the mini-golf course on the west side of town. All mileages for climbing areas are given from this intersection with Highway 2. The brown roadside mile markers in Icicle Canyon aren't 100% accurate, but can be helpful in getting your bearings. As you travel up most of the canyon, the road heads northwest; for the sake of simplicity in description, Icicle Creek is always south of the road, and points down canyon are always due west. The best way to find the bouldering areas in Icicle Canyon is to read the area directions and then use the mileage to locate some sort of landmark. Unfortunately, the best landmarks for some areas are adjacent areas; between-area mileages are provided for this purpose, though they won't be precise enough for the tough-to-find areas. With time, each spot will become obvious and you'll be able to impress your friends by rattling off area after area as you zoom down the canyon.

Icicle Canyon is the center of Leavenworth's vibrant outdoor recreation scene, and can feel downright crowded on summer weekends. Hikers, backpackers, kayakers, mountain bikers, trad climbers, bird watchers, campers, and others all use the Icicle for their outdoor pursuits. Midweek and during the winter, however, the canyon is much quieter, even to the point of seeming empty. The Icicle is also home to yuppie vacation homes, hippy-types dwelling in yurts, and the ubiquitous drunken bubbas. I've even met one young man who had made an extended trip to Icicle Canyon to prospect for gold. The ability to absorb so many different people and present such an isolated feel is part of what makes the Icicle so special. Please be respectful of others in the canyon, keeping in mind that you represent just one of a wide range of user groups.

ICICLE CANYON MILEAGE TABLE

ICICLE CANYON	Mileage from Highway 2	Mileage from Snow Creek Trailhead	Mileage from Previous Area
The Fridge	3.40	-0.90	3.40
The Bond Boulders	3.40	-0.90	
Upper Bond Boulders	3.40	-0.90	
Starfox	3.60	-0.70	0.20
Y.F.A.W.	4.30	0.00	0.70
Fern Gully	4.50	0.20	0.20
The Moudra	4.50	0.20	
Watercolors	4.80	0.50	0.30
Sleeping Lady	5.10	0.80	0.30
Mad Meadows	5.10	0.80	
The Airfield	5.10	0.80	
The Fist / Rob's Corral	5.20	0.90	0.10
Mitchell Flats	5.20	0.90	
Clamshell Cave	5.20	0.90	
The Zapper	5.30	1.00	0.10
Chiefed Joseph Boulder	5.50	1.30	0.20
Barney's Rubble	5.50	1.30	
Forestland	5.70	1.45	0.20
The Locksmith	5.70	1.45	
The Domestic Boulders	5.70	1.45	
Muscle Beach	5.70	1.45	
The Lonely Fish	5.80	1.55	0.10
Hook Creek Boulder	6.00	1.80	0.20
Straightaway Boulders	6.00	1.80	
Icicle Buttress Boulders	6.30	2.10	0.30
Bulge Boulders	6.80	2.60	0.50
Rat Creek Boulders	6.90	2.70	0.10
Blister Boulders	7.00	2.80	0.10
JY Boulders	7.10	2.90	0.10
The Washout	7.25	3.05	0.15
Carnival Boulders	7.40	3.20	0.15
Jess Campbell Memorial	7.50	3.30	0.10
Pretty Boulders	7.70	3.50	0.20
Orange Wall	8.00	3.80	0.30
Twisted Tree / AJ / Ice Cube	8.10	3.90	0.10
420 Boulders	8.10	3.90	0.00
Little Bridge Creek Wall	8.50	4.30	0.40
BCFS / BDE / Tiger Lily	8.50	4.30	
The Saber	8.50	4.30	

	Mileage from Highway 2	Mileage from Snow Creek Trailhead	Mileage from Previous Area
The Machine Gun	8.70	4.30	0.20
The Sword	8.80	4.60	0.10
Scat Boulders	8.80	4.60	
Egg Rock	9.00	4.85	0.20
Fuzz Wall	9.20	5.00	0.20
Tin Man	9.30	5.20	0.10
The Daydream	9.40	5.30	0.10
Mighty Mouse	10.50	6.40	1.10
Jack Creek	16.7	12.5	6.2

THE FRIDGE BOULDER

The Fridge Boulder is the closest Icicle Canyon bouldering spot to Leavenworth, and one of the most historic. Its proximity to town as well as to the road make it a popular evening spot for those looking to get in a quick session after work or a day of route climbing. The boulder is in a south-facing corner that receives some winter sun, but the shady side is where the goods are. *The Fridge Left* (V7), *Center* (V4), and *Right* (V4) lines are aged Leavenworth classics, must-ticks for any visiting boulderer. Access to the Fridge and its surrounding area was permanently secured in 2005 as part of the Sam Hill purchase by the Trust for Public Land and the Chelan-Douglas Land Trust, thanks largely to the efforts of local climbers and the Washington Climbers Coalition.

The Fridge is located 3.4 miles from Icicle Junction, and visible on the right side of the road. Park in the pullout on the left just before the boulder – it is the pullout directly after a left hand pullout with a gate marked "US Property - No Trespassing." Please cross the road carefully and help keep this popular, high-visibility spot clean.

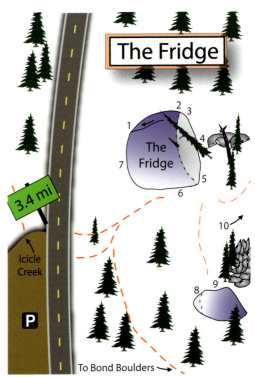

❒ 1. Cool Down V0- ★
Traverse up and left on the juggy rail and crack. This is the standard downclimb for the boulder.

❒ 2. Cellar Door V3 ★
Climb over the undercut seam on the right side of the corner.

❒ 3. Fridge Right V4 ★★★
Climb the slopey arête from a stand start. Make a tough barndoor move to a good hold on the corner, then finish up and left on greasy slopers. A great sandbag.

❒ 4. Fridge Center V4 ★★★
Start on crisp pinch/crimps in the center of the face. Maneuver to jugs on top of the huge block and top out.
Variation (V5): Begin as for Fridge Center and make an iron-cross move to the good corner hold on Fridge Right, finishing up that problem. Very reach-dependent.

❒ 5. Fridge Left V7 ★★★
Start with your left hand on the arête and a your right hand on a gaston edge on the face. Slap to a good sloper on the right face, then climb to a high left-hand crimp around the arête. Classic!

❒ 6. Fridge Door V2 ★
Start on the right side of the tall thin face, climbing straight up to grasp the left arête, finishing with an easier top-out. Great balance practice.
Variation (V1): To use the slabby footholds with a good 'railing,' begin on the left side of the face and follow the arête up and right to the top.

❒ 7. Fridge Slab V0 ★★
Climb the high slab on the roadside face of the boulder. Can you do it in sneakers? With no hands?

❒ 8. The Lizard V4
Start crouched with two low opposing edges. Paste your feet on, slap up to the crimp and top out straight up.

❒ 9. Jumping Spiders V4
Start on two opposing sidepulls in the middle of the face and lunge for the lip. It's closer than it looks.

❒ 10. Timeline V9 ★
Start on the left end of the tall face uphill from the fridge with a high left-hand sidepull. Climb up and right on poor edges over a sloping landing. Top out up crack. F.A. Kyle O'Meara

AREA

Cole Allen glides up the slopers of *Fridge Right* (V4).

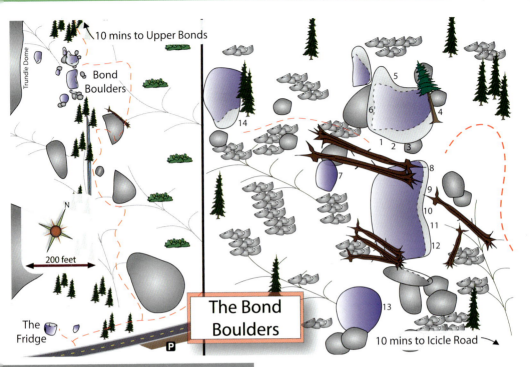

10 mins to Upper Bonds

Bond
Boulders

Trundle Dome

14

5

6

4

1 2 3

7

8

9

10

11

12

N

200 feet

13

The
Fridge

**The Bond
Boulders**

P

10 mins to Icicle Road

THE BOND BOULDERS

The Bond Boulders got their name capriciously, but it somehow stuck, and it fits. The area sports a high concentration of difficult climbs on salt-and-pepper granite rife with
angular features, clean swooped faces, and hard moves with
little hope of 'cheater' beta. If Pierce Brosnan were a rock,
he'd look a lot like the From Russia With Love face; if Sean
Connery were a boulderer in his youth, you'd have found
him projecting the clean, pure testpieces at this secluded
hillside area before reclining with a martini and a cigar.
The Bond Boulders are an awesome close-to-town 'secret,'
and are well worth the visit if the classic moderates on The
Fridge leave you wanting more.

*The Bond Boulders are 10 minutes above The Fridge, nestled
in a shady gully just below the popular Trundle Dome crag.
From The Fridge, follow the well-worn trail along the faint
ridge back towards Leavenworth for roughly one minute to
a fork in the trail just before a big low-angle slab. Take the
left fork, following the trail uphill through a series of switchbacks on the right side of a small creek, eventually climbing
the right side of the gully and passing a few smallish erratics
before crossing back left toward the boulders.*

❒ 1. **Goldfinger V7** ★★
Climb the blunt arête from a stand start matched on a sloper
left of the arête. Climb straight up using heel hooks and the
"Goldfinger" hold, a small two-finger right-hand sidepull.

❒ 2. **License to Kill V6** ★
Stack pads or jump to a high flat crimp
and climb straight up the vertical face.

❒ 3. **Sean Connery V6** ★★
Climb the faint dihedral feature from
a high start off the adjacent boulder
with a good right-hand gaston. Make a
few tenuous moves with poor feet to a
sketchy mantle.

AREA

❒ 4. **Moonraker V7** ★
Start standing just right of the tree with a sharp left-hand
sidepull and a right-hand squeezing the arête. Slap up to the
overhanging lip and top out straight up.

❒ 5. **Shaken, Not Stirred V4/5** ★★

Start matched on the chest-high
shelf. Heel hook and slap up the
overhanging prow feature to an
easy top-out on the left. Awesome!

❒ 6. **Project**
Climb the cramped roof from underclings in the flared crack. May
be too cramped to ever go…

❒ 7. **Underground Lair V2**
Climb the good right-leaning rail.

❒ 8. **From Russia With
Love V9** ★★
Start on the right side of the wide, scooped overhang.
Climb up and left on crisp edges to slopers at the lip and an
awkward mantle. Starting with a right-foot heel or toe hook is
helpful, but adds a bit of reachiness. F.A. Kyle O'Meara.

❒ 9. **Oddjob V11ish** ★★
Start standing above the large log with two left-facing sidepulls. Dyno to the lip. Powerful! F.A. Johnny Goicoechea.

❒ 10. **Pierce Brosnan V9** ★★★
Start in the obvious flared dihedral with a flat left-hand
crimp and a tiny right-hand sidepull. Dance up the overhanging scoop to a tensiony slap for the lip, then move left to a
jug in the seam and an easy mantle. Fantastic. F.A. Johnny
Goicoechea.

❒ 11. **Roger Moore V5** ★
Start a few feet left of Pierce Brosnan with a good incut pod in
the horizontal seam. Climb straight up to an easy top-out.

□ 12. Jaws V6 ★★
Climb the curved arête from a head-high scoop using heel hooks and a poor crimp on the face.

□ 13. Pussy Galore V3 ★
Two boulders over from the From Russia With Love face, climb this arête from a stand start with slopers on the left. Move right to an incut ear hold, then top out straight up.

□ 14. The Bulldozer Dyno V6 ★★
Roughly 25 yards above the From Russia With Love boulder, start with a good triangular pinch on the right (downhill) side of the overhang and dyno to a good sloper at the lip. F.A. Kyle O'Meara.
Variation (V7): Start on good crimps in the overhang and move directly right to the pinch on the arête without dabbing.

□ 1. Project
Climb the curved, slightly overhanging face.

Drew Schick on an early ascent of *Sean Connery* (V6).

THE UPPER BOND BOULDERS

The Upper Bond Boulders are perched on a plateau several hundred yards above the Bond Boulders. Though the Upper Bonds have not yet been fully developed, they are already home to Johnny Goicoechea's highball masterpiece *Against the Grain* (V8) and the crisp, uncompromising blade of Drew Schick's *Bury the Hatchet* (V10), both of which are well worth the grueling approach. With panoramic views of the Lower Icicle, the Bond Boulders get abundant sun and are one of the first areas to thaw in the early spring.

The Upper Bond Boulders are at the top of the steep, rocky slope directly above the Bond Boulders. Follow the Recital Wall trail past Shaken, Not Stirred through a wooded patch to the base of the hillside. Hike along the left side of the steep, rocky face, staying just right of the overgrown gully. Roughly 50 yards uphill, follow a right-trending ramp to a series of switchbacks up a steep and exposed game trail, more or less following the USFS national forest boundary marked by small yellow and black signs. Top out onto the Upper Bond plateau roughly 10 minutes above the Lower Bonds.

□ 2. Unknown V?
A climb may have been done up the center of the crumbly quartz face.

□ 3. Unknown V2 ★
Climb the right arête of the whitish face on chunky sidepulls. Most will drop from the lip; the top-out is not for the faint of heart, and is the only way down from the top of the boulder without a rope!

AGAINST THE GRAIN

□ 4. Against the Grain V8 ★★★
Climb the center of the tall face from an obvious right-facing sidepull in the crack and a tiny left-hand crimp. Cryptic moves on holds that all seem to face the wrong direction lead to a scary mantle way off the deck. This climb alone is well worth the hike! F.A. Johnny Goicoechea.

□ 5. Unknown V4 ★
Climb the high arête from a stand start with a flat right-hand edge and a sharp left-hand sidepull.

□ 6. Unknown V7 ★
Start sitting under the bulge just right of the huge Ponderosa Pine with two low sidepulls. Climb through small incut edges to a delicate top-out on slopers. Climbs better than it looks.

□ 7. Unknown V1
Start on the low, diagonal crack ledge and climb the short face under the huge log. Top out awkwardly between the branches.

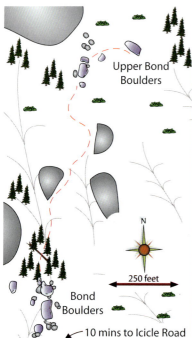

Upper Bond Boulders

Bond Boulders

250 feet

← 10 mins to Icicle Road

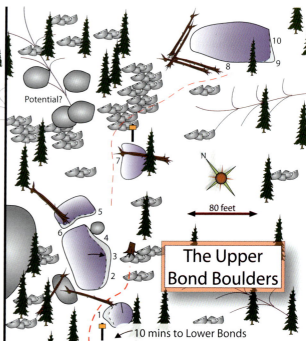

Potential?

80 feet

The Upper Bond Boulders

10 mins to Lower Bonds →

❏ 8. Unknown V2 ★
Climb the center of the face from a very high crimp. You may need to stack pads…

❏ 9. Bury the Hatchet V10 ★★★
Climb the steep arête on the boulder's downhill face from a stand start with a high right-hand sloper and a high right foot. Hard!

❏ 10. Unknown V0 ★
Climb the right side of the black slab using the arête.

BURY THE HATCHET

Johnny Goicoechea bearing down on the second ascent of *Bury the Hatchet* (V10).

STARFOX

Starfox sits all by itself in the talus just up canyon from Mountaineer's Dome, a popular beginner/class crag. Starfox is a beautiful overhanging dihedral with crisp flat edges… but unfortunately the crux is sneaking around the edge of an adjacent boulder without dabbing.

Park for Starfox in the Mountaineer's Dome pullout on the left 0.2 miles past the Fridge, 3.6 miles from Icicle Junction. Starfox is 60 yards uphill on the back side of an obvious triangular, slabby boulder with a dead log perched on top.

1. Starfox V6 ★

Get in the hole and start on a flat crimp rail on the left side of the dihedral. Climb back and forth between positive crimps until you latch a beefy left-hand sidepull. Keeping your rump off of the rock behind you, climb up to the jug, dyno for the lip, and top out.

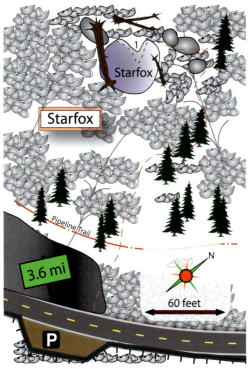

YOUR FRIENDS ARE WATCHING

Your Friends Are Watching is another stand-alone climb a little ways up the hill in the lower Icicle.

Park for YFAW on the left side of the road 4.3 miles from Icicle Junction. It is the first pullout after the Snow Creek trailhead, and is a popular spot with Enchantments hikers who don't want to shell out the cash for a USFS Northwest Forest Pass. The trail to YFAW starts roughly 20 yards further up canyon. Follow the rough trail up a steep talus slide on the left side of the large buttress. YFAW is on a stout boulder 100 yards uphill in an alcove just behind a huge tree. The Fern Gully boulders are in a hidden valley directly above this hillside perch.

1. Your Friends Are Watching V6 ★

Start sitting on the left side of the flat platform with a good edge. Climb the overhanging face on nice crimps to a jug at the lip.

2. Nobody's Watching V5

Climb the narrow overhanging face from a chest-high jug. May need a little cleaning…

THE GOVERNMENT BOULDERS

The illicit "Government Boulders" are just below the pullout for Your Friends are Watching. These boulders are unfortunately off-limits due to their being on Icicle Irrigation District Property—they can't have people running amok around the intake for the irrigation canal. Included here for historical purposes only, the Government Boulders are home to *The Pumphouse* (V2), a classic old-school problem that dates to the 1970s, as well as newer poaches like *Filibusted* (V8) and *Where the Swamp Donkey Lies* (V9).

The Government Boulders are located just downhill from the row of small white signs reading "No Trespassing, Icicle Irrigation Div." Sadly, vehicles parked at this pullout do attract attention, and Sheriff's deputies have been spotted peering down the hill looking for trespassers. Try pleading ignorance on that one…

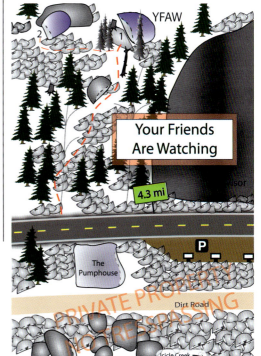

FERN GULLY

Fern Gully sits atop the cliff formation across the street from the Snow Creek Parking lot, home to Tom Moulin's over-the-road masterpiece *The Visor* (5.13+). The area was first "discovered" by Kyle O'Meara in 2005, but did not see development until the summer of 2013. The area is home to a small array of nice moderates as well as Drew Schick's unique instant classics *Chubby Fairy* (V4) and *Indigenous* (V9). The approach to Fern Gully is short and steep, and is much more pleasant on a cool, shady day than in the heat of the summer sun.

The approach to Fern Gully begins roughly 0.2 miles past the Snow Creek lot, beginning from the same parking area as the Moudra boulder. Park in the large pullout with a bulletin board on the left side of Icicle Road 4.5 miles from Icicle Junction. From the east end of the parking lot, walk across the road and up a short, steep trail towards the Moudra, but break right and cut across a short, steep wash about half-way to the cluster of boulders. Walk roughly 30 yards down canyon until the hillside opens up and a short, light green telephone marker is visible downhill at the edge of the road. Follow the faint climbers' trail straight uphill for roughly 200 yards, following the left edge of the hillside, until a forested plateau becomes visible roughly 100 yards to your right. Follow the ever-fainter trail right and slightly uphill to the secluded valley that is home to the Fern Gully boulders.

1. Unknown V0
Climb the chunky seam, topping out up and left.

2. Wood Nymph V3
Climb the short bulge from a stand start with edges at the juncture of two seams to the left of the arête.

3. Unknown V1
Climb the tall dirty face.

4. Chubby Fairy V4 ★★
Start matched on a juggy horn in the center of the roof and climb big moves up and left to an involved top-out.
Variation (V6): Start on crimps up and right from the start of Chubby Fairy and traverse left into the top-out.

5. The Choir Boys Project
Not remotely like Choir Boys…

6. Indigenous V9 ★★★
Start standing under the suspended boulder with your left hand on an undercling and your right on a small edge on the lip. Swing your right foot to a high hold in the face, then bump and compress your hands to the lip. Finish up and right with meatwraps along the top of the sloped ridge.
F.A. Drew Schick.

7. Mini Mountain V0
Start with the obvious calcium jug and climb straight up.

AREA

LEFT Andrew Philbin navigates the technical compression moves of *Indigenous* (V9).
BELOW Drew Schick eyes the top of the *Hexxus* project.

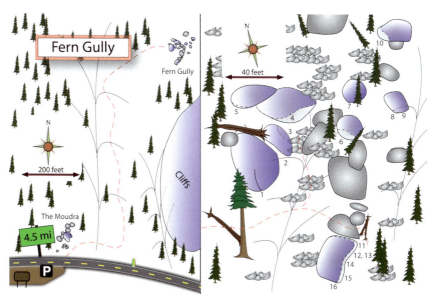

Fern Gully

Fern Gully

40 feet

N

Cliffs

200 feet

N

The Moudra

4.5 mi

P

5
4
3
6
2
1
7
8 9
10
11
12, 13
14
15
16

❒ 8. Unknown V0 ★
Climb nice features up the shallow groove.

❒ 9. Unknown VB
Climb the featured, dirty slab.

❒ 10. Project

❒ 11. Unknown V2 ★
Climb the short arête from a stand start with sidepulls.

❒ 12. Do You Believe in Fairies? V1 ★
Climb the shallow scoop using incut sidepulls and a neat triangular dish foothold.

❒ 13. Fairy Slipper V4 ★
Start with a high left-hand sidepull to the left of DYBIF, climbing up and right on opposing sidepulls to top out above the scoop.

❒ 14. Hexxus Project
Start with your right hand on the high start crimp of Fairy Slipper. Climb up and left to the sloping orange sidepull, then finish up and right on poor crimps.
Variation (V5): Start as for Hexxus and climb directly left from the orange sidepull into the finish of Mount Warning.

❒ 15. Mount Warning V3 ★★
Climb the left side of the tall face from a high right-hand sidepull.

❒ 16. Batty Koda V6 ★★
Start sitting matched on the low flake on the left arête of the boulder. Make a few full-span moves to gain opposing sidepulls above the bulge, then climb up and right, finishing on the same holds as Mount Warning. The stand start with opposing sidepulls is roughly V4.

LEFT Dmitry Kalashnikov getting athletic on *The Moudra* (V4).
RIGHT Johnny Goicoechea on the first (known) boulder ascent of
Watercolors (V5).

THE MOUDRA

The Moudra is a small roadside area developed in 2012 by
Cole Allen. Though it sports only two problems as of this
writing, they are worth the short walk. The Moudra also
marks the beginning of the steep hike to the Fern Gully
area.

The Moudra is directly across from the large pullout with a
bulletin board on the left, 4.5 miles from Icicle Junction and
0.2 miles from the Snow Creek trailhead. From the east
end of the parking lot, walk across the road and up a short,
steep trail to the obvious cluster. The Moudra is on the
uphill side of the large boulder.

❏ 1. **Ain't Nothin' but a Hueco Thing V6**
Start on low right-facing sidepulls and crimp up and left across
the short, steep face. Top out up and left in an awkward
corner.

❏ 2. **The Moudra V4** ★★
Start squeezing the overhanging arête feature. Slap up the
right-hand rail and reach to high pinches on the arête. Follow
the jug rail all the way right to top out in the corner next to
the suspended boulder.

❏ 3. **Project**
Start on low incut crimps and climb straight up the extremely
thin face.

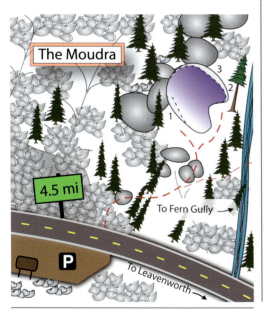

WATERCOLORS

Watercolors is the Sleeping Lady's intimidating older sister, a
hidden, gorgeous highball that is both very obscure and very
close to the road. Just a few hundred yards below the Mad
Meadows pullout, Watercolors sits in a tall, slightly overhanging scoop that is not visible from the road but literally
tops out over the Icicle. Though this climb has been scouted
by boulderers for many years, the first known unroped
ascent occurred in the summer of 2014, with the FA of *The
Impressionist* (V9) following a few weeks later. Needless to
say, this is a low-water boulder!

Park for Watercolors in large left-hand pullout 4.8 miles
from Icicle Junction, roughly 0.3 miles before the Mad
Meadows pullout. The pullout is marked by a pair of west-
facing signs reading "Rough Road Next 1/2 Miles," roughly
150 yards upstream of the obvious cable suspended across
the creek. The short, steep, and loose hike down begins just
down canyon from a small group of trees clustered around
the signs, then traverses directly upstream at the bottom of
the hill. Please take care when descending the hill, and be
aware of your impact, both physical and on the experience
of others in the canyon, if you're considering doing any
trailer-hitch rappelling…

❏ 1. **Watercolors V5** ★★★
Start standing in the center of the streaked scoop with a
slopey left-hand pinch and a small right-hand gaston. Paste
your left foot on a small, ill-placed edge and stab to a good
crimp above. Finish along the seams up and left, making a dis-
concerting move sideways – and away from dry land – to the
prominent basketball-sloper-jug before hitting the lip above.
Truly classic, and committing! Starting one move in is roughly
V3 and is equally good.

❏ 2. **The Impressionist V9** ★★★
Climb the amazingly sculpted slashes up the right side of the
face, trending awkwardly over the adjacent boulder as you get
higher. F.A. Drew Schick

MOUDRA

WATERCOLORS

Joel Campbell earns a top dinner on the first ascent of La
Hacienda (V5). [Photo] Max Hasson.

THE SLEEPING LADY / LA HACIENDA

The Sleeping Lady is quite possibly the best climb in the Universe, a gorgeous line of river-polished jugs overhanging the turbulent rapids of Icicle Creek. Like the placid resort a few miles closer to town, *the Sleeping Lady* gets its name from a vague resemblance in the ridgeline of Wedge Mountain at the southern mouth of Icicle Canyon. *La Hacienda* (V5) and its burly neighbor *Wildfire* (V12) are relatively recent additions that are well worth the dodgy river crossing required to access them. The woods above *La Hacienda* are also home to a small cluster of boulders below the Dog Dome crag (not included on map) that are worthy of a visit when they can be reached: these are seasonal areas. *The Sleeping Lady* is inaccessible during the greater part of each spring, and during high flooding years can be almost 100% submerged. La Hacienda, as well as the boulders below Dog Dome, are only accessible during the warmest part of the summer when the water is low enough to allow passage across the Icicle. Regardless of the season, this scenic hang is a great first stop in Little Bavaria, and a good way to orient yourself to Icicle Canyon.

The Sleeping Lady is nestled beside the pullout for the Mad Meadows area, 5.1 miles from Icicle Junction. Park on the left side of the road roughly 20 yards before a brown wooden sign containing USFS fire information for Icicle Canyon (this sign contains various messages during the summer months, but is typically blank during the winter). A short trail leads down to the Sleeping Lady from the east end of the pullout. To reach La Hacienda and the boulders below Dog Dome, walk a bit further up canyon and look for the easiest way to hop across.

SLEEPING LADY   LA HACIENDA   DOG DOME

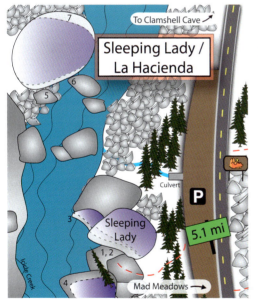

"A rare view of a wonderful climb." Adam Healy climbs the *Sleeping Lady* (V2). **[Photo]** Max Hasson

⌐ 1. The Sleeping Lady V2 ★★★
Climb down to the little platform at the edge of the stream, grab the head-high polished shelf, and make increasingly larger moves up the overhanging blocks. After a committing lunge to a rounded horn, climb right to jugs, then top out slightly left. A fall from anywhere on this climb could potentially be fatal.

⌐ 2. Sound Asleep V2 ★
Start as for The Sleeping Lady, but traverse right at the second flat shelf instead of lunging straight up. Move right to a thin flake in the scrunched corner and finish with a nice mantle. A good alternative for the faint of heart.

⌐ 3. Sleeping Lady Extension V3 ★
Scramble down the upstream side of the Sleeping Lady to access the start of this problem. Begin with a good left-hand sidepull on the corner overhanging the stream and climb around the lip to the start of The Sleeping Lady. Finish as for the Sleeping Lady, or for full pump value, continue right to Sound Alseep. A late summer problem, and another good one not to fall off.

⌐ 4. The Pee Problem V2
Carefully traverse left from the middle of the descent to the Sleeping Lady to a small platform. Climb straight up the sloping shelves to a slightly insecure top-out. What's that smell?

⌐ 5. Born Sinner V6 ★★
Start standing with an undercling in the sloping shelf on the left side of the large slab. Climb over the bulge and top out straight up the slab above.

⌐ 6. La Hacienda V5 ★★★
Step off the adjacent boulder onto the lowest part of the tall slab. Climb up and left into the shallow groove. One who successfully completes a "La Hacienda challenge" gets a free dinner at the eponymous Mexican restaurant in Gold Bar... Don't fall!

⌐ 7. Wildfire V12 ★★
Start sitting under the overhang on the upstream side of the La Hacienda boulder with opposing sidepulls. Climb up to a huge move for a tiny crimp, then top out up and right. F.A. Johnny Goicoechea.

DOG DOME BOULDERS
There are a number of fun problems in the woods above La Hacienda. One of the closest boulders offers a fun V3 that uses a cool beer-can-sized pinch to climb its overhanging downhill face. Further uphill, there is a nice wide overhang facing the river that sports three tough crimp problems; the line that starts in the center with a double-undercling and goes up and left is *Traumatized* (V9). Ask around for beta, or just explore—all of the established problems below Dog Dome are within three minutes of La Hacienda.

It's a bird, it's a plane . . . No, it's Drew Schick on *Superman* (V9).
[PHOTO] Max Hasson

MAD MEADOWS

Mad Meadows is one of Leavenworth's premier bouldering areas, a series of stepped plateaus that are home to bunches of classic moderates as well as some of the area's best hard problems. Lower Mad Meadows is home to a concentration of old-school hard problems like *The Sail* (V9), *The Peephole* (V10), *Cloaca* (V11), and *The Ram* (V11/12), all within a roughly 10-yard radius of each other. Further uphill lies a cluster of classic moderates including creatively-named classics like *The Pocket* (V4), *The Rail* (V3), *The Undercling* (V4), and *The Hole* (V5), as well as the Hanta Man roof, which climbs like it was imported straight from Hueco Tanks. A few minutes further down canyon, the majestic *Pimpsqueak* (V8/9) stands alone, one of the proudest and most sought-after hard climbs in the Icicle. Mad Meadows offers something for everyone. Mad Meadows gets all-day sun in the summer, and snakes are commonly observed on the approach and in the upper boulders below the Playground Point crag.

Finding Mad Meadows is easy. Park on the left side of the road 5.1 miles from Icicle Junction, just before the brown USFS fire information sign that also marks the parking for The Sleeping Lady. Start up the steep hill across from the parking, following well-worn switchbacks for roughly 50 yards to the level ground above. Follow the trail directly right (toward Leavenworth) through an open 'meadow,' crossing a seasonally-swampy area before eventually emerging onto an open, gentle hillside. The Lower and Upper areas are visible straight ahead, stretching up the shallow gully to Hanta Man. It's about a five minute walk to the Lower area, and about 10-12 minutes total to Pimpsqueak.

The Airfield

Playground Point Crags

N

100 yards

Upper Mad Meadows

Pimpsqueak

Lower Mad Meadows

5.1 mi

Mad Meadows Overview

AREA

← Sleeping Lady

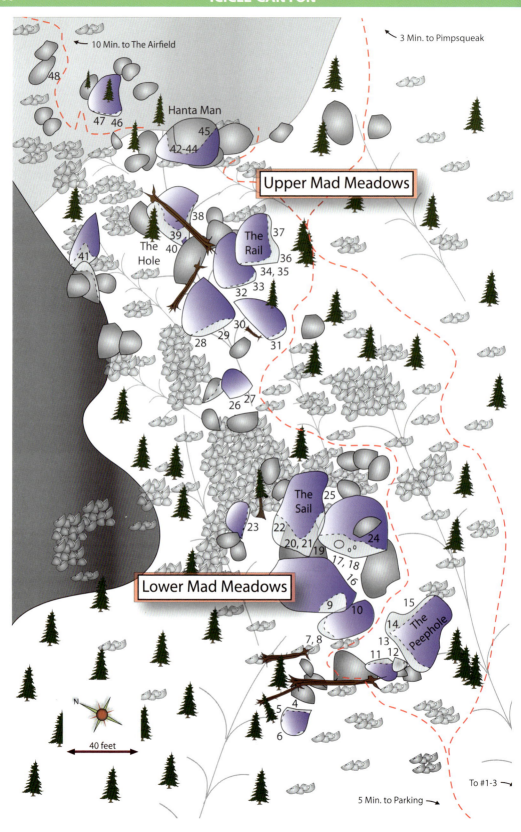

10 Min. to The Airfield

3 Min. to Pimpsqueak

48

47 46

Hanta Man

45

42-44

Upper Mad Meadows

38

39

40

The Hole

The Rail

37

36

34, 35

41

33

32

30

28 29

31

26 27

The Sail

25

23

22

24

20, 21

19

17, 18

16

Lower Mad Meadows

9

10

15

14

The Peephole

13

11 12

7, 8

N

4

5

6

40 feet

To #1-3

5 Min. to Parking

Andrew Deliduka projecting Heartbreaker Low (V9) before Jeff Parmenter eked out the first ascent in the spring of 2014. **[PHOTO]** Hayley Zanol

❐ 1. The Great Pierogi 5.11 ★

The Great Pierogi boulder is visible downhill from the trail one or two minutes before you reach the Lower Mad Meadows area. The left-trending, sandy crack of The Great Pierogi was listed in an earlier version of Viktor Kramer's route guidebook as a 5.11 toprope; it's unclear whether it has been bouldered. Definitely does not see much traffic…

Variation (Project?): Sit start as for The Heartbreaker and climb into The Great Pierogi.

❐ 2. The Heartbreaker V7 ★★★

Start standing with your left hand in the right side of the obvious slot and your right on a sidepull. Make a big move to the mailbox slot up and right, then climb to the cool meatwrap on the lip and make a tough – heartbreakingly tough – mantle. An awesome addition to the area that was amazingly first climbed in 2014! F.A. Jeff Parmenter.

Variation: *Ladykiller* (V8): Start in the slot and climb straight up the arête to a very high finish pinching the narrow arête. Bring some pads! F.A. Drew Schick.

❐ 3. The Heartbreaker Low V9 ★★

Start sitting with a flat right-hand sidepull and a sharp crimp around the left side of the arête and climb into the start of The Heartbreaker.

Variation (V9): Start as for Heartbreaker Low and finish as for Ladykiller.

❐ 4. Pocket Rocket V3 ★

Climb the short overhang from a sit start on the slab with low crimpers. Cool holds!

❐ 5. Hairy Spotter V5

With the torched tree at your back, climb up and right on sloping edges in the faint seam.

❐ 6. Squarepusher V3

Climb the short, blocky arête on the downhill side of the boulder, finishing straight over the grainy lip after a cruxy lunge.

❐ 7. Flounder V2 ★

Start sitting on the right side of the blunt overhang, climbing straight up on slopers to a thrutchy finish onto the slab above.

❐ 8. Swordfish V4 ★★

Start sitting on slopers as for Flounder and climb up and left on fun grips to a lefthand crimp around the corner. Stick the lip and finish on the left side of the arête.

❐ 9. Project

The cramped roof behind Swordfish. Someone may have climbed this?

❐ 10. Alpine Feel V0 ★

Climb the stepped slab on the left as you scramble into the Peephole corridor. Several variations can be done to make this a nice warm-up.

❐ 11. The Lamb V3

Start sitting, matched on the low flat hold in this little overhang, climbing a few stout moves up both arêtes to finish straight up. Can you do it in sneakers?

❐ 12. Drugstore Cowboy V3 ★★

Start sitting with two shallow pockets just right of the wild bulge of the Peephole. Climb up and right with a big foot ledge to rough jugs in the crack, finishing steep pumpy jugs between the boulders. The stand start is a great problem on its own, and can be made more difficult by eliminating the boulder on the right.

❐ 13. Future Trippin' V12 ★★

See description on next page.

❐ 14. The Peephole V10 ★★★

Start matched on the 'peephole' jug under the teardrop overhang, climbing up and out on pinches to match the big undercling in the steepest part of the roof. Steep, technical climbing leads up and right through tricky crimps to a final dyno to the lip. One of the best problems in Leavenworth, this problem has seen a surprising lack of interest in recent years. F.A. Cole Allen—back in the day!

Kelly Sheridan squeezing hard on The Peephole (V10). **[PHOTO]** Max Hasson

🗖 15. Occum's Razor V5 ★
Start matched on quartzy sloping crimps in the shallow corner left of the Peephole, climbing a few tenuous moves to an easier finish straight up. Slippery, and harder than it looks.

🗖 16. V0 ★
From the inside of the Hueco Route room, climb the left-trending crack to top out as for #10.

🗖 17. The Hueco Route V1 ★★
Start sitting on the left end of the steep swiss-cheese wall in the sheltered room. Climb up and right on juggy huecos to two pockets roughly halfway up the face. Drop off from here, or kick your feet onto the boulder behind you, finishing 'Fred Nicole style' on the other rock. Stays dry all winter.

🗖 18. Cloaca V11 ★★★
Start as for The Hueco Route, but from the final two pockets, make difficult moves straight up to gain the lip. Morpho, and probably not possible for climbers under 5'6" or so. One of Leavenworth's most striking lines, this climb was a project in *Central Washington Bouldering*. F.A. Johnny Goicoechea.

Johnny Goicoechea campusing the first move of *The Ram* (V11/12). **[PHOTO]** Brian Sweeney

Kyle O'Meara on an early ascent of *Cloaca* (V11). **[PHOTO]** Max Hasson

🗖 19. Barnacles V1 ★★
On the left side of the second 'room,' climb incut ripples up the vertical wall behind the Sail. Stemming off of the other boulder is poor style, but many will welcome its help during the tricky mantle.

🗖 20. The Sail V9 ★★★
This super-steep, super-cool line climbs directly out the steep bulge of this suspended boulder. Pull on with a decent left-hand pinch and a poor right sloper, slapping twice to a formerly-square-cut, now rounded, edge on the right side of the bulge. Grab the incut slot in the face, and climb straight to jugs on the arête to finish. F.A. Johnny Goicoechea in the late 1990s.

🗖 21. The Ram V11/12 ★★★
Start underneath the bulge, climbing The Sail to the right-hand edge before making a wide slap to an incut crimp on the blank left face of the boulder. Squeeze and slap to bring your right hand onto the left face and finish up the sloping edges above. Or, skip all that work and simply campus straight to the left crimp from the start like Johnny G! This problem is gener-

ally climbed to the lip as a drop-off, F.A. Cole Allen, but was first topped out by Kyle O'Meara.
Variation (V6): Climb The Ram using the boulder below for your feet. Seriously!

🗖 22. The Jib V8
Start with a sharp right-facing crimp on the left side of the steep face, pull on, and stab to the hidden jug up and left. Finish up and right as for The Ram. F.A. Johnny Goicoechea.

🗖 23. Unknown V6 ★
Find this short, square boulder just past The Jib. Climb the face from gastons in a seam on the right, moving to small crimps and an easier top-out.
Variation (V7?): Start on crimps in the center of the face and finish as above.

🗖 24. Flex the Matrix V5
This neat flake of granite sits on top of the Hueco Route boulder. Start sitting with two tiny crimps and chuck to the flat shelf above. Take care not to fall off the landing!

🗖 25. The Rudder V1 ★
Climb the face and left arête on the uphill side of the Sail boulder. Might need some cleaning.

🗖 26. Wooly Mammoth V0
Climb the left arête of the first boulder reached walking up from the lower cluster, making use of the seam as you go.

🗖 27. The Dish V1 ★
Climb the center of the short face on neat sloping huecos.

🗖 28. Dr. Doom V2
Around the left side of the tall pocketed face, climb the crack from a grove of bushes to a high, easy finish.

🗖 29. The Pocket V4 ★★★
Climb the center of the tall face on bubbly huecos and pockets to a high, crimpy finish at the boulder's apex. Very good.

🗖 30. Madvillian V2 ★
Climb the right arête, using holds on the face when necessary. Finish just right of the nose on jugs.

❑ 31. Heir Apparent V0
Traverse up and right with big ledges on the trailside lip.

❑ 32. Bushmen V3 ★
The short overgrown face around the corner from The Rail. On the left side of the overhang, grab a small crimp, step on, and dyno for the lip. Tree dab.

❑ 33. Pruning Shears V1
Climb the right arête of the overgrown face from a good incut at head height.

❑ 34. The Crack V2 ★★
From the blocky ledge in the little alcove, climb up and slightly left to the incut crack. Finish straight up with a strenuous mantle to the right of the tiny corner. Great fun.

❑ 35. The Crimp V5 ★
Starting on the blocky ledge as for #34, grab the crimp on the face and make a big move right to the arête. Finish straight up with big moves on the juggy corner. The Crimp has long since broken off, making this one solid for the grade.

❑ 36. The Rail V3 ★★★
Start sitting with two low opposing sidepulls and a good heel hook on the corner. Cross back to 'the rail,' a good pinch on the arête, match, and finish straight up the arête with a fun rock-over. Good, safe fun.

❑ 37. The Scoop V2 ★★
Start sitting in the left side of the obvious polished scoop right of The Rail. Climb up and right in the cool seam to an incut crimp and good holds over the lip. Funky.
Variation (V4): Start as for The Scoop, but climb slightly left and over the lip on little crimpers.

❑ 38. The Undercling V4 ★★★
Starting with a big, smooth hueco in the narrow alcove, climb to a flat undercling blade to reach the top of the slightly overhanging face. Finish up the left side of the slab over the sketchy landing. Awesome!

❑ 39. The Hole V6 ★★★
Start sitting in the hole under the overhanging face, matched in a huge undercling in the hueco. Climb straight out the short, steep overhang with some foot trickery, finishing up the easy slab above. This climb can be super-technical or super-burly, but never easy.
Variation (V6): Continue left along the lip to top out as for the The Flake.

❑ 40. The Flake V5/6 ★★
Start standing at the base of the adjacent boulder with a good left-hand sidepull rail and a tiny right-hand gaston flake. Toe hook in the start of The Hole, slap to the lip, and top out up and right with a few great moves up the prow. Great fun, with the poor landing being the only detractor.
Variation (Project): Sit start as for The Hole and climb directly into the start of The Flake.

❑ 41. Foot Fumpkin V4 ★★
Roughly 30 yards up and left from The Hole, this problem climbs out a hidden cave on the right side of the jumbled alcove under the obvious suspended block. Start with tufa huecos in the deepest part of the cave and climb out to a cramped top-out. Amazingly, this hidden gem was just discovered in 2013 by Leavenworth locals Andrew Deliduka and Shaun Johnson.

HANTA MAN
The next several problems are on a small plateau just above the main Upper Mad Meadows zone. The Hanta Man cave is on the back side of the large, rounded boulder roughly 50 yards above The Undercling.

❑ 42. No Pain No Grain V5 ★
This near-horizontal crack climb starts with two hand jams in the deepest part of the roof, climbing straight out to the lip on painful locks in the low fissure. F.A. Jens Holsten.

❑ 43. Hanta Man V7 ★★
Starting matched in the crack in the deepest part of the cave, climb through a right-hand undercling to a good crimp near the lip of the cave, finishing right and up via the two grainy cracks. Fun and technical, this would be a much better climb if not for the small boulder in the cave.

❑ 44. God is in the Details V11/12 ★★★
Start as for Hanta Man, but once you have gained the incut crimp, grab a small undercling with your right hand and make a heinous couple of moves left into the start of Superman. This is a long-time fantasy line that was finally realized by Dave Thompson.

HANTA MAN

45. Superman V9 ★★★
Start crouched on the left side of the cave with a small, incut left-hand crimp and an obvious right-hand sloper. Muscle your feet onto the wall, slap to the lip, and make easier but strenuous moves up and right to top out up the right side of the arête. There may be a knee bar somewhere on this climb…

46. Spongebob Squarepad V3 ★★★
Climb the square arête just above the Hanta Man cave from a stand start, slapping and hugging your way to an easier finish. Super fun. Can be made more difficult by eliminating holds on the left face.
Variation (V6): Start sitting.

47. The Octopus V3 ★
Starting in the sweet hueco pockets on the face left of Spongebob Squarepad, climb straight up to the juggy crack and top out.

48. Unknown V3
Climb the right side of the tall, grainy face. Does not see many ascents.

PIMPSQUEAK AREA
To find Pimpsqueak, continue traversing down canyon from The Rail boulder, maintaining roughly the same elevation as you pass a small balanced boulder. After a minute or two, the mini-crag on the backside of the Amphitheater will be visible on the right. Follow the trail up and left over the small ridge, then dip into the shallow drainage. This portion of Mad Madows can be a bit confusing, but just keep walking back toward town—you'll know Pimpsqueak when you see it.

1. The Amphitheater V3 ★★
Start on the two chest-high pods on the right side of this secluded scooped face. Climb to a teensy crimp, then bust to the flat ledge above and mantle. Dynoing directly from the pockets adds a grade or two.
Variation (V0): Start on the chest-high pods, but move right to the crack and follow it to the top.

2. Crank V1 ★
Climb the crack on the left side of the scooped face to a juggy top-out. More strenuous than one might expect.

3. Winterbottom Arête V3 ★
Climb the short arête left of Crank from a sit-start, slapping up slopers and face edges to a mellow finish.

4. The Kiddie Pool V1 ★★
Just down from the Ampitheater, you'll find another scooped face sporting this fun traverse. Start on the right end of the sloping ledge, traversing left on good holds next to the tree. Drop from here or mantle out of the 'pool' onto the dirty, low-angle face above.

5. 30 Seconds V4
That's about as long as this one will entertain most people… Start sitting in the middle of the low face with your right hand on a sidepull crimp in the incipient crack. Pull on over low smears and fire for the ledge, finishing up the dirty slab above.

6. Unknown V0
The tallish face on the downhill side of the Amphitheater boulder has a couple of easy topropes that can be bouldered.

7. Tweedle Dee V0
On the small 'corridor' boulder between the Amphitheater and Pimpsqueak, climb to the lip from a head-high jug and top out.

8. Tweedle Dum V0
The rightmost crack on the boulder. Start on scooped sidepulls down and left in the discontinuous crack, moving right to layback up the short flake.

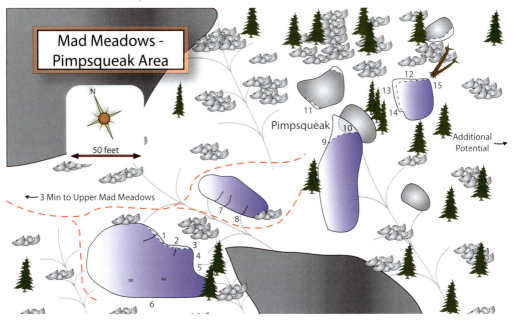

Mad Meadows - Pimpsqueak Area

N

50 feet

3 Min to Upper Mad Meadows

Pimpsqueak

Additional Potential

9. Pimpsqueak V8/9 ★★★

One of the coolest features around.
Start up the clean right arête to a jug
at the edge of the cave, then head
straight out the horizontal prow,
squeezing between the slopey lip
and better holds under the roof. This
problem has become much more
difficult since the departure of the thank-
God jug on Greg Collum's '*Pipsqueak*,'
though it is still one of the best lines in Leavenworth. **NOTE:**
Please do not build fires or camp underneath the Pimpsqueak
boulder, as it has a big impact on the area and has been
noticed by the Forest Service—you are not in the "middle of
nowhere!"

PIMPSQUEAK

10. Crimpsqueak V8 ★★

Start in the deepest part of the cave with sloping hueco features in the roof. Using strange heel hooks and slopers, climb
to the lip opposite Pimpqueak and a good crimp on the face.
Chuck to a good left-facing sidepull and top out.

11. Unknown V2

Start sitting under the tiny roof, mantle, and rock over the lip.
Silly but fun.

12. Dog Log V2 ★

Climb the scooped face on friable edges from a high right-
leaning crimp rail. A one-move exercise in pain tolerance; at
least it's a cool move.

13. Size Wise V4

Start crouched on the right side of the short, steep arête
spread wide between the toothy left arête and a low right
undercling. Slap to a jug on the corner and finish straight up.
Morpho.

14. V13s Don't Have Kneebars V1 ★

Start standing with a low left-hand undercling and a right
hand on the edge of the sharp right-facing corner. Work
around the small bomb-bay corner with (optional) weird kneebars to mantle straight over the bulge.
Variation (V2): Start sitting on the right arête.

15. The Firefly V1 ★

Climb the short arête on the back of the smallish boulder.

Jessica Campbell pimping the toe hook
on *Pimpsqueak* (V8/9).
[PHOTO] Matthew Hall

Unnamed, mixed media. Jessica Campbell (2014).

Kelly Sheridan on *The Airfield Arête* (V7).
[PHOTO] Max Hasson.

THE AIRFIELD

First developed in the spring of 2011, the Airfield is a concentrated cluster of boulders high above Mad Meadows. The Airfield pairs its airy views with a nice circuit of moderates on a diverse variety of stone, including *The Airfield Arête* (V7), *Tombstone* (V4), *Agape* (V3), and *Punxsutawney Phil* (V6). The Airfield is also home to Johnny Goicoechea's testpiece *The Shadow* (V10), a striking and powerful dyno problem on impeccable salt-and-pepper granite that is one of the best new additions to the Icicle in recent years. The Airfield offers sweeping views of the lower Icicle and is one of the first areas to thaw in the early spring.

The Airfield is above Mad Meadows. Park as for Mad Meadows (previous chapter) and hike to the Hanta Man / Superman cave. Follow the trail straight uphill past the Spongebob Squarepad boulder and to the right along the edge of the cliffband. After a minute or two, take a sharp left switchback near a short overhang and follow the trail up and left below the second set of slabby cliffs that comprise the Playground Point crag. Pass a steep bottleneck after roughly three 'sections' of cliff, then cut sharply to the right around the back of the fourth and final section. Follow the trail up through shallow valleys, reaching The Snail area roughly five minutes after the last switchback. The Airfield is few minutes further at the head of the valley, nestled below a large white dome with prominent rock scars. Dip through a small thicket just before reaching the Airfield Arête boulder. The hike should take no more than 15 or 20 minutes from Upper Mad Meadows.

THE SNAIL

The Snail is a short, round boulder nestled against the right side of the valley roughly five minutes below the Airfield proper. The problems described here are listed from left to right when viewed from the trail.

❑ 1. **Umbilicus V2**
Start on the "V" in the center of the face on the Snail boulder. Climb up and right on slopers.

❑ 2. **The Snail V3** ★
Start matched on a low crimp rail below the arête. Move right to a blocky rail and top out straight up the arête on flat edges.

❑ 3. **Table Top Pop V5** ★
Climb the short cliffband to the right of the Snail from crimps under a rounded head-high shelf. Move to slopers on the lip and top out straight up. Better than it looks.

❑ 4. **Black Peter V4** ★★
Climb the right side of the smallish cliffband in front of a broken tree. Start on head-high sidepulls, power up to a unique sidepull pocket, then top out straight up on small edges. Good.

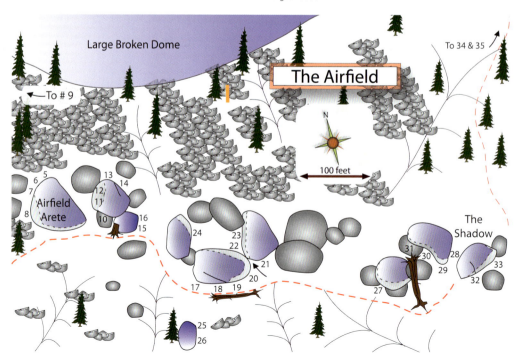

Large Broken Dome

The Airfield

To 34 & 35

To # 9

N

100 feet

Airfield Arete

The Shadow

❐ 5. The Tray Table V1
Climb the left arête from a crouch start on a good ledge.

❐ 6. Landing Gear V2 ★
Start with a head-high sloper and an incut crimp and climb straight up. The crouch start with a left-hand crimp and a right-hand sloper adds some fun.

❐ 7. Prepare Cabin for Arrival V0 ★
Climb the center of the face from head-high ledges with a boulder at your back. Top out to the right on questionable rock. The sit start adds one very hard move.

❐ 8. The Airfield Arete V7 ★★★
The prominent curved right arête of the first boulder at the Airfield. Start squeezing the sloping arête with a left-hand crimp on the face. Climb straight up the arête using heel hooks and small crimps on the face. Mantle slightly left of the arête. F.A. Drew Schick.

❐ 9. Drew's Folly V3 ★
Climb a tall, downhill-facing, vertical face in the talus over a jumbled landing (just outside of map area).

❐ 10. Unknown V3
Climb the tallish face over an uneven landing.

❐ 11. Project
Start crouched in the cave with a good left-hand sidepull and a right-hand sloper with a triangular thumb catch. Climb up and right through the bottlecap hold to top out as for #10.

❐ 12. The Mole V5 ★★
Start as for #11 but climb left and top out through the tunnel. Move left along the edge of the boulder to a tough match on poor sidepulls, then top out straight up near the left arête. Pretty good for a hole-climb!

❐ 13. Unknown V1
Climb the slab from a stand start with the left hand on a diagonal seam and right on the arête.

❐ 14. Unknown V1
Climb the tall cracks over the poor stepped landing. The low start in the pit is a project.

❐ 15. The Croissant V1 ★★
Climb the tallish arête from a crouch start with opposing incut jugs. Very good.

❐ 16. Turnover V4 ★
Start with chest-high jugs on the face, move right to a sidepull in the vertical seam, then perch and use small crimps to reach the horizontal slot below the lip.

❐ 17. Unknown V1 ★
Climb the left side of the orange face from a high start with a flake crimp.

❐ 18. Orange Face V2 ★
Climb the tallish orange face using crimps in the left-trending crack.

❐ 19. Unknown V7 ★
Start in undercling pods in low bomb-bay corner. Muscle to a sloper on the lip, then top out up and right with poor slopers on orange rock.

❐ 20. Moth Music V6 ★
Start crouched with a low edge and either dyno up and right to a big ledge or climb straight up on techy pinches.

❐ 21. Unknown VB
Climb the featured slab to the right of the entrance to the cave.

❐ 22. Tombstone V4 ★★
Enter the cave through a narrow corridor. This problem climbs the steepest wall of the cave from a good triangular ledge near the entrance. Climb up and right to a good jug at the six-foot level, then make a big move to a left-hand crimp below the lip and top out.

❐ 23. Unknown V2
Climb the short face from a sit start.

❐ 24. Agape V3 ★★
Climb the tall overhanging prow from a crouch start with a gaston meatwrap in the left side of the cave. Very good.

CROISSANT

LEFT Joel Campbell sticks the crux crimp on *Tombstone* (V4).
RIGHT TOP Close Encounters of the Granite Kind: Joel Campbell on the steep roof of *The UFO* (V8).
RIGHT BOTTOM The *"Drive On Project."*

LOWER AIRFIELD

LANDING GEAR

The next two problems are on a tall squarish boulder thirty yards downhill from the Orange Face boulder (not quite to scale on the map).

❑ 25. **Landing Gear V2** ★
Climb the right arête.

❑ 26. **Project**
Climb the tall face.

❑ 27. **Unknown V5** ★
Start next to the adjacent boulder with a high crimp. Campus to slopers, then make a tough press move onto the face.

❑ 28. **Six More Weeks V1** ★
Climb the tall face on incut rails.

❑ 29. **Punxsutawney Phil V6** ★★★
Climb the steep arête from a stand start with a tiny left-hand flake and a right-hand undercling around the corner. Slap left to a sloper rail then compress to the top. Excellent. F.A. Drew Schick.

❑ 30. **The Shadow V10** ★★★
Start crouched with bad slopers on a faint shelf in the overhang. Dyno up and right to the sloping shelf and match, then throw a heel up and make powerful moves up and right on edges to top out. F.A. Johnny Goicoechea.

❑ 31. **Early Spring V5** ★
Start sitting on the boulder above The Shadow with a good incut jug. Climb up and left on crimps.

❑ 32. **M.I.G. 9 V2**
Climb the left side of the short face from a stand start with sidepulls in the dirty crack.

❑ 33. **The Dogfighter V4** ★
Start with arms spread between a high right crimp and a low left undercling. Dyno to the axe-head hold on the lip and top out straight up.

THE UFO

The UFO is five minutes uphill from the Smoke boulder. Hike straight up the hillside until it begins to flatten, then trend slightly left toward a large, undercut boulder with a sloped landing.

❑ 34. **The UFO V8** ★★
Start crouched with opposing slopers at the edge of the orange-tinted roof. Slap to a good edge around the lip, then climb right along the edge of the roof to a tall top-out. F.A. Joel Campbell.

❑ 35. **Project**
The *"Drive On Project."* The landing of this climb will probably need some work...

U.F.O.

THE FIST / ROB'S CORRAL

The Fist is a rounded, fist-shaped boulder that nearly overhangs the road just past the pullout for The Sleeping Lady and Mad Meadows. The Fist and the boulder in the neighboring mini-cluster of Rob's Corral offer a small circuit of easy to moderate climbs, as well as the absolutely heinous one-move-wonder *More Cushin' for Your Tushin'* (V12). The trail to Clamshell Cave passes directly through The Fist / Rob's Corral area.

The Fist can't be missed. Drive 0.1 miles past the brown USFS fire information sign that marks the pullout for Mad Meadows and The Sleeping Lady and park on the left, 5.2 miles from Icicle Junction, directly across from the obvious fist-shaped boulder next to the road. About as short an approach as you could ask for!

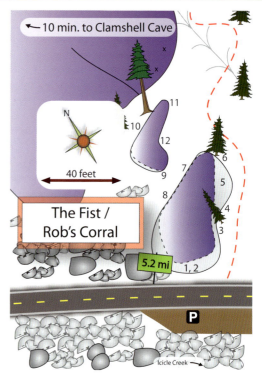

☐ **1. The Fist 5.10(?)**
Start standing on the jumble of boulders under the overhang with a high right hand jam in the crack. Climb straight out and over the bugle, finishing with big sandy ledges on the left face. Committing, dirty, and rarely done; the grade for this one is likely a guess that has been passed down through generations…

☐ **2. Project**
Start matched in the seam where you begin The Fist, but climb directly right on horizontal cracks up the steep face. Finish straight over the lip with the left arête.

☐ **3. Unknown V3**
Start on a high crumbly edge left of the tree and mantle using a sharp foot pocket.

☐ **4. More Pushin' V3**
Start matched on small edges on the lip four feet right of the tree. Traverse right along the lip until you can reach the higher lip and rock over.

☐ **5. More Cushion for Your Tushin' V12 ★**
Start matched on the axe-head undercling flake in the steepest part of the roof. Paste your feet on nothing and dyno to the lip. Starting with toe hooks on the arête is "cheating." This problem became significantly more difficult in 2007 when a tiny, but crucial, foothold broke. F.A. Cole Allen (V10 pre-break), Joel Campbel (post-break).

☐ **6. Less Cushion V2**
Start matched on the thin lip by the tree. Climb left around the corner and mantle.

☐ **7. Unknown VB**
Several variations climb the low-angle slab.

☐ **8. Unknown V5 ★**
Traverse up and right along the straight lip, topping out straight up the corner. Technical.

☐ **9. Unknown V1**
Start matched on the grainy lip and traverse up and right. Top out at the first opportunity.

☐ **10. Unknown V0**
Traverse up and left along the low-angle lip.

☐ **11. Unknown V3 ★**
Climb the tall arête on the right side of the face. Usually pretty dirty.

☐ **12. Unknown V0**
Start in the left-trending seam, get your feet up, and make your way to the lip.

Joel Campbell on the project on the Fist boulder.

AREA

SEATTLE BOULDERING PROJECT

MITCHELL FLATS

Mitchell Flats is a small area nestled on a hidden plateau between Clamshell Cave and Mad Meadows. Mitchell Flats, A.K.A. Central Park, is named for Leavenworth local Scott Mitchell, who discovered the area in 2007. Mitchell Flats offers a number of fun moderates in a quiet, secluded setting where you're more likely to see a deer, coyote, or bear than another boulderer. There is potential for new problems on the plateau above Mitchell Flats and, as always, above that...

To find Mitchell Flats, park in the same pullout as for Clamshell Cave, across from the obvious Fist Boulder on the right 5.2 miles from Icicle Junction (0.9 miles past the Snow Creek Parking lot; 0.1 miles past the Mad Meadows pullout). Follow the well-worn Clamshell Cave trail past the Fist and left, trending uphill. When the trail dips into a small drainage and crosses a small creek, stay on the east side of the creek and follow faint switchbacks straight up the gentle incline. Continue straight uphill, passing a first plateau marked by two large trees, to a second plateau marked by a big, flat slab and two round boulders. Walk directly east along the second plateau for roughly 100 yards to a small cluster of tall boulders below a scruffy cliffband.

⌐ 1. **Kelp V1**
Start matched on the flat rail, move to the lip and top out.

⌐ 2. **The Squid V2**
Start on the flat calcium-coated hold and climb up and left to the lip. Top out either left or continue along the lip to the top.

⌐ 3. **The Whale V3 ★**
Start on a sloping rail above the awkward boulder. Climb up and left through cool rails and edges. Recently broken, may be somewhat harder.

AREA

4. The Crab V3 ★
Start as for #3 but move right through sloping edges to a neat right-hand fin-crimp and cross to a jug straight above.

5. Brine V2
Climb the right arête. Top out to the left on jugs.

6. Cole's Crack V5 ★★
Climb the slanting crack from a crouch start with your right hand in the crack and your left on a thin crimp. Follow crack straight up and right. The detached ledge is on for your feet. Much better than it looks! F.A. Cole Allen.

7. Whip It Good V4-6 ★
Several height-dependent variations can be climbed on edges on the right side of the tall face.

8. Mr. DNA V3 ★★
Start on edges just right of the obvious knob, climbing through underclings with heuco feet to a big move for a sloping seam. Top out straight up.

9. Mr. Kamikaze V2 ★★
Climb the tall corner feature from two slopers in the left-facing seam. Awesome!

10. Strange Pursuit V4
There is a small, slabby boulder on the left a few minutes before Mitchell Flats proper that has a short bulge/face problem on its rear side.

LEFT Cortney Cusack stretches out on *Kelp* (V1).
BELOW Jens Holsten grapples with *The Crab* (V3).
[PHOTO] Max Hasson.

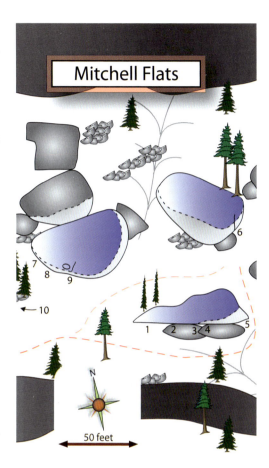

Mitchell Flats

50 feet

CLAMSHELL CAVE

Clamshell Cave is a small, popular crag on the hillside above Icicle Creek that is also home to modest collection of quality boulder problems. Older highball classics on The Cube, a large square-cut boulder at the base of the cliff, are supplemented by several cool 'new-school' problems such as *Crimp, Crimp, Slap, Throw* (V4), and *The Octopus* (V7) and the truly new-school problems #16-18. Clamshell Cave itself is a sheltered room created by a giant hueco in the undercut bottom of the cliff. Sadly, the rock quality in this neat hangout isn't quite what it could be. Marking the beginning of Clamshell's uphill trudge is The Fist and the neighboring Rob's Corral, home to a couple of interesting problems of their own. The boulders at Clamshell get a good amount of sun but can be comfortable even in summer heat with a nice breeze… Don't expect too much solitude in return for your legwork, however, as Clamshell Cave is quite popular with novice craggers.

The hike to Clamshell Cave begins 100 yards past the brown fire information sign that marks the approach to Mad Meadows, 5.25 miles from Icicle Junction. Park across from The Fist, a large fist-shaped boulder that nearly overhangs the road, and Rob's Corral, a tiny cluster of boulders and short cliffs just above it (see previous chapter). Follow the well-worn trail left and up a short hill, directly left through a flat meadow, then across a small stream and up a series of steep, dusty switchbacks. The trail drops you on a gently-sloped plateau just below the crag after about 10 minutes of hiking.

Alternatively, Clamshell Cave can be reached from Upper Forestland. From the Ruminator boulder, follow a faint trail east and slightly uphill for roughly 75 yards, then drop into a small gully and traverse straight across the hillside for another 75 yards. The trail ends at a dense cluster of trees next to Crimp, Crimp, Slap, Throw.

"Pirate Max Hasson poised to attack *The Octopus* (V7)."

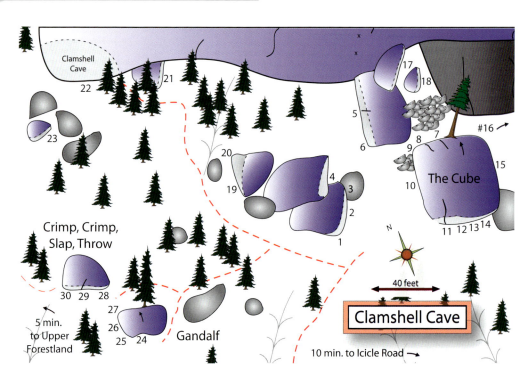

CLAMSHELL CAVE

□ 1. The Octopus V7 ★★
This dynamic problem climbs the right arête of the first boulder at Clamshell. Pull on using a good pinch/crimp on the arête and a small lefthand sidepull on the face. Slap to the grainy sloper and finish up the corner. Stiff for the grade.
Variation (V3): Start with your right hand on the arête and jump to the sloper.

□ 2. Pentaphobia V5 ★
Climb the scooped vertical face on tiny edges. May feel a bit tough 'till you warm up to it…

□ 3. Cornucopia V2 ★
Start on a jug at head-height in the cramped corner and climb the blunt arête on slopers.

□ 4. Slice of Tea V3 ★★
Start in the hole between the boulders behind Cornucopia. Climb the left-leaning flake to a cruxy move for the lip. Best not to fall off this one!

□ 5. Playback V1 ★★★
A strenuous layback up the obvious right-facing flake in the middle of the overhanging face. Finish straight up with a committing mantle onto the slab. Really good.

□ 6. Terminal Traverse V2
Start on the downhill side of the overhanging face, traversing left on slopers on the lip to mantle as for Playback.

□ 7. The Segment V0 ★
Climb the short hand crack just right of the tree. A great climb for beginners or kids.

□ 8. Tron V0
Climb the intermittent crack a few feet right of The Segment.

□ 9. Rubick's Arête V0 ★
Climb the north arête of The Cube on big, loose holds to good incut crimps. Quite easy but a tad exposed.

□ 10. The Cube V3 ★★★
Climb delicate face moves up left-facing flakes in the middle of the tall face. A cryptic section on sharp incuts leads to better holds and a high finish. Classic! A true sandbag.

□ 11. Cube Crack 5.7 ★★
Climb the obvious hand/fist crack.
Variation (V2): Start sitting in the small hole under the start of the crack. "Be a boulderer."

□ 12. Shallow V1 ★★★
Climb the tall face right of the crack on big holds, moving left to good holds, then back right on small sidepulls. Finish straight up.
Variation (V2): Crouch start with a sidepull jug on the low lip.

□ 13. Cube Traverse V1
Starting with underclings in a whitish scoop on the right side of the face, traverse left along the undercut fact to finish up Cube Crack.

□ 14. Under the Bleachers V5 ★★
Climb the right arête of the tall face from an undercling at waist height. The small boulder to the right is a bit awkward, but the moves are great. Top out straight up the arête.

□ 15. Unknown V5 ★
Climb the tall vertical face over a terrible landing from a low start on the left of the face with a tree at your back. Will likely need cleaning…

□ 16. Unknown V6 ★
25 yards east of the crack boulder, climb the short, steep prow from a low sloper on the right arête. Grade unconfirmed.

AREA

□ 17. Thimbleberry V7 ★
Climb up the rocky gully above the Cube boulder (on the back of Playback) to a small cluster of trees roughly halfway up the cliff. This climb ascends the right side of the tall, flat face to the left of the trees. Start in a small alcove with a tiny triangular left-hand hold and a low, sloping right-hand sidepull. Follow the tiny crimps up and right to an obvious flat edge, then top out by rocking over the right side of the lip.

□ 18. Unknown V4 ★
Climb the east side of the round boulder behind #17 from a flat crimp edge at waist height with an obvious calcium deposit in the middle of the face. Use tiny crimps to gain the juggy calcium seam above, then top out straight over the boulder's apex.

□ 19. Scram V2 ★★
Traverse up and left on the grainy lip, finishing with a fun mantle on the left side of the point.

□ 20. Unknown V0
Climb the short arête on the left side of the Scram boulder from a stand start.

□ 21. Project
This project is set into the cliff along the faint trail to the actual Clamshell Cave. Dyno / run and jump to a jug at the top of the face. Would make a good American Ninja Warrior obstacle…

□ 22. Project
Start on the right side of the cave and traverse along the steeply overhung lip (V4/5 on its own) to a stopper move for an obvious finish hold a few feet up the face.

□ 23. Bowl Weevil V3
Start with two head-high gastons in the tiny overhang. Slap to the lip and mantle… More fun than it looks.

24. Gandalf V2 ★★
Climb the left arête of the tall scooped slab. Exit left to better holds at the notch in the arête, or continue to the top up the dirty slab if you're "feeling saucy."

25. Greed V2
SDS on the foothold of #26, climbing up and right on edges to finish up the right arête.

26. Elfen Magic V1 ★
Start in the middle of the slab with a good edge foothold, climbing straight up to finish up the tall slab on sloping holds.

27. The Hobbit V2 ★
Climb the short corner from a sit-start. Look around for the good holds! Descend next to the tree.

28. The Goods V3 ★
From high edges on the right end of the lip, traverse left on slopers, eventually mantling on good holds near the left arête.

29. Cleaver Crack V1 ★
Climb the obvious hand crack in the middle of the face, jamming, laybacking, or pinching the side like a true boulderer…

30. Crimp, Crimp, Slap, Throw V4 ★★★
Can I get some beta here??? Climb the left arête of the modest boulder from a stand start with two small crimps, gaining the jug on the lip with a fun toss. Awesome!

31. Terminal Gravity V10 ★★
This hidden gem sits about 5 minutes up and left from Clamshell Cave in the drainage down and right from The Locksmith. Climb the short, steep overhanging prow from a sit start. F.A. Cole Allen.

Andy Knepshield tops out *Cube Crack* ("5.7")
[PHOTO] Aaron Matheson.

THE ZAPPER

The Zapper is a small roadside cluster just past the Fist boulder and the start of the trail to Clamshell Cave. Though many climbers have checked out this cluster in years past, the first known problems established at the Zapper area were put up by Chumstick local Joe Treftz in 2013.

The Zapper is roughly 50 yards after the obvious Fist boulder. Park at the far end of the big pullout 5.3 miles from Icicle Junction and follow a faint trail uphill to the short overhanging face of the left side of the dark, short crag set into the hillside.

❒ 1. **Road Warrior V1** ★

Climb the perched boulder with prominent calcium streaks next to The Zapper. Start on the right side of the face and climb straight up to a second ledge and easy top-out. Exposed! Grade unconfirmed.

❒ 2. **The Zapper V5/6** ★

Start on the right end of the fractured white face with a small left-hand crimp and your right hand on a blocky jug. Move up to the horizontal crack, then traverse left with poor feet to top out in the dirty crack around the corner. Morpho.

❒ 3. **Project**

Start as for The Zapper but transfer to the undercut face above and climb straight up. Will need some serious cleaning.

AREA

The Zapper from Icicle Road.

CHIEFED JOSEPH

The Chiefed Joseph boulder sits on the south side of Icicle Creek, directly across from Barney's Rubble and the Forestland parking area. Though a number of boulderers had been lured across the river to check out this overhanging prow over the years, it was first climbed in 2012 by Leavenworth local Joe Treftz and has only seen a few repeats. This mini-area is difficult to access, but should be at the top of your list when Icicle Creek is low.

The Chiefed Joseph boulder is best accessed by crossing Icicle Creek near the Sleeping Lady / La Hacienda area at low water, then traversing west along the roughly 0.5 miles of open hillside. Icicle Creek is occasionally low enough to cross directly below Barney's Rubble, but only very rarely. Accessing the Chiefed Joseph boulder from the Hook Creek Bridge to the west requires crossing private property and is not recommended. No map is provided for this area, but use the topo photo to identify the boulder before hiking, and the GPS coordinates to navigate to it once you're across the creek.

Drew Schick contemplating how high he can go on *Silhouette Arête* (V6). Icicle Road is visible in the background.
[PHOTO] Max Hasson.

❒ 1. Unknown V3/4 ★★
There is a moderate face climb roughly 25 yards downhill and west of Chiefed Joseph that is difficult to see from the north side of the road.

❒ 2. Chiefed Joseph V4 ★
Climb the center of the downhill face of the Chiefed Joseph boulder.

❒ 3. Silhouette Arête V6 ★★★
Climb the obvious overhanging arête on the boulder's west corner from a high right-hand sidepull.

AREA

❒ 4. V0 ★
Climb the slab on the back of the boulder.

Chiefed Joseph

Chiefed Joseph
as viewed from the Barney's Rubbble parking

No. 1

⌐ 23. **Mad Bush V12** ★★★

Start crouched on the obvious jug rail on the right side of the face and climb through poor sloping pods and tiny crimps to an obvious right-hand sidepull rail. Top out with finesse… F.A. Jimmy Webb.

Variation: *Firebelly* (V7): The stand start from the right-hand sidepull rail was done in 2007 by Kyle O'Meara.

⌐ 24. **V5**

From the Barney's Rubble parking area, hike downhill and left toward this obvious large boulder some 40 yards from Bruce's Boulder. Climb the right side of the undercut arête from a stand start. The sit start, if there is one, is a project…

⌐ 25. **Alfalfa or Spanky? V5**

★★★

Climb the dihedral in the middle of the tall downstream face. Special beta can transform this problem from something frustrating into something fun…

⌐ 26. **Musk V9** ★★

Start on high sloping crimps at the bottom of the slight scoop on the right end of the face. Climb either up and left using delicate footwork, or dyno up and right to a sloping crimp. Guile-dependent. F.A. Joel Campbell.

⌐ 27. **Lowpers V3**

Start crouched in the small overhang with two flat opposing rails. Slap to the lip and finish up and left.

⌐ 28. **Therête V0**

Climb the uphill arête.

⌐ 29. **Joel's Jump Start V8** ★

Make a desperate jump to a high sloper on the lip and top out in the dirty right-facing corner above. Like Swiftwater's *Chicken Man* (V8), the difficulty of this one fluctuates annually with the sand level. Most of us will have to wait for a good year to get this one…

⌐ 30. **The Fin V7** ★★

Start sitting, hugging the polished fin of rock with hands and feet. Stab to a left-hand crimper and continue up the blunt arête with some involved heel-hooking. A classic problem on unique river-polished granite.

THE FIN

Inspired by the spot from Ryan Paulsness, Charlie Barrett throws conservative values to the wind on the first ascent of *Cremation of Care* (V10)
(PHOTO) Max Hasson

"Forestland has been Icicle Canyon's premiere bouldering area in recent years . . . This is one of Leavenworth's most popular bouldering areas, and several parties can typically be found here on spring and fall weekends." Central Washington Bouldering. *Several parties indeed - these words couldn't ring more true today!*

FORESTLAND

Forestland is the Icicle's largest and most popular bouldering area, and deservedly so. In terms of concentration and the quality of problems, Forestland is probably Leavenworth's 'best' area. Forestland is divided into three tiers, the "Lower," the "Upper," and the "Upper Upper," each of which are described in further detail below. Please take note: With the explosion of Leavenworth bouldering's popularity over the past several years, Forestland has seen an enormous increase in annual user-visits. This traffic has brought joy to many and has fostered the development of the Upper Upper Forestland talus, but the high level of impact caused by so many people has also made Forestland the focal point in the increasingly-relevant debate about bouldering access in Leavenworth generally. Please do your part to keep access to Forestland open by acting responsibly when you visit the area: Though it should go without saying, please pick up *any* trash you see, stick to trails as best as you can, and never, ever have fires in the boulders. Rattlesnakes are also frequently observed in Forestland throughout the summer; pay special attention on the trail from the parking lot, as well as in the talus of the upper areas.

Access Forestland via a dirt driveway on the right side of the road 5.7 miles from Icicle Junction, the only of its kind in the area. Follow the drive a couple hundred yards back toward Leavenworth to a large parking area, directly above Barney's Rubble, which was formerly a staging area for firefighting efforts during the 1994 forest fires. A well-worn trail leaves the northeast end of the parking lot by a few small boulders. Follow this trail for about 100 yards, and cross the small stream (note: the log bridge over this stream recently washed out, and efforts to negotiate a replacement with the USFS are currently underway). After crossing the bridge, there are two options: Most boulderers headed to Lower and Upper Forestland will continue straight, following the trail for another 150 yards, over a smaller stream, to the obvious cluster of boulders. Those headed for The Monarch or The Teacup, or those seeking direct access to Upper Upper Forestland generally, should turn left and follow the faint trail uphill along the east side of the stream. After about 80 yards, the trail breaks slightly right, trending across an open vegetated area toward the obvious dark overhang of The Monarch and, above it, The Teacup.

LOWER FORESTLAND

Lower Forestland, the first cluster reached from the parking lot, offers a quality circuit of easy-to-moderate problems with flat, even landings. In addition to a handful of nice warm-up problems, Forestland is home to classic moderate sandbags like One Summer (V5), The Real Thing (V4), and Feel the Pinch (V4) that complement higher, harder classics like The Shield (V7) and Busted (V8). Paul Nadler's 2012 addition to the area, Autopilot (V11), is an instant classic that is the area's testpiece.

☐ 1. Lock and Pop V3 ★

Start sitting matched on the trailside jug, climbing the arête and right side of the short face. Finish straight up in the shallow groove. Better than it looks.

☐ 2. Squeezer V3

Stand start from a high, flat edge. This climb has somehow been done from a low start. A bit silly, but it's there…

☐ 3. Runner V0 ★

Climb the center of the slab on small edges. Alternatively, discard all technique and hop to the finish from a running start.

☐ 4. Marathon Man V0 ★

Climb the right side of the slab using smears and small edges.

☐ 5. Slabstraction V0

Climb the short slab around the corner from Marathon Man.

☐ 6. Lock and Load V4 ★

Start on the left side of the rounded bulge with a high knob in the seam. Climb straight up on slopers to a devilish mantle. An old-school line that rarely gets done these days.

Variation (V6): Start on small head-high edges down and left of the knob, climbing right along the lip into Lock and Load. Finish as above.

☐ 7. Backdoor Ass Attack V7 ★★

Start hanging from a nice head-high jug next to the trail. Throw your heel next to your hands and rock up on poor slopers to an insecure mantle finish.

Variation (V9): Start sitting with a sloping right-hand sidepull and a small left undercling. Make a powerful chuck to the jug and finish as above. One very tough move.

☐ 8. Project

Sit start on a right-facing sidepull and climb up through poor slopers. This problem was listed as a project in *Central Washington Bouldering*, and has resisted the few efforts it has seen since…

☐ 9. Breadline V1 ★★★

Climb the fatty right-facing flake to finish straight up with some delicate footwork.

Variation (V2): Start as for Breadline, but finish up and right on the flat sloper of One Summer.

Variation (V8): From the start hold of Breadline, traverse straight right to top out as for The Real Thing.

☐ 10. One Summer V5 ★★

Start standing with small crimps, step high and lunge to the obvious flat ledge. The crouch start down and left with an incut crimp trades an extra grade for a star.

☐ 11. The Real Thing V4 ★★★

Climb the vertical face using small edges and a prominent left-facing sidepull, which has unfortunately crumbled slightly in recent years. Great technical face climbing.

Greg Adams sticks the dyno on *One Summer* (V5).
[PHOTO] Matthew Hall.

⌐ 12. Concavity V2 ★
Start crouched, matched on an undercling under the shelf, move to the juggy crack, and finish up and right. Starting with the crack is a fun V0.
Variation (V2): Start as above, but climb up and left through loose edges on the scooped face.

⌐ 13. Arrested Development V4 ★★★
Hop to a good square-cut hold on the left arête, then climb up and right with holds on the face to a committing finish high on the corner. Already tall and imposing, this line became significantly more difficult in the winter of 2013/14 when a key sidepull flake broke.
Variation (V6): From the right-hand starting holds, climb up and right to a right-leaning gaston on the face and finish straight up.

⌐ 14. The Shield V7 ★★★
Grab two wide sidepulls in the center of the face, paste your feet on, and dyno to an incut right-hand sidepull at the ten foot level. Move slightly left to finish with a small notch on the lip. A classic Leavenworth move that has retained its character despite occasional crumblage.

⌐ 15. Bedroom Bully V8/9 ★
Start with two head-high crimps on the right side of the face and stab to the incut fingerlock up and right. Hit the lip and mantle straight over. You might want to tape a finger for this one… Starting with the fingerlock and mantling is a fun V2/3.

⌐ 16. The Drill Sargeant V8 ★
Climb the short corner just right of Bedroom Bully from two low sidepulls. The stand start to this one clocks in around V2/3.

⌐ 17. Feel the Pinch V4 ★★★
Start crouched on a sloping rail on the right side of the face. Climb up and left through another sloper to a neat-o pinch and gaston crimp, topping out a few feet right of the tree. A definite must-do, and *way* hard for the grade.

⌐ 18. Fiend it Like Crack V4 ★★
Start crouched with the sloper as for Feel the Pinch, but climb up right on sloping holds along the bottom edge of the crack. Round the corner and finish straight up the right side of the arête with quartz holds in the seam.
Variation (V5): Start sitting with a low, sloping flake on the right side of the arête as for Busted and climb up and left into the standard start.

⌐ 19. Busted V8 ★★★
Climb directly up the overhanging arête from a sit start matched on the low, flexing flake. Use slopers for your left hand and crimps for your right to set up for a powerful move to the high sloping ledges of Fiend it Like Crack.
Variation (V7): Start two moves in, with the lowest left-hand sloper and an incut right-hand sidepull. All of the glory with none of the butt-dragging…

⌐ 20. Autopilot V11 ★★★
Start cross-matched on an incut crimp in the center of the clean face. Move to a high left-hand micro-pinch, then ratchet up the body tension and crimp strength to climb up and left through seemingly-blank territory. Nobody will call this one easy. F.A. Paul Nadler.

⌐ 21. Cruise Control V6 ★★
Start in the center of the overhang, with a left-hand gaston on the right-hand start hold of Autopilot. Move right through cryptic sidepulls to finish on the short corner. This one's all about the feet…

⌐ 22. Power Steering V2 ★
Start sitting on the short corner and climb straight up to finish as for Cruise Control.

⌐ 23. Dredge V1 ★
Climb the slab left of the tree on small edges to a flat jug near the top.

⌐ 24. Hearthstone V0
Start with high jugs on the right side of the lip, mantle, and climb to the top.

⌐ 25. Silly with an S V0
Start sitting on the left side of the trailside slab and mantle.

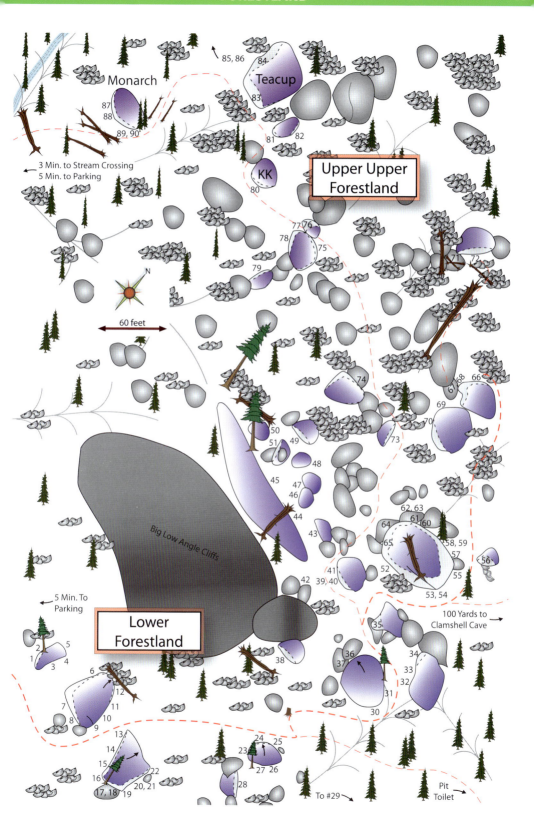

Monarch

87
88
89, 90

85, 86

84

Teacup

83

81
82

KK
80

3 Min. to Stream Crossing
5 Min. to Parking

Upper Upper Forestland

77 76
78
79
75

71
72

N

60 feet

74

67 68
66

69
70

73

50
51
49
48

45
47
46

44

43

Big Low Angle Cliffs

62, 63
61
64
60
65
58, 59
57
56
52
55
53, 54

41
42 39, 40

5 Min. To Parking

Lower Forestland

35

100 Yards to Clamshell Cave

38

36
37

34
33
32

31
30

6
12
7
11
8
10
9

13
14
15
16
17, 18 19
22
20, 21

24 25
23
27 26
28

To #29

Pit Toilet

2 5
1
3 4

Cortney Cusack gettin' physical like Olivia Newt on *The Physical* (V4)

□ 26. Cowardly Lion V0 ★
Climb the slight scoop on the right side of the face to mantle onto the arête and top out.

□ 27. The Scarecrow V1 ★★
Climb the thin face just right of the tree, climbing from tiny crimps to good right-facing ledges below the lip.

□ 28. Toto V4
Start matched on a flexing sidepull flake in the small alcove to the left of The Scarecrow. Bust to the lip and top out. Highball!

□ 29. V1-3
From the back of the Scarecrow boulder, walk downhill and toward town for about 25 yards to find this smallish boulder. A few fun variations climb the downhill face.

UPPER FORESTLAND

The boulders of Upper Forestland sit on a rambling plateau a couple hundred feet above Lower Forestland. There is a nice warm-up circuit among the first boulders reached, but as you hike further, classic moderates like *Lovage* (V3) and *The Physical* (V4) yield to harder and harder problems. The ultra-mega highball *The Ruminator* (V5) and its unruly cousin *Cremation of Care* (V10) are two of Leavenworth's highest problems, but with a flat landing, they are accessible to mere mortals. A small cluster of even harder problems, like the techy bulge of *The Practitioner* (V11) and the powerful crimpers of *Chunky Vanilla* (V10) lie further uphill.

To reach Upper Forestland, follow the obvious trail straight the short hill above the Scarecrow boulder. After passing the first cluster and rounding The Physical, the trail splits on either side of the Ruminator boulder. To get to the problems on the backside of the Ruminator, the Practitioner, and Chunky Vanilla, follow the trail to the right around the back of The Physical and keep to the right of the Ruminator. To get to Sunny and Steep, Bad Moon Rising, and the trail to Upper Upper Forestland, continue straight past The Physical and curve around the far side of Sunny and Steep.

□ 30. Unknown 5.11 ★
There is an old toprope on the right side of the tall face to the left as you reach Upper Forestland that has been bouldered in recent years. Follow edges just left of the arête to a prominent lip block one body length below the lip. Top out up and slightly left.

□ 31. Unknown V1 ★★
Climb the left side of the tall, slabby face, finishing on easy ledges. Your pad is probably better used for the jump-down descent…

□ 32. Fedge V2 ★
Start on the corner with a small triangular crimp, climbing up to an incut sidepull and a tiny two-finger divot on the slab. Start down and right on small gastons for a fun variation.

□ 33. Slickfoot Holiday V1+ ★
Start on the big rounded edge 10 feet left of the corner, climbing up and right on small edges to the high slab finish of #32. A sneaker testpiece!

□ 34. Lovage V3 ★★
Start sitting matched on the big ledge on the left end of the face. Climb straight up to the hidden jug on top of the corner and top out. Morpho, more like V4 for shorter climbers.

□ 35. The Physical V4 ★★★
Start this muscley problem on the slab below the flying arête. Punch up and left using opposing holds on either side of the bulge. Great movement and a high commitment factor make this a must-do.

□ 36. Unknown V3
Climb the short arête with the boulder at your back.

□ 37. Unknown V2 ★
Start standing on the scooped slab and climb the right side of the face on sidepulls.

□ 38. Unknown V3
Climb the grainy bulge from a high, incut hueco.

□ 39. Sunny and Steep V2 ★★★
Climb the left side of the beautiful featured face on rounded jugs. Feel free to add a grade in the summer heat!

□ 40. Funny and Cheap V4 ★
Start as for Sunny and Steep, but climb directly right to a low sidepull and a big undercling. Bust for rounded slopers up and right, then climb straight to the lip on flat edges.
Variation (V2): Skip the low move – climb straight up, then right to the slopers, finishing as above.

□ 41. Unkown V7
Start crouched with low right-facing sidepulls in the seam left of Sunny and Steep. Climb up and left to an incut triangular crimp, finishing straight up.

□ 42. Unkown V0
Climb the low-angle arête of the smallish boulder behind Sunny and Steep.

□ 43. Tahitian Moon V0 ★
Start on a big jug on the left side of the small boulder and traverse the right along the lip to mantle just before the corner. A good child/beginner climb.

□ 44. Bad Moon Rising V2 ★★
Climb the clean black water streak just to the left of the fallen tree. Beautiful friction climbing.

□ 45. Moondog V0 ★
Fifteen feet right of the fallen tree, follow the mossy ledges up the slab. The most convenient downclimb for Bad Moon Rising.

□ 46. Project
Climb the steep, blunt arête from two very low edges. Ouchie!

□ 47. Death to Rednecks V2 ★
Climb the tricky slab by the base of the fallen tree.

□ 48. V3
Climb the vertical face with right-facing edges.

Cole Allen on a pre-break ascent of *The Coffee Cup* (V10, now V8). **[PHOTO]** Brian Sweeney.

49. Unknown V2 ★
Hike downhill from Bad Moon Rising and through a cluster of smaller boulders to find this pleasant, slightly overhanging face. Start with a head-high shelf and climb to the lip. The low start on edges bumps the grade a few notches.

50. Unknown V0
Climb the short slab.

51. Unknown V5
Start crouched with a low crimp rail. Lift yourself off the adjacent boulder and climb a few moves on slopers to mantle and top out. Grade unconfirmed.

THE RUMINATOR

52. Project
This climb is in a sheltered alcove several yards left of The Ruminator. There is a start hold…

53. The Ruminator V5
★★★

THE RUMINATOR

You may have to think about this one for a minute… Climb the steep left-leaning crack up the middle of the huge overhang. Long moves between big holds in the 45-degree crack lead to an insecure mantle at the lip. One of the area's proudest; take a look at the top before you set off.

54. Cremation of Care V10 ★★★
OMG. Start as for The Ruminator, but once you hit the prominent triangular ledge about 2/3 of the way up, move left to the blunt arête and top out by squeezing straight out the bulge. Bring, like, lots of pads. F.A. Charlie Barrett.

55. Cole's Jump V7 ★
On the right side of the Ruminator overhang, two terrible crimps are perennially chalked in the hopes they can provide V-sick passage to the slopers above. While the stand remains an impossi-proj, the jumpstart to the lip goes.

56. Noggin-Banger V7 ★
Start crouched with low jugs in the horizontal crack. Climb straight out the low horizontal arête to a good edge on the lip. Top out straight up the arête… Leavenworth's tougher version of the classic Squamish lowball The Cutting Edge.

57. Unknown V6 ★
Start sitting with slopers a few feet right of the trees. Traverse right along the lip into the mantle of Dangle.

58. Dangle V7 ★★
Start sitting with a flat, low edge on the left side of the steep overhang. Make a hard move to the obvious incut flake three feet above, then hit the slippery lip and press out the crux mantle.

59. Hypertrophy V10 ★★
Do the first move of Dangle and keep traversing right on edges to a prominent right-hand sidepull just past the tree. Bust to a good hold under the lip, then finish up and right with a tough mantle. Get this one while you can; it will soon be obscured by trees. F.A. Johnny Goicoechea.

60. Kobe Tai V8 ★★
Roughly 20 feet right of Dangle and Hypertrophy, climb the overhanging face over the gap between the boulders. Start from a rounded right-hand crimp and a low left-hand undercling. Harder and harder moves on beautiful crisp edges lead to a heady lip encounter.

61. Curtis Suave V4 ★
Climb the blunt arête from the top of the boulder a few feet right of Kobe Tai, starting with a big move to the lip from a right-hand sidepull.

62. The Cro-Magnon V6 ★
Start with a good right-facing sidepull on the undercut orange face and dyno to the lip. Moving to the right arête and up is a less-contrived V1.

63. Unknown V3 ★
Climb the arête left of The Cro-Magnon on nice rounded ledges.

64. Clod-Hopper V2
Start sitting with slopers on the very low corner, moving up and left to a jug and mantle. Finishing way up and left would be quite scary…

65. Bananas V8 ★★
Start standing at the edge of the rocky cave, matched on a sloping rail at head height. Pull on, chuck to a small, sloping crimp below the lip, and hold it together for the top-out. This problem is most easily accessed from the backside of Sunny and Steep.

THE COFFEE CUP / PRACTITIONER

Find the Coffee Cup / Practitioner boulder by following the trail straight uphill from Dangle. Trend slightly left, then hard left, staying high as you round the uphill side of the small, unassuming cluster.

66. The Coffee Cup V8 ★★★
Start matched on the obvious sloping rail on the left side of the steep face. Kick your left foot to a high sloping foothold at the end of the rail, stick the crimp above, and move to the lip. An old-school testpiece that unfortunately broke shortly after the publication of *Central Washington Bouldering*, becoming significantly easier. Your first V10?

67. The Practitioner V11 ★★★
Start under the steepest part of the square roof with a good undercling in the seam. Climb up and right out of the roof, then squeeze and slap straight up the blunt corner to a difficult dyno for the lip. This uber-classic bulge was a longstanding project until visiting Colorado hardman Herman Feissner dispatched it in 2006. "Leavenworth's hardest – so far." – *Central Washington Bouldering*.

PRACTIONER

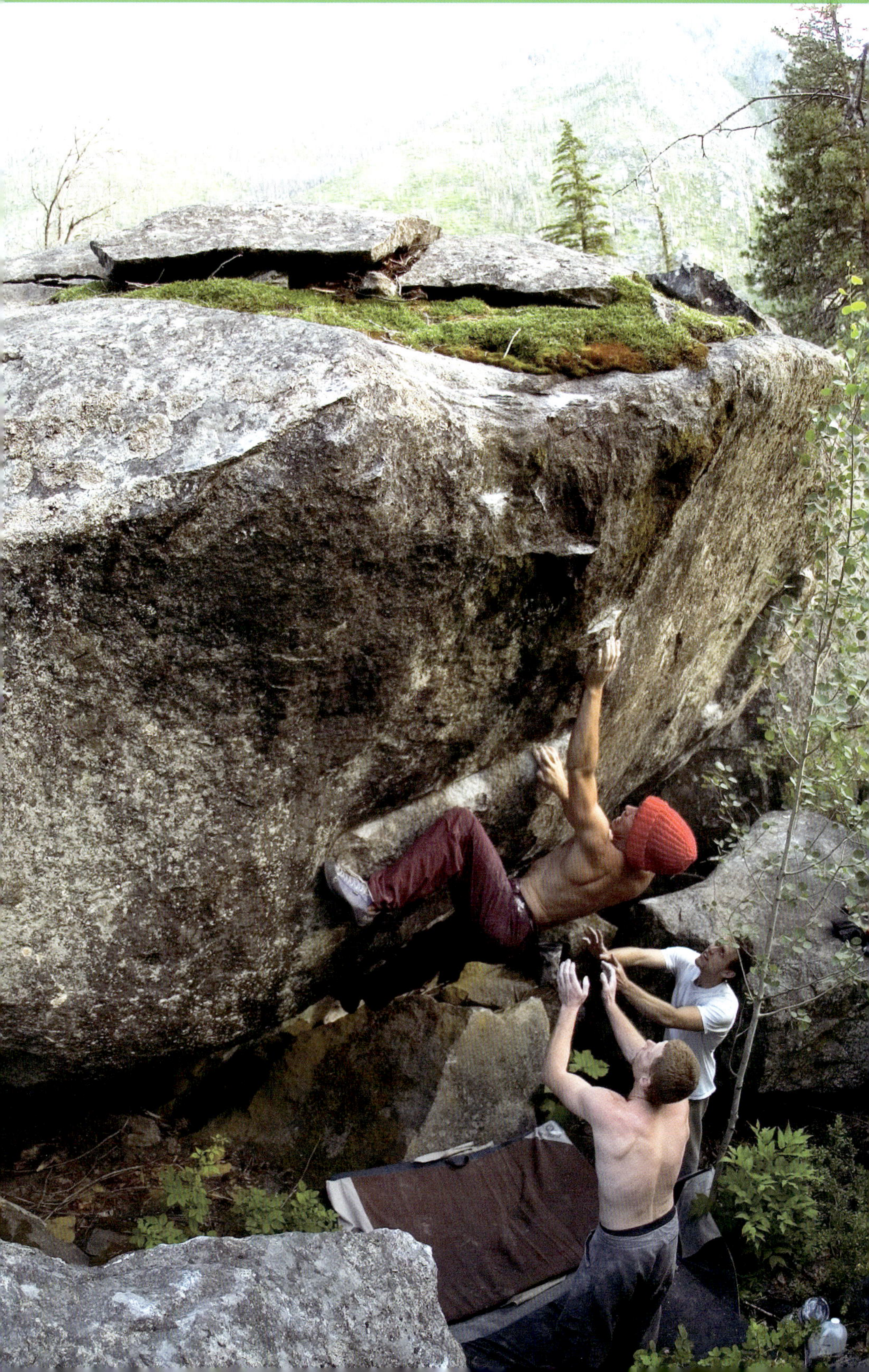

Ryan Paulsness tops out #63 (V3). **[PHOTO]**
Max Hasson.

❒ 68. Unknown V9 ★
Start as for The Practitioner, but climb up and right along underclings in the faint seam to gain a good right-hand crimp over the bulge. Top out by climbing up and back left, rocking over onto the finishing sloper of The Practitioner. If you judge by the number of ascents, more difficult than its popular neighbor... F.A. Joel Campbell.

❒ 69. Unknown V1 ★
Climb the tall slab. Rarely climbed.

❒ 70. Unknown V6 ★
Climb the tall orange face from a stand start with high edges. Obscure but good.

❒ 71. Mano a Mono V5 ★
To reach this boulder, climb onto the flat-topped boulder behind the Practitioner, hop onto the narrow rock directly behind it, and walk roughly 20 yards uphill on the huge log to the squarish, slightly overhanging face. This problem starts matched on an obvious sloper on the left side of the face. Slap to the deep mono to the left of the corner and finish straight up with edges around the lip.

❒ 72. Chunky Vanilla V10 ★★
Start squatting on the flat boulder beneath the face, matched on a grainy, flat, right-facing edge. Climb up and right to two sidepull crimps, then dyno to the lip. Fingery and hard. F.A. Johnny Goicoechea.

UPPER UPPER FORESTLAND

Upper Upper Forestland is the dispersed talus field that stretches uphill and west from Upper Forestland. The talus of Upper Upper Forestland was not included in *Central Washington Bouldering*, but the area is not new. Upper Upper Forestland classics like *Abstraction* (V10), *Kobra Kon* (V9), and *The Teacup* (V13) have been climbed on for years, while a number of the area's grainy moderates have seen dozens of 'first ascents.' Though the rock in Upper Upper Forestland becomes sandier and more friable the further you hike, there is still potential for new problems in the jumble above The Teacup.

The easiest way to access Upper Upper Forestland is to follow the faint trail leaving from behind the Sunny and Steep boulder. Walk west and slightly uphill around the short, dark, overhang of #73, then traverse an open area to the obvious orange rock of #75. To reach the Teacup from Kobra Kon, follow the trail up and over a small adjacent boulder and around the corner, staying left/below the cluster of larger boulders. Alternatively, approach Upper Upper Forestland via the Monarch boulder by turning left off of the Lower Forestland approach just after the stream crossing. Please take care to stay on the trail in the vicinity of The Monarch and The Teacup to avoid damaging the fragile riparian vegetation.

❒ 73. Unknown V1
Climb the short, curved overhang from a stand start. Top out to the left or the right.

❒ 74. Unknown V2
Start standing on the adjacent boulder with a good high edge and climb straight up.

❒ 75. Unknown V3 ★
Start sitting matched on the obvious shelf and climb up and left on grainy edges to the lip. Top out up and right with jugs on the arête.

❒ 76. Abstraction V10 ★★
This unique problem climbs the far side of the diamond-shaped suspended block next to #75. Begin with a decent left-hand pinch and opposing right-hand sloper at roughly the same level (i.e., at the part of the arête closest to the adjacent boulder). Paste your right foot super high and slap up the double arêtes. Top out slightly to the left. F.A. Johnny Goicoechea.

❒ 77. Dave's Problem V11 ★
Just right of Abstraction, start crouched with two opposing sidepulls on a diamond-shaped flake. Make a hard move to the grooved sloper, then top out with edges up and right. Rarely (never?) repeated. F.A. Dave Thompson.

❒ 78. Project
Edges in the dark overhang.

❒ 79. Unknown V5 ★
Climb the suspended face from a stand start with crimps, moving up and right through poor slopers. Grade unconfirmed.

❒ 80. Kobra Kon V9 ★★★
Climb the tall overhanging face from a good left-hand sidepull and a high right-hand edge. Move through sidepulls to slopers, topping out just left of the boulder's apex. They don't get much more striking than this...

❒ 81. Unknown V2
Climb the short, chossy face from a stand start.

❒ 82. Unknown V5
Climb the scooped overhang from loose edges at head height. A lower start may have been done. Grade unconfirmed.

Isaac Howard finagles the angles on *Trickle of Silence* (V9).

⊓ 83. **The Teacup V13** ★★★

For many years, The Teacup was Leavenworth's crown jewel and its hardest problem, a position just recently usurped with Carlo Traversi's first ascent of the legendary Ladder Project. Start sitting underneath the obvious prow with a right-hand sloper and a decent left-hand sidepull crimp. Climb to a flat left-hand edge and a positive right-hand crimp, then make a huge move up and left to a sloper, finishing left of the flying prow. F.A. Dave Thompson.

⊓ 84. **Unknown V4** ★★

This problem climbs the often-overlooked roof behind the Teacup from a stand start with a good left-hand crimp and a right-hand sloper on either side of a small prow. Move up and left to the groove, then rock over using the prominent rail. Traverse left to the end of the rail for full value.
Variation (V7): Climb straight up the prow, topping out to the right. Grade unconfirmed.

⊓ 85. **Unknown V2**

Problems #85 and 86 are on the obvious white boulder roughly 10 yards west of The Teacup. This problem traverses left along the grainy lip until you can rock over.

⊓ 86. **Project**

Climb the low roof and top out as for #85.

⊓ 87. **Sponge Bob Scott Pants V3** ★

Start with low opposing sidepulls and climb straight up the mini-bulge on the left side of the face.

⊓ 88. **The Monarch V10** ★★

Start with two low, left-facing sidepulls. Climb to a terribly sloping right-hand pinch, then either dyno or lock off to the obvious edge above. Formerly V8, this problem used to involve a dyno to a unique doorknob-shaped knob that has since broken off…

⊓ 89. **Trickle of Silence V9** ★★★

Start matched on a waist-high fin sloper on the right side of the face. Climb up and left on sloping edges to a hard dynamic move for a good crimp on the left side of the prow. Intricate and body-tensiony movement.

⊓ 90. **Unknown V4**

Climb up and right from the sloping start of Trickle of Silence, finishing by squeezing up the short arête. This problem has not seen much traffic in recent years, probably because of the large tree leaning against it…

THE TEACUP

Cole Allen sticks a heinous V8 dyno at The Locksmith.

THE LOCKSMITH

The Locksmith is a small cluster of boulders perched several hundred yards up and slightly right from Upper Forestland. Along with The Upper Bond Boulders, The Airfield, The Scab, and a handful of isolated boulders, the Locksmith represents the new breed of Leavenworth areas that have popped up in the last couple years and are a sign of great things to come. Though the Locksmith is only home to a few established problems and one or two projects, it makes one think about what you might find, anywhere in the Icicle, if you just hiked a little further uphill…

To find the Locksmith, hike up and slightly right from the Ruminator boulder on a faint game trail. Follow the trail straight up, then sharply right at the top of a steep rise, then uphill again towards the large square overhang roughly 50 yards above (#2). Hike uphill just left of this boulder to a second, small overhang roughly 50 yards above (#3). From here, walk up and right at a 45-degree angle around the cliffband and toward the huge overhanging prow that makes up the downhill side of the Locksmith boulder. The hike should take roughly 10 minutes from Upper Forestland; no map is provided, and it's suggested you use the GPS coordinates for your first visit.

JOHNNY'S PROW   AREA   DYNO

SECOND CLUSTER

❒ 1. Johnny's Problem
V10 ★★

This isolated problem sits on a small shelf roughly one third of the way to The Locksmith. Follow the faint trail uphill from The Ruminator for roughly five minutes until you're even with the top of a small low-angle cliff band to the left. Cut directly left near two large fallen trees, then traverse the top of the cliff face to the obvious west-facing prow. Start squeezing between a small sidepull crimp for your left hand and a low sloper on the arête for your right. Climb to the good flat hold at the seven-foot level, then top out on the right side of the corner. Rarely attempted, and even more rarely climbed! F.A. Johnny Goicoechea

❒ 2. Project
Climb the huge right arête of the obvious perched boulder near the trail roughly two thirds of the way to The Locksmith. Chossy.

❒ 3. Unknown
Roughly 50 yards above #2, there is a small overhanging cave that may or may not have been climbed.

❒ 4. The Locksmith V8 ★★
Start standing under the steep dihedral, matched on a poor sloper. Climb up the techy flared seam to jugs near the lip and rock around right to top out. Very groovy!
Variation (project): Start matched on slopers two feet lower in the dihedral.

❒ 5. Project
Any climb up this larger-than-life prow would be incredible…

❒ 6. Joel's Problem V5 ★
On the right side of the corridor behind The Locksmith, start with head-high gaston crimps on the overhanging face. Pop to the grainy right-hand crimp and top out straight up.

❒ 7. Unkown V8 ★★★
Roughly 50 yards east of The Locksmith, this burly problem climbs the left side of the steep, undercut UFO roof. Start matched on an undercling crimp, establish on the left-hand sidepull above, then dyno to a brick-pinch jug on the lip. Traverse 10 feet left to top out around the corner. Really?

❒ 8. Project
Climb straight out the right side of the steep roof on gastons and sidepulls. Wicked.

There are a few other established climbs on the boulders in between The Locksmith and #s 7-8, and the tall arête slightly downhill of #8 is still a project at time of writing.

THE DOMESTIC BOULDERS

The Domestic Boulders is a medium-sized cluster of blocks strewn about the top of the Domestic Dome crag, directly above the beginning of the driveway to the Forestland parking lot. Developed in late 2009 by Kyle O'Meara and others, the Domestics are home to a nice concentration of classic moderate-to-hard problems, including *Bootin' Dookie* (V6), *Coprophobia* (V7), *Domestic Violence* (V7), and *No-Contact Order* (V6). The Domestic Boulders get good late-day sun, and are one of the first Icicle Canyon areas to dry out in the early spring.

Reach the Domestic Boulders by turning off of Icicle Road onto the dirt driveway to the Forestland parking lot, 5.7 miles from Icicle Junction. Park at the top of the short hill (before turning right to Forestland) and follow the well-worn trail past the "675 feet" sign toward the cluster of large boulders below the cliff. Skirt the uphill side of the cluster, climb through some talus, and curve left up the sandy trail at the far end of the cliff.

PARKING

　　Once on top of the cliff, follow the fainter trail directly west, then northwest and up a steep hill to the Bootin' Dookie boulder. The hike should take no more than 10 minutes total.

❏ 1. **Unknown V4** ★★

At the east edge of the cluster below Domestic Dome, there is a tall, vertical face at ground level that is home to two fun problems. This line climbs the center of the face from a head-high right-facing sloper. Tall, with a committing move to the lip! Would be three stars if not for the rock quality.

Drew Schick tops out the jump start to the right of *Bootin' Dookie* (V8).
[PHOTO] Max Hasson.

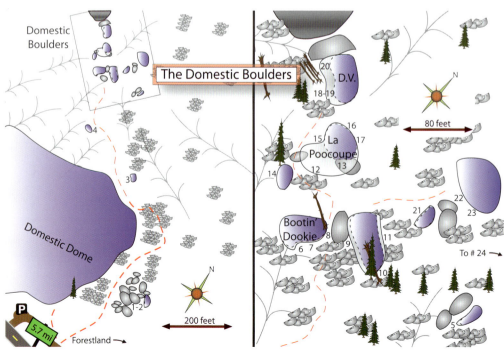

9. **Ginopapacino V9** ★
Climb the short overhanging face with
the slab at your back. Start crouched and
cross-matched on two good incuts, climbing up and left on small incut edges to a
tricky lip encounter.

Drew Schick sticks the lip on *Ginopapacino* (V9).
[PHOTO] Max Hasson.

Kyle O'Meara gets a spot on *No Contact Order* (V6). **[PHOTO]** Max Hasson.

BOOTIN' DOOKIE

❐ 2. Unknown V3 ★
Climb the right side of the face on crumbly crimps.

❐ 3. Unknown V2 ★
Climb the center of the scooped slab to the right as you crest the top of the cliff. Typically dirty.

❐ 4. Unknown V2
The smallish boulder just below the final uphill push to the Domestic Boulders proper has a nice climb on its left arête.

❐ 5. Unknown V5 ★★
Climb the hidden overhanging arête from a stand start with an incut right-hand crimp and a high left-hand sloper. Committing!

❐ 6. Bootin' Dookie V6 ★★★
Start sitting in the overhanging corner feature with a good left hand on the arête and an incut sidepull for your right hand. Climb straight up the corner using the flat crimp on the left face and a sloping right-hand pod in the seam. Finish with a tricky mantle and a few slab moves. Named for an unfortunate habit of Kyle O'Meara's spaniel Kona…

❐ 7. Unknown V8 ★★
Start standing on the arête right of Bootin' Dookie with a sloping right-hand pinch. Jump start to the lip and top out up and right.

❐ 8. Unknown V0 ★
Climb the textured ledges up the slightly overhanging corner.

❐ 9. Ginopapacino V9 ★
See photo description, previous page.

❐ 10. Project
Climb the blunt overhanging arête to the right of the large log.

❐ 11. Unknown V1 ★
Start standing in the hole with a high right-trending seam. Move to another seam and top out straight up.

❐ 12. Coprophobia V7 ★★
Start sitting on the low boulder on the left side of the roof with an incut right-hand gaston, your left hand pinching a low rail, and your left foot on a low incut on the arête. Climb cryptic moves up and right along the lip to top out straight up from two curved jugs, roughly 10 feet right of the start.
Variation (V8): Climb Coprophobia, but instead of topping out at the jugs, move down and right to an incut gaston and finish with the crux mantle of La Poocoupe.

❐ 13. La Poocoupe V6 ★
Start matched on the detached boulder under the right side of the wide overhang. Gain an incut left-hand sidepull in the roof, match, and bust for the lip, finishing with a difficult mantle.

❐ 14. Unknown V1
Climb the short slab just below Coprophobia.

❐ 15. Unknown V3
Start sitting on the flat rock, matched in the seam. Move to the lip and top out.

❐ 16. Unknown V3 ★
Start crouched in the small alcove on the right side of the face. Climb up and left on nice flat edges until you can rock up to the lip.

❐ 17. Unknown V1
Stat matched on head-high edges on the left side of the short, flat wall and climb straight up.

❐ 18. No-Contact Order V6 ★★★
Start standing, matched on the right arête. Climb up and left along the arête to top out as for Domestic Violence. Proud!

❐ 19. Project
Start inside the cave and climb into Domestic Violence. V16?

❐ 20. Domestic Violence V7 ★★★
Start next to the rectangular slab, squeezing between a high left-hand sloper and a high, flat right-hand crimp. Make unique, gymnastic moves through a curved incut crimper to top out straight up the arête.

❐ 21. Unknown V1
Start on the low, loose flake and climb up and left along the sloping arête.

❐ 22. The Ear Slab V5 ★★
Climb the center of the tall vertical face from a high crimp.

❐ 23. Project?
Climb the right side of the tall face.

❐ 24. Unknown V7 ★
This short problem climbs the far side of a squat boulder roughly 50 yards up and right from #22 and 23. Start crouched, slap to a sloping hueco dish and top out. Grade unconfirmed.

MUSCLE BEACH

Muscle Beach is a smallish riverside dome on Icicle Creek just past the entrance to the Forestland parking area. Though primarily a toprope crag, Muscle Beach is home to *Annie's Climax* (5.10+), Leavenworth's only deep-water solo. Hit this area on a sunny summer day when the frigid water will feel refreshing (it's called Icicle Creek for a reason!). Muscle Beach is a neat hang, even with the large home directly across the river.

Access Muscle Beach via a faint trail entering the woods on the left roughly 10 yards past the entrance to the
Forestland parking area, roughly 5.8 miles from Icicle Junction. Follow the trail through open trees, along the bottom of a low-angle slab, and then down a steep rocky section to reach the (climber's) right side of the crag. Annie's Climax climbs the far (again, climber's) left side of the crag from the ledge some 20 feet above the

AREA

creek. Consult Viktor Kramar's Leavenworth Rock for more precise beta (see p. 131 for a killer photo of John Stordahl cruising the climb), and be careful. Though people have jumped into the creek from the top of this cliff, this is not Mallorca, water levels vary greatly, and an uncontrolled fall could be very dangerous.

THE LONELY FISH

The Lonely Fish, a.k.a. Another Roadside Attraction, is the large roadside boulder just past the turn for the Forestland parking area. Along with the Millennium Boulder across the road, the Lonely Fish area is home to a high concentration of hard and unique problems. The area is home to a trio of striking, hard traverses, the *Lonely Fish* (V8), the *Millennium Traverse* (V8), and *Droppin' the Kirschbaum* (V10), so if you enjoy traverses but don't feel like scraping along in the dirt, you'll find sideways heaven here. The Millennium boulder is a nice warm-up spot with several moderate problems on crisp salt-and-pepper granite. Visit this area in the spring and fall when the temps will make the sun refreshing.

The Lonely Fish is visible on the right side of the road 5.8 miles from Icicle Junction, 0.1 miles after the turn to For- estland parking. Please park completely off the roadway on the right side of the road. The Millennium boulder is visible directly across the road from the Lonely Fish, though a bit more distant. The Millennium boulder is directly adjacent to private property, so please stick to trails, maintain a low profile, and always be respectful in interactions with the landowner.

The Lonely Fish from the road.

❑ 1. **Squeaky Clean V2** ★
Climb the mini-corner feature to the left of Dirty Dude from a stand start. The top out is tall but easy.

❑ 2. **Dirty Dude V10** ★★
Start on an incut left-hand sidepull and a high right-hand gaston. Move to the good edges high above and top out with the right arête. This problem has broken and become significantly harder since the publication of *Central Washing- ton Bouldering*.
Variation: *Dirty Dude Low* (V11): Start with both hands on incut left-facing sidepulls and make a difficult move to the high gaston. Finish as above. F.A. Joel Campbell (pre-break); Johnny Goicoechea (post-break).
Variation (Project): Start sitting down and left and climb into Dirty Dude Low. V16?

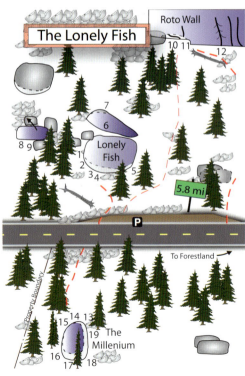

Lizzy Asher shows just the slightest bit of try-hard as she sticks the ninja-kick move on *The Lonely Fish* (V8).

3. Sorrow Bird

V9 ★★

Establish on the high crimp rail using the boulder below and the sloping hueco in the face. Make a big move to a sloper on the lip and top out straight up with the vertical rail. F.A. Johnny Goicoechea.

4. The Lonely Fish

V8 ★★

Establish on the high crimp rail and traverse right to an axe-head pinch. Ninja-kick your foot out right and haul yourself into an easy top-out in the high dihedral. The crimps at the beginning of this problem have broken several times to no huge effect. A classic testpiece. F.A. Joel Campbell.
Variation (V8): Start on the footholds to the right of the dihedral and finish as above.

THE LONELY FISH

5. Caught Red-Handed **V3** ★

Climb the Right side of the tall face from a an overhead start on a good sidepull jug. Work to the obvious incut seam, then up you go!

6. Unknown **V5** ★★

Establish on tiny edges on the face then work right to an airy finish with the jug on the arête. An old toprope that has become a fun modern highball. A photo of this climb was featured in *Climbing Magazine* No. 279.

7. Project

Tiny edges on steep face.

8. Easy One **V0** ★

Climb the tallish face on good holds. Usually done in sneakers. Variation (V1): Start on the arête to the left and climb into Easy One.

9. Easy Two **V0**

Grab the good jug at head height and use the juggy corner to mantle and top out.

10. Droppin' the Kirschbaum **V10** ★★★

This one-time longstanding-project is located on the left end of Roto Wall, approximately fifty yards uphill from the Lonely Fish. Start in the middle of the wall on low right-facing holds. Punch left out the overhanging rail on sloping crimps, then traverse back right across the entire lip on perfect granite to top out in the wide crack. "A mammoth endeavor, although there are no stopper moves." F.A. Kyle O'Meara.

Kyle O'Meara had to don his superhero costume – or at least the mask – to do the first ascent of *Droppin' the Kirschbaum* (V10).

Kori Carlton gets a trad climbing spot from James Lucas as she sets off on the upper half of #6. Unknown (V5). **[PHOTO]** Max Hasson

11. Bombs Away V7 ★

Jump start to the slanting crimps at the 9 foot level on the right end of the alcove. Climb up to the lip and move right to the crack to top out.

12. The Canyon Life 5.11 ★

Climb the tall dihedral on the left end of Roto Wall proper. Careful! F.A. Jens Holsten & Max Hasson.

MILLENIUM BOULDER

13. The Corner V2

Start on the left corner of the round boulder with your left hand on a good crimp and your right on a low sloper. Climb up and right on edges, eventually mantling onto the corner.

14. Millennium Mantle V1 ★

Start matched on the sloping shelf with good footholds. Mantle. Eliminate the crimpers up and left or try it in sneakers for more of a challenge.

15.1999 V2 ★

Start on the low arête with your left hand on a good sloper and your right on a teensy crimp on the face. Slap up to a crimp and top out straight up. Great fun.
Varation (V?): Start on the uber-low flake and move into 1999.

16. 2001 V4 ★★

Start with a sharp left-hand sidepull and sloping right crimp on the blunt arête. Paste your feet high, hit the crimps above, and rock up to an edge high on the face. Burly and balancey.

17. Washington Apples V10 ★★

Intricate face climbing on sharp, tiny edges to the left of the tree. "How you like them apples??" F.A. Johnny Goicoechea.

18. Project

Bad holds on the steep arête.

19. The Millennium Traverse V8 ★★

Start next to the boulder on the right side of the face with a sloping pinch. Make a tough first move left to the dark divot, and continue across the lip to a good edge. Kick your foot up high and slap to the flat shelf to top out.
Variation (V?): Climb straight up the sloping bulge from the start of the Millennium Traverse.

THE MILLENNIUM TRAVERSE

BEN HERRINGTON

Six months into climbing I moved from the mecca of Utah to Washington. I had no knowledge of climbing in Washington outside of alpine climbing. About a month after being here, I was reading through a climbing magazine when I saw an obituary for the late Damien Potts. In his obituary it stated that he had authored a bouldering guidebook to Leavenworth, Washington. The next weekend I was in Leavenworth with my new guide ("*A Cheesy Guide to Pleasing Rock*"). That first season was awesome. So many aesthetic, stand alone, and perfect granite lines right by the road. It felt like I had the whole place to myself. The only other boulderers I ever saw were Kelly, Kyle, and Cole. The first time I met Kyle, I was sleeping on the side of the road with my crash pad under the car. Kyle noticed the pad and stopped and chatted for a bit. He gave me a copy of a video their crew had made of all the new stuff they were putting up called Northwest Connection. I watched that video many times. Watching Cole do the FA of *The Peephole* V10 really stood out to me. The line has a jug start, cool features, and is intricate and classic Leavenworth climbing with holds that are barely there. At the time I wasn't that great of a climber, but I loved hiking around, looking at hard lines and projects, and fantasizing about the day I can put them together (and still do). It felt good to come back years later and put *The Peephole* down. It is still one of the hardest V10s I have done.

Leavenworth really made me the climber I am today. It was a great proving ground, with small feet, and tensiony, powerful, and techy climbing. I jumped in the Granite deep end and learned how to climb. It really felt like Leavenworth bouldering was having its golden age and I wanted to be a part of it. Over the years, I have climbed like crazy working my way through the classics and then the test pieces. Now I am leaving behind my own lines. I went from thinking 'how could anyone climb this' to climbing many of the lines I had fantasized about. I can't wait to put up more beautiful hard lines for others to get psyched on, the same way I got psyched by Cole, Johnny, and Dave's lines.

Leavenworth is the gift that keeps on giving, and the golden age is still going strong. There are problems getting put up five minutes from the road, hiding in plain sight. All you have to do is wander up hill and search for your own Granite bliss. There are patches of boulders everywhere. Just wait until you find out about the rest of Washington.

THE HOOK CREEK BOULDER

The Hook Creek Boulder, a.k.a. the Rat Creek boulder, is one of first developed bouldering spots on the south side of Icicle Creek, in no small part because it is the easiest to access. The Hook Creek Boulder is home to several old-school topropes, as well as the classic lowball testpiece *Atomic Energy* (V9) and a few other worthy link-ups and moderates. Unfortunately, after decades of problem-free access to this block, the parcel on which it sits was finally developed in 2013, and the boulder is now within several yards of a private residence. **Please respect the landowner's privacy by avoiding the Hook Creek Boulder until the access situation is solidified; the information provided herein is for historical purposes only.**

This large, square-cut boulder sits on private property 50 yards downstream of the bridge directly below the Alphabet Wall pullout 6.0 miles from Icicle Junction; this same pullout marks the start of the Straightaway Boulders.

❒ **1. Atomic Hole V4** ⋆
Start with a chalked sloper under the left side of the overhang on the boulder's concave east face. Climb left to a neat hueco on the corner, then traverse the lip rightwards to finish straight up the tall face.

❒ **2. Atomic Energy V9** ⋆⋆
Start on the innermost crimp in the right wall of the overhang, making several steep moves across the beautiful low seam to jugs on the corner. Climb up and left to finish straight up the tall face as for Atomic Hole. Soft for the grade but no gimme. F.A. Cole Allen.
Variation (V9): Start as for Atomic Hole and move right into the start of Atomic Energy.

Kelly Sheridan leads with the feet on *Atomic Lama* (V10).
[PHOTO] Cortney Cusack.

❒ **3. Dalai Lama V8** ⋆
Grab two small crimps at the eight foot level in the center of the lip. Either campus, dyno, or use a high foot chip to gain a better hold up and right and top out.

❒ **4. Atomic Lama V10** ⋆⋆
Climb the beginning of Atomic Energy, but once you reach the jugs on the corner, instead of climbing straight up, move left along the lip on crimps to the right starting hold of Dalai Lama, finishing up that problem. Abe Linkem'! F.A. Kyle O'Meara.

❒ **5. Sweenis V3** ⋆
Start hugging the small boulder next to the Atomic Energy alcove from a sit start. Slap up opposing holds, finishing out left along the juggy lip. Low but fun.

Several toprope climbs on the Hook Creek boulder also make for fun boulder problems. The descent with huecos on the right side of the south face is 5.6 or so, and the obvious layback flake on the left side is 5.10ish. The "Thermal Energy" project, which has unfortunately exfoliated significantly in recent years, is more or less directly across from the Alphabet Wall pullout, roughly 100 yards above the bridge.

Cortney Cusack on *Atomic Hole* (V4).

THE STRAIGHTAWAY BOULDERS

The Straightaway Boulders are a spread-out cluster scattered on both sides of the road, stretching from the large Alphabet Wall pullout to the base of slabby Icicle Buttress. The Straightaway Boulders give credence to exaggerated boasts that one could park their vehicle every 50 yards in Icicle Canyon and find a gorgeous roadside boulder… That said, this is not a place to look for high problem concentration, nor does it provide much in the way of warm-ups. The Straightaway Boulders contain some of the best harder problems in the Leavenworth Area, from the savage power climbing of *Beautification* (V11) and *The Cotton Pony* (V10) to the iconic *WAS* (V8) and the staggeringly beautiful *Turbulence* (V11/12). The biggest prize of them all, however, was climbed at the time this guide was in production: the longstanding "Ladder Project," an independent line of widely-spaced edges and shelves up a sheer 20-foot overhang became *The Penrose Step* when it was climbed by Carlo Traversi in the fall of 2013 at the astronomical grade of V14.

For warm winter sun and somewhat more accessible difficulty, check out the south-facing classics *The Icehouse* (V4), *Taller* (V6), and Leavenworth's granitic answer to Hueco's *Babyface*, *Answer Man* (V6). The sneaker climb *Forget Your Rubbers* (V0) is a fun oddity and one of the few warm-ups in the Straightaways. Many of the Straightaway Boulders are in the sun during most of the day; check out the Icehouse and the Cotton Pony for a few shadier climbs.

The Straightaway Boulders begin just after the large lefthand pullout 6.0 miles from Icicle Junction, and just past 6.2 miles at the base of Icicle Buttress. The approaches at The Straightaway Boulders tend to be short and steep, and all the boulders mentioned here are within 50 yards of the road. The easiest way to locate all the Straightaways the first time through is on foot: Park either in the Alphabet Wall pullout (directly across from the six mile marker) or the Turbulence pullout across from the beginning of Icicle Buttress. Each area has a small landmark, though none are too obvious, especially if you're whipping by in your car. Just past the Straightaway Boulders, below and adjacent to the cliff, are The Icicle Buttress Boulders (next chapter).

ALPHABET WALL BOULDERS

Alphabet Wall is home to a number of fine cracks and the rad sport climb Return to the *Womb* (5.10+). The main trail to the crag leaves from the South side of the left-hand pullout at 6.0 miles. The faint trail to Forget Your Rubbers leaves from the middle of the pullout, and the trail to Beautification heads towards the creek from the North end.

❒ 1. **Beautification V11** ★★★

Beautification is an incredible riverside testpiece that was established by Dave Thompson in 2007. Start sitting with two shallow pockets on the left side of the steep upstream face. Move into two opposing sidepulls and stick a brutal move to the good ledge above. Top out straight up. Basically a perfect boulder problem. Seasonally submerged and/or blocked by snags.

❒ 2. **More Fun Than Beer V6** ★

Start on left-facing sidepulls in the crack and move up and right to slopers over the adjacent boulder. Much more exciting than it would appear. F.A. Joel Campbell.

❒ 3. **Project**

Climb the tall arête from the big rail on the face.

❒ 4. **Forget Your Rubbers V0** ★★★

Follow the faint trail up the hill to the shallow amphitheater on the far left side of Alphabet Wall. Climb juggy huecos and pockets to a high finish, then traverse left along the ledge and downclimb the crack in the corner. You can leave your climbing shoes in the car… Most recently re-discovered by Joe Treftz.

THE ICEHOUSE

The Icehouse is the first large boulder visible on the right after the Alphabet Wall parking area. 50 yards after the six mile marker, there is an orange pole on the right marking a buried telephone cable. Leave the road here and follow the trail uphill and slightly left from the mini pullout. The featured face of the Icehouse is clearly visible at the top of the steep incline, 20 yards above the pavement.

❒ 5. **The Freezer V3** ★

Directly below the Icehouse, this hidden block has a nice climb on its river-facing side. Start squeezing the double arêtes with a high foot, spanning between good slopers until you can slap to the edge of the lip. Top out straight up. It is unclear whether this boulder lies on private or public land; exercise care when visiting the area and always comply with all posted signage.

❒ 6. **The Freezer Right V4** ★

Start on the right side of the arête with a low right foot and a good left foot edge, holding the arête with your left hand and a low crimp with your right hand. Set your feet up and bust to a nice incut handle on the right side of the lip. Top out straight up.

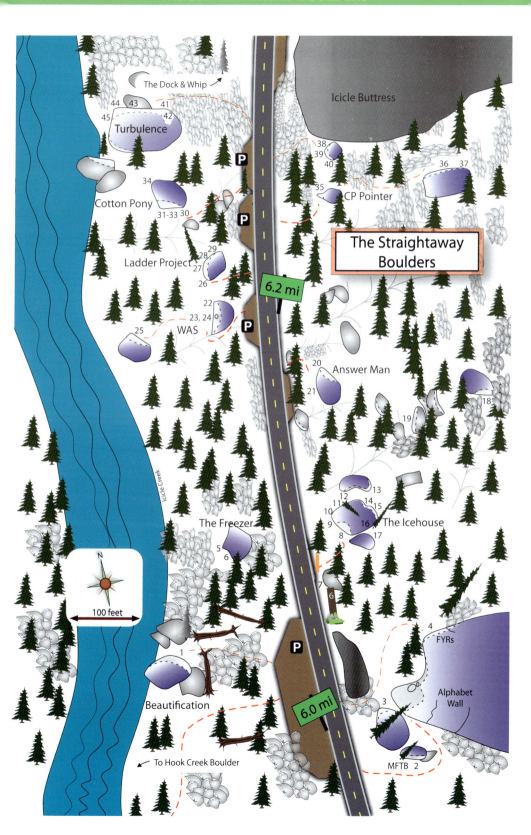

The Dock & Whip

44 43 41
45 42
Turbulence

Icicle Buttress

38
39
40

36 37

35
CP Pointer

The Straightaway Boulders

34
Cotton Pony
31-33 30

Ladder Project
28 29
27
26

6.2 mi

22
23, 24
25 WAS

20
Answer Man
21

19

18

Icicle Creek

12 13
11 14 15
10
9 16 The Icehouse
8 17

The Freezer
5
6

N

100 feet

7
6

4
FYRs

1
Beautification

6.0 mi

0
3
Alphabet
Wall

MFTB 2

To Hook Creek Boulder

Jessica Campbell on *Tall Boy* (V5). **[PHOTO]** Max Hasson.

❏ 7. Project
Climb the roadside bulge from a matched start on a poor sidepull on the left side.

❏ 8. The Icehouse V4 ★★★
Start on low crimpers on the right side of the scooped face. Climb past the unique tufa-like pinch to a jug, and finish straight up the technical face.

❏ 9. Tall Boy V5 ★★
Begin with a right-hand sidepull on the right arête of the tall slab. Climb left, then up past a sloping rail and tiny crimps. Excellent.

❏ 10. Ice Age V5 ★
Begin on a low right-hand undercling and climb the off-vertical arête to a gripping finish. Technical and hard for the grade.

❏ 11. Ice Grip V4 ★★
Climb from a high right-hand sidepull to sloping shelves in the shallow dihedral. A nice mix of power and technique.

❏ 12. Fat Lip V3 ★
Begin with sloping edges on the left end of the low boulder next to the Icehouse. Traverse right along the lip to the cool fin and finish around the corner. Silly but fun.

❏ 13. The Icicle V2 ★★
Climb the small bulging arête from low opposing sidepulls. Great climbing for such a tiny rock.

❏ 14. Little Bear V3 ★★
Start crouched with low holds on the corner and make a big move up and left to the basketball sloper. Slap straight up the small prow to finish.

❏ 15. Bear Hug V5 ★★
Begin with your arms spread between the left arête and the opposing rail underneath the bulge. One burly move for flat edges above leads to a thrutchy finish.
Variation (V6): Start with your right hand on the lowest rail and do one or two moves into Bear Hug.

❏ 16. Claustrophobia V3 ★
Climb the vertical face between the tree and the other boulder. A bit sandy, and harder than it looks.

❏ 17. Bearly V0
Climb the dirty little face.

❏ 18. Blood Diamond V9 ★★
The diamond in the rough! To find Blood Diamond, walk roughly 50 yards directly uphill from the Icehouse, following the faint trail up a narrow gully until you reach a mini-cliff on the right. When you crest the steep hillside, walk directly left to the obvious cluster of large boulders. Blood Diamond climbs the right side of the dark, tall, diamond-shaped face from a crouch start with a good left hold and a sloping right hand in the head-high seam. Establish on two tiny crimps above, then dyno to the left-facing gaston crack. An incredible addition to the Straightways' pantheon of hard problems. F.A. Ben Herrington.

❏ 19. Project
There is a short, steep face in the cluster of boulders fifty yards up and left from the Icehouse that has not been climbed. Harder than it looks.

Joel Campbell mines for the perfect beta on *Blood Diamond* (V9).

23. WAS V8 ★★★

Jump to the basketball-hoop hueco in the middle of the face, and climb to the top using the left arête. An incredibly pure line that is one of Leavenworth's finest. This climb "was" a project…
F.A. Johnny Goicoechea.

Andrew Philbin teching through the crux of WAS (V8).

ANSWER MAN
"CAN YOU ANSWER? YES I CAN, BUT WHAT WOULD BE THE ANSWER TO THE ANSWER MAN?"
- ROBERT HUNTER, ST. STEPHEN

ANSWER MAN

Answer Man is roughly 6.1 miles from Icicle Junction, on the north side of the road about 100 yards past the Icehouse. A small, blank roof nearly overhanging the right side of the road marks the beginning of Answer Man's steep, faint approach. The boulder's eponym is a tall overhanging arête that can vaguely be seen from the road. Bring some determination and a friend to spot.

❐ 20. **Answer Man V6** ★★
Sit start on the small boulder with two flat edges. Climb the tall arête on opposing sidepulls to an insecure finish over an uneven landing.

❐ 21. **Taller V6** ★★★
Climb the high face from chest-high crimps. Wide, powerful climbing on perfect chunky edges leads to a big bump move to a jug below the lip. Fantastic.

WAS & THE PENROSE STEP

WAS is on the left side of Icicle Road, roughly 100 yards past Answer Man. Look for a low blob of rock on the left side of the road as you drive up; this is actually the top of the WAS boulder. WAS may be the most difficult boulder to find in the Straightaway Boulders, but is well worth the mission. The large overhang 20 yards up the road and a bit more downhill than WAS is the Penrose Step, a.k.a. the Ladder Project, itself a landmark that is home to several fun climbs and Leavenworth's proudest problem. The faint trail to the Ladder Project descends from the mini pullout just west of the boulder's steep face.

❐ 22. **Maybe V4** ★
Climb the left arête of the tall scooped face from a small incut sidepull. Work up the arête to good edges on the left face, then mantle to the dirty lip and top out.

❐ 23. **WAS V8** ★★★
See description on previous page.

❐ 24. **IS V7** ★★
Begin in the hueco as for WAS, but climb up and right on sloping crimps to a wide reach for good edges near the arête. Make an awkward mantle onto the slab around the corner to finish.

❐ 25. **Hemp V3** ★
Follow the faint trail to the water's edge from WAS to this scenic riverside problem. From a good slot edge under the overhang, climb left to the lip. Pop right to the good rail, and mantle; descend via the ramp.

❐ 26. **Rex Flex V3** ★
From high jugs on the right side of the Ladder Project boulder, climb up and left on good but sketchy holds and press it out. Scary!

❐ 27. **The Penrose Step, a.k.a. The Ladder Project V14** ★★★
Climb the tall, clean overhanging face from two high crimps in the shallow groove. The stopper first move is the easiest on this ridiculous testpiece... F.A. Carlo Traversi.

❐ 28. **Dog Named Rehab V4** ★★
Start on the right side of the featured scoop left of the tree with an incut left-hand sidepull and a right sidepull at the bottom of the ramp. Slap up the mini-bulge, then make a long move to the lip and press out the mantle. Not bad at all.

❐ 29. **I Know, Dyno! V9** ★
Start on a decent head-high crimp around the corner from Dog Named Rehab and dyno to the notch up and right. Grade unconfirmed – it's not entirely clear this one has been done.

THE COTTON PONY & COTTON PONY POINTER

The Cotton Pony is located on the left side of the road another 80 yards past WAS. Named for a certain canine's predilection to retrieve roadside litter for her owner, whether appreciated or not. Park in the second medium-sized pullout on the left, directly across from the Cotton Pony Pointer, a small spike of rock on the opposite hillside. Follow the trail downhill and slightly left from a cluster of small trees to find this super-steep overhang. For the Cotton Pony Pointer, follow faint switchbacks up the steep slope directly above the pullout.

❐ 30. **The Pony Ride V4** ★★
Begin low on the right side of the steep face. Follow the shrinking crack up and left until you're forced to make a big move left to the notch and top out with some powerful squeezing. Awesome.

❐ 31. **The Cotton Pony V10** ★★★
See description, next page.

❐ 32. **The Cotton Pony Low V11/12** ★★★
Begin sitting with a low undercling on the left arête of the sheer face. Traverse right along small crimps to the minus bar, continuing into the dyno of the Cotton Pony. Steep and unrelenting, this line was a longstanding project until its first ascent in 2007. As with the higher start, a hold on this line has mysteriously improved recently, but the overall difficulty and quality remain roughly the same. F.A. Johnny Goicoechea.

❐ 33. **The Cotton Pony Left V10**
This climb was done by Cole Allen in the summer of 2014. No beta is available.

❐ 34. **Tampax Arête V4** ★★
Climb the tall arête around the corner from The Cotton Pony. Super-cool jugs at the start lead to scarier climbing above the sloping landing. Finish to the left on top of the bulge and walk off the slab to descend.

Adam Healy powers up for the crux dyno of *The Cotton Pony* (V10).
[PHOTO] Max Hasson.

31. The Cotton Pony V10 ★★★

Start on the horizontal 'minus bar' rail in the middle of the roof. Move up to the Star Trek pinch and small right-hand crimp, then dyno to the V-shaped groove at the lip (V9/10 on its own). The footholds for this problem have mysteriously improved since the publication of *Central Washington Bouldering*, easing the difficulty a touch. Powerful and hard! F.A. Joel Campbell.

THE COTTON PONY

"THE MOVE, AS MEASURED BY BOB BUCKLEY, IS FOUR FEET EIGHT INCHES LONG."
- TERRY COWAN, A.K.A. KIXROX

35. The Cotton Pony Pointer V9 ★★

Start sitting on a boulder under the right side of the overhanging prow with a good right-hand sidepull. Move through sharp crimps to an insecure top-out above a rocky landing.
F.A. Johnny Goicoechea.

36. Joel's Problem V6 ★
Start matched on a flat edge in the middle of the vertical face and climb through edges to top out. Grade unconfirmed.
F.A. Joel Campbell.

37. Unkown V0 ★
Climb the shallow dihedral.

PROJECT BOULDER

There is an obscure boulder hidden above the road at the far eastern edge of Icicle Buttress. Park as for The Swiss Project Boulder and walk roughly 20 yards further up the road to a short, steep, and loose trail a few yards before the edge of the cliff. This boulder sits in a shallow bowl roughly 25 yards above the road.

38. Project
Start matched on the half-pad edge and throw for an incut left hand. A lot harder than it looks!

39. Project
Start crouched under the steep arête with a sloping left-hand underling and a right-hand sidepull. Squeeze to the lip, then top out up and right on slopers.

40. Project
Climb the cramped face from a low right-hand gaston.

THE SWISS PROJECT BOULDER

41. The Mothermilker V9 ★★
Start matched on a left-facing undercling with a high left foot ledge, slap to a high sloper on the lip and work your way over. Powerful! F.A. Joel Campbell.

42. The Cougarmilker V10 ★★
Start matched in a low shelf under the roof and climb sideways into the start of The Mothermilker. Very hard. F.A. Johnny Goicoechea.

43. Turbulence V11/12 ★★★

Start on a head-high jug on the right side of the swooped overhang and climb up and left onto the face. From two left-facing sidepulls, make an improbable all-points-off dyno to a sloper on the lip and mantle over, or use the new-school beta and heel hook to a tiny crimp below the lip. Formerly known as the longstanding "Swiss Proj." due to its riverside location and its perfect form. Simply one of a kind. F.A. Johnny Goicoechea.
Variation (V12): Start sitting and climb a few moves on wide edges into the start of Turbulence. F.A. Ben Herrington.

44. Upright Position V4 ★
Start on the big jug start of Turbulence and climb up and right on incut cracks and jugs to a high top out. Quite fun.

45. Puddlebutt VSploosh ★★
Climb onto the riverside slab from the adjacent boulder. A cruxy dyno to a jug about halfway leads to an easier top-out. Watch out for the sploosh! F.A. Joel Campbell, who says he'll buy dinner for anyone who repeats this problem.

Kyle O'Meara demonstrates perfect form on *The Mothermilker* (V9). **[PHOTO]** Max Hasson.

Keri Carlton climbs the *Tampax Arête* (V4).
[PHOTO] Max Hasson.

ICICLE BUTTRESS BOULDERS

There are a couple of easily-overlooked boulders scattered at the base of Icicle Buttress, a low-angle roadside cliff that is home to a number of fun beginner trad climbs. Batman was previously included in *Central Washington Bouldering*, but The Dock and Whip boulders are relatively-recent additions, as are the roadside oddities of *Throwin' the Houlihan* (V4) and *The Impossible Problem* (V8/9). Check out the Icicle Buttress boulders when you're craving something new but don't feel like walking far for it...

The Icicle Buttress Boulders are located along the side of the road just past the Straightaway Boulders, between 6.3 and 6.4 miles from Icicle Junction. Batman is visible from the road as you drive past, as is the top of The Whip directly across the road.

1. The Dinghy V5 ★

Start with edges close to the adjacent boulder, climbing straight up to a good flat crimp then making a harder move to the hole. Top out by rocking slightly left.

2. Fish & Chips V6 ★

Start with a chest-high edge, tick-tack up and left on crimps to the hole, then top out by rocking up and left.

3. Starboard Arête V5 ★★

Start standing with your left hand on an incut sidepull and your right hand on the arête. Slap up the arête and sidepulls to a ledge on the arête three feet below the lip, then bust to the top. Committing.

THE DOCK

4. Ghostride the Whip V5 ★

Start standing on the adjacent boulder with an orange shelf. Move to the big calcium sloper, then to crimps. Finish straight up with a horn over the stepped landing.

5. Cool Whip V10 ★★

From a crouched start matched on sloping underclings, gain two opposing sidepulls and jump to the ball hold at the top of the bulge. Use heel hooks and trickery to climb right and top out on the slopers of Miracle Whip. Powerful!

6. Miracle Whip V7 ★★

Start matched on the protruding meatwrap spike. Move up and left to the sloper, then climb technical off-balance moves straight up right-facing slopers on the faint arête.

7. Pussy Whip V3

Start on the lower-angle face and climb up and right on edges.

8. Tuxedo on a Turd V3

Start with a left-hand sidepull and a right-hand pinch at the bottom of the detached block. Move to the shelf and finish straight up.

9. Batman V8 ★★★

Start on the right end of the overhang with your left hand locked in the incipient crack and your right hand on the low sloping shelf. Cross up to poor holds on the lip and traverse left until you can slap to the faint depression in the slab above. Mantle and walk off the slab to the left. Classic!

10. Batman Begins V9 ★★

Start sitting on the far right end of the overhang. Traverse left along the sloping shelf for a move or two, then stab to the lock in the crack and top out as for Batman.

11. Throwin' the Houlihan V4 ★★

Find Throwin' the Houlihan by walking roughly 80 yards past Batman until you can see a wide, squat boulder roughly 40 yards downhill from the road. The start to the trail is roughly 30 yards past a small brown sign that reads "Leaving Private Property." Start sitting on the right side of the uphill face. Squeeze the angular block, working through sharp edges to finish atop the short slab above. Tricky and unique.

BATMAN BEGINS

Johnny Goicoechea on Batman Begins (V9).
[PHOTO] Max Hasson

Megan Lewis on *Starboard Arete* (V5)
[PHOTO] Max Hasson

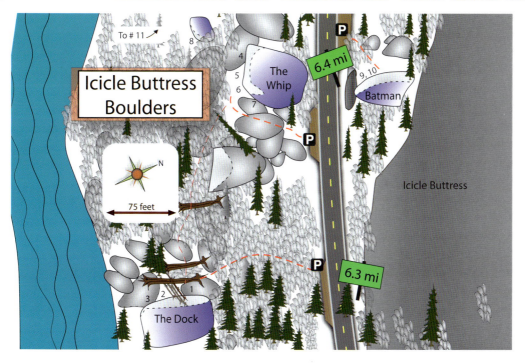

To # 11

8

4

5

6

7

Icicle Buttress Boulders

N

75 feet

The Whip

9, 10

Batman

P

6.4 mi

P

P

6.3 mi

Icicle Buttress

3 2 1

The Dock

THE BULGE BOULDERS

The Bulge Boulders is a small cluster of newly-developed boulders that are visible from the Icicle Road. Though it's likely that many boulderers checked these boulders out in years past, the first problems at the Bulge Boulders were established in the spring of 2013. While there aren't that many problems here, the quality of the rock and the movement on the area's two harder problems, *Kelly's Bulge* (V8) and *Johnny's Bulge* (V9) makes the area well worth a visit.

The Bulge Boulders lie 6.8 miles from Icicle Junction and are visible from Icicle Road. Park in a small pullout on the left just after some roadside talus and follow the still-faint trail uphill to approach the obvious cluster from the right.

☐ 1. **Drew's Bulge V3** ★
Start sitting with a low left-hand sidepull and a sharp right-hand crimp. Climb straight up and follow the arête right to top out. Odd.

☐ 2. **Unknown V1** ★
Start sitting at the right end of the sloping rail. Climb up and left to slopers on the lip and mantle.

☐ 3. **Kelly's Bulge V8** ★★
Start sitting with a left hand-heel match on the low rail and your right hand on a sharp crescent-shaped crimp. Climb up and right to match inset slopers on the lip, then climb straight right on Squamish-esque slopers to a dynamic move for a good crimp and an easy top-out. Really good movement. F.A. Johnny Goicoechea.

☐ 4. **Kona's Bulge V9** ★★
Start as for Kelly's Bulge but finish straight up from the start with high crimps. F.A. Kyle O'Meara.

☐ 5. **Johnny's Bulge V9** ★★
Start near the left lip of the deep overhang with your left hand on the lower incut crimp and your right hand on a sloper on the lip. Climb straight up using wide-open compression moves. Rad. F.A. Johnny Goicoechea. Variation (project): Start lower.

Isaac Howard on Kelly's Bulge *(V8).*

AREA

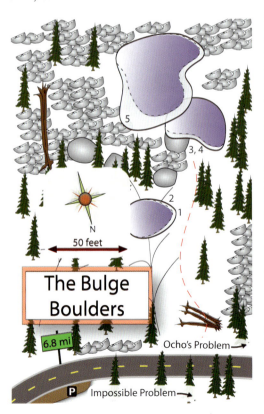

Dimitry Kalashnikov grappling for the poor slopers on The Impossible Problem (V8/9).

THE IMPOSSIBLE PROBLEM

The Impossible Problem sits on a small shelf directly below the parking for the Bulge Boulders. Start hiking downhill roughly 25 yards down canyon from the parking, just up-canyon from the edge of the cluster of boulders. Follow a well-worn trail straight downhill, then cut right through the dense brush to the nice, river-facing overhang.

❏ 6. **The Impossible Problem V8/9** ★★
Start standing at the edge of the riverside bulge with a tweaky left-hand pocket and a head-high two-finger right-hand crimp. Tech and slap your way up the blunt arete to an incut pocket two feet below the lip. Top out straight up. F.A. Joel Campbell.

❏ 7. **The Impossible Project**
Start sitting matched on the horizontal rail down and right from the start of the Impossible Problem. V15?

❏ 8. **Hot Holds V0** ★
Climb the faint low-angle dihedral on the uphill side of the boulder.

❏ 9. **Cool Holds V0**
Climb the short slab on the up-river face.

OCHO'S PROBLEM

To find the Ocho's Problem boulder, walk 75 yards back down canyon from the parking for the Bulge Boulders and enter the woods directly across from the start of a 50-yard long cluster of small boulders on the south side of the road. Walk straight into the woods and follow a faint trail slightly west along a small incline. The boulder is only 20ish yards from the road, but is obscured by dense undergrowth.

❏ 10. **Ocho's Problem V5** ★★
Climb the left side of the tall east-facing slab from a stand start spread between two sidepull crimps. Slap to a neat textured pinch on the face, then tech your way up the tall, handhold-less slab.

❏ 11. **The Rainmaker V8** ★★
Start standing around the arête left of Ocho's Problem with a sidepull sloper on the arête and an angular left-hand gaston. Climb delicate vmoves up and left along the sloping lip to top out on the corner. Very nice. F.A. John Stordahl.

❏ 12. **Project**
Start standing in the center of the face with a terrible left-hand sloper and an incut right-hand gaston.

IMPOSSIBLE PROBLEM

OCHO'S PROBLEM

THE RAT CREEK BOULDERS

The Rat Creek Boulders is a complex of several spread-out areas across Icicle Creek, roughly half a mile down canyon from Eightmile Campground. Though the Rat Creeks are impossible to access during most of the year, and at best difficult to access during the late summer, the area has seen sporadic development by boulderers over the past decade. The Lower Rat Creeks are a dozen or so boulders scattered throughout a flat, open area that still shows signs of the fire that swept the area in 1994. The Upper Rat Creek Boulders are perched on a plateau several hundred yards above the river in a jumbled talus field visible from the road, and were not developed until roughly 2010, with a spike in activity during the summer of 2013. Check this area out when the river's low and you're itching for some exploring. No map is provided; bring good hiking shoes and a light load, as you'll be doing plenty of walking!

The Rat Creek Boulders are very difficult to access, as the former trail across the Hook Creek bridge and along the river's edge is now a private driveway. The best bet seems to be to park on the left side of Icicle Road 6.9 miles from Icicle Junction, 0.2 miles before the Eightmile Campground, in a pullout across from a large creekside white boulder. Hike down the steep slope and look for the path of least resistance. An alternative crossing can also be made between Throwin' the Houlihan and The Impossible Problem, roughly 0.1 mile further down canyon. The obvious white boulder marks the western edge of the Lower Rat Creek cluster, which extends to the southeast toward the prominent Rat Creek Dome.

To reach the Upper Rat Creeks, head straight up the left-side of the steep hillside just above the large Rat Creek Boulder, which is home to a few obscure topropes and gear climbs. Once you crest the plateau, trend uphill and right to the large cluster. Total hiking time for the Upper Rat Creeks is about 15 minutes from Icicle Creek.

Drew Schick gains an appreciation for Kyle O'Meara's *Required Taste* (V10). **[PHOTO]** Max Hasson

Rat Creek Boulders
as viewed from 100 yards above parking

Upper Rat Creeks

Rat Creek Dome →

Lower Rat Creeks

← River Crossing

P

Kyle O'Meara works through moves on one of the nice boulders at the Upper Rat Creeks area.

Rob Lewis at the Upper Rat Creek Boulders.
[PHOTO] Max Hasson

The Upper Rat Creek Boulders.
[PHOTO] Max Hasson.

RIVER CROSSING   BUBBLE BOY   LOWER RAT REEK   UPPER RAT CREEK

THE BLISTER BOULDER

The Blister Boulder sits alone on the hillside a few hundred yards down canyon from the popular JY Boulders. Though it's a long hike for just one problem, the Blister Boulder has some of the most unique stone in Leavenworth. Nearly every hold is a knob is a knob!

Park for the Blister Boulder in a small lefthand pullout 7.0 miles up Icicle Road, roughly 0.1 mile before the entrance to Eightmile Campground. Find the well-worn Upper Eightmile Buttress trail that begins in a faint, wooded wash on the right side of the road and zig-zags past the short Stone's Throw crag. Pass a fun seam problem (V3) after roughly five minutes. After 10 minutes of slogging uphill, the trail meanders right past the Veteran's Club crag and two obvious short sport climbs, Nose Job (5.9+) and Face Value (5.8), into an open area. The Blister Boulder is the large boulder roughly 40 yards right of the trail, perched on the edge of a small plateau at roughly the same level as the Veteran's Club.

❒ 1. **Unknown V3**

This smallish problem sits to the right of the trail, roughly halfway to the Blister Boulder. Start crouched in the small corner and climb up and right in the steep seam to a dirty top-out.

❒ 2. **Dick Blisters V6** ★★

Start standing with high sloping knobs on the bottom of the tall, angled arête.

Paw your way up and left on knobs to mantle onto the slab roughly 2/3 of the way up. A new-school classic!
F.A. Andrew Deliduka.

AREA

An unknown climber snags an early ascent of *Dick Blisters* (V6).
[PHOTO] Scott Mitchell.

JY BOULDERS

The collection of boulders below the popular JY Crag hosts a nice mix of quality problems in a beautiful meadow setting. The striking *Yosemite Highball* (V4) is one of the best for its grade in Leavenworth, while the powerful and steep *Nosebleed* (V7), *Mad Max* (V8), and *The Strainer* (V8) are big favorites with the weekend-warrior crowd, and for good reason – they offer some of the most thuggy, dynamic bouldering at the grade in the area! More recent additions like *Green Lung* (V11, sit V12), *Thunderdome* (V9, sit V11), and *Hong Kong, a.k.a. Johnny Appleseed* (V10) have attracted the elite ranks to the JYs as well. Though the JY Boulders have received more attention in the past few years, they still see less traffic than the Icicle's other, larger areas, and they still retain a quiet and peaceful feel. Only five minutes above the JY Boulders proper, the Upper JYs offer an even more of an off-the-beaten path feel, and still have potential for new problems. With nice late-day sun, the JY Boulders are a pleasant spot in the spring and fall, but can feel a bit warm in the summer when the sun begins to bake the area in the early afternoon. The Gamecube, Green Lung, and the Mad Max cave, however, stay shady nearly all day.

The JY boulders are located on the hillside directly across from the entrance to Eightmile Campground. To access Green Lung, Yosemite Highball, and Mad Max, park on the right 7.1 miles from Icicle Junction, roughly 20 yards past the brown Forest Service sign across from the campground entrance. Follow the climber's trail up and right past the diminutive XY Crag, up and right toward the Green Lung boulder, then left again to the Yosemite boulder. To access Nosebleed directly, or to access the Upper JYs, park another 0.1 miles past the entrance to Eightmile Campground and follow the climber's trail up the far side of a small jumble of boulders. Hike directly east (right) once you crest the short rise, then follow switchbacks up the open hillside for a few minutes to the Nosebleed boulder.

1. German Acres V0
Climb the short arête 10 yards downhill from Nosebleed from a loose sidepull.

2. Geoff's Mantle V4?
On steepest part of the downhill face of the Nosebleed boulder, start on two high crimps and mantle over the deceptively hard bulge. Woot.

3. Unknown V2 ★
Climb the blunt, low-angle arête from a high incut foot. Actually really good!

4. Gradisfaction V2 ★
Start standing roughly 10 feet left of the obvious 'nose' hold with underclings in the overlap. Climb up and left to a big reach for slopers on the arête, topping out as for #3. This problem has cleaned up remarkably well in the last couple of years.

5 Nosebleed Left V7 ★
Start matched on a sloper in the V roughly six feet left of Nosebleed, move up to the chunky left-facing pinch jug, then make a couple of wide bump moves to the 'nose' hold. Morpho – V9 if you're under 5'9"?

6. Nosebleed V7 ★★
Start sitting with low opposing sidepulls, slap to the nose, and make a tough press move to stand up with the left arête in hand. The one-move-wonder that isn't!

7. Sassy Chipmunk V3 ★
Start sitting with the low, loose rail 10 feet right of the nose, make a big rock-over move up and right to the jug and finish with an easy mantle. The stand is a much more enjoyable V0.

8. One-Mover V2 ★
Start on two high, wide crimps on the small boulder, chuck to the lip, and top out.

9. Right Angles V8 ★★★
Start sitting by the square corner on the left side of the tall face. Slap up and right to the cool gaston/sloper and bump up the vertical, left-facing rail until you can stand up and reach for the jug. Very good.

10. The Yosemite Highball V4 ★★★
Start sitting on the left end of the tall face as for Right Angles. Do the big move up and right to the sloper, then continue right along the shelf to an incut flake. Make a big move straight to the lip, then finish up and left with the obvious jug and an interesting mantle. Beautiful.

11. Nosemite V4 ★
Climb the overhung bulge on the right side of the Yosemite Boulder. Sharp, and usually pretty dirty.

12. The Strainer V8 ★★★
Start crouched at the right edge of the small overhang directly above the trail with a good right-hand crimp on the arête and a sloping left-hand sidepull in the face. Pop to the left-facing sloper, then compress and slap your way up and left to top out next to the adjacent boulder. Though too short to be a true five-star problem, this one tops out this guide's three-star scale because of the pure quality of the pebble wrestling…

Jessica Campbell on *Nosebleed* (V7).
[PHOTO] Max Hasson

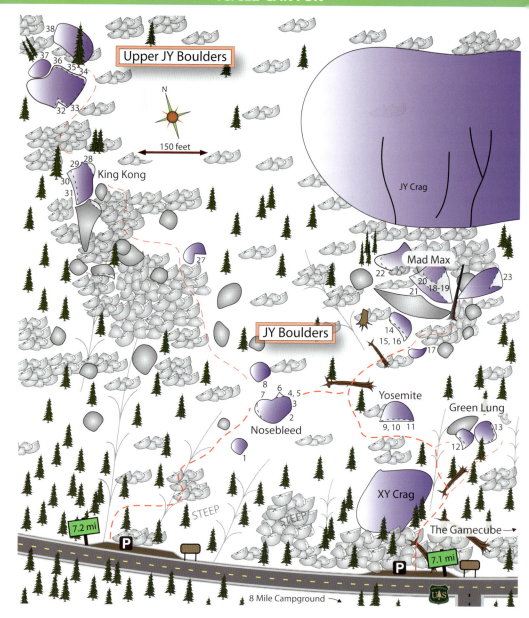

Upper JY Boulders

N

150 feet

King Kong

JY Crag

Mad Max

JY Boulders

Yosemite

Green Lung

Nosebleed

XY Crag

The Gamecube →

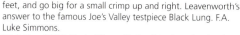

7.2 mi

P

STEEP

STEEP

7.1 mi

P

8 Mile Campground →

---

13. Green Lung V11 ★★

Start standing in front of the dark, blunt arête with a decent right-hand sidepull and a tiny, crescent-shaped left-hand crimp. Establish on a high foot (hard in itself), then move to the shallow pocket up and left, readjust your feet, and go big for a small crimp up and right. Leavenworth's answer to the famous Joe's Valley testpiece Black Lung. F.A. Luke Simmons.

Variation (V12): Start sitting with the flat crimp that is a key foot for the stand. As if it needed to be any harder! F.A. Ben Herrington.

14. The White Traverse V7 ★

Sort of like the Peak District's famed Green Traverse, but on sharp white granite… with painful granite crimps. Start on the left end of the short face and climb right on the strange incuts, avoiding the lip. Top out on the right arête.

Variation (V2/3): Slap to the lip from the start and traverse right to top out.

15. Max Attacks V3 ★

Start on the chest-high rail a few feet left of the arête. Climb straight up on sharp holds to an engaging mantle.

16. The White Arête V5 ★★

Start as for Max Attacks but move right to the arête, stab to the chunky square crimp on the corner and power to the lip, finishing with an awkward mantle. Great fun.

17. **Private Pile V1**

Climb the short arête in the sheltered corridor from two chest-high edges. Or don't.

18. **Mad Max V8** ★★★

Start wedged in the lowest part of the cave with your left hand on a low sloper, your right hand on an equally-low left-hand sidepull, and most of your weight on a far left heel hook. Punch up through slopers and pinches to a tough move for a left-hand sidepull and an even tougher compression move to crimps over the lip. Finish up the tallish slab. Wildly steep for featured granite, this climb became significantly more difficult when the jug for the move to the left-hand sidepull broke significantly in the spring of 2014. This is the only problem the author has established twice…

19. **Thunderdome V9** ★★★

Start crouched, matched on the left-facing sloping rail on the right side of the cave. Make a few compressiony moves out the steep roof on flat crimps to a good jug just below the lip, then top out up and right with a long and sequential traverse between jugs on the face and the sloping lip. The first ascent of the problem was, impressively, flashed by Johnny Goicoechea.

Variation (V4): The finish from the flat jug is a fun problem in its own right.

Variation (V11): Start as for Mad Max and traverse right along the sloping rail into the start of Thunderdome. Epic, though the Thunderdome moves are still the crux… F.A. Johnny Goicoechea.

20. **Project?**

There are two start holds that are perennially chalked on the short, blunt arête on the right as you exit the tunnel below Mad Max. It's unclear whether this problem has been climbed.

LEFT Adam Healy crushes *Thunderdome* (V9).
[PHOTO] Max Hasson

BELOW Jimmy Webb makes an impressive flash ascent of *Thunderdome Low* (V11).
[PHOTO] Aaron Matheson.

21. Project
Climb the mega-tall arête from a jump start. The longstanding vision of Portland hardman Adam Healey, this climb *will* be done someday!

22. Project
Climb the blunt overhanging arête. Anyone have a seven-foot wingspan?

23. Guano Slap V1 ★★
Just uphill from Mad Max, start this reachy problem on head-high slopers at the edge of the cave. Climb to the calcium-coated jug and stand tall to reach the lip. Really good! Extra points if you can grab the lip, turn around, and top out by turning upside down like Cole Allen…
Variation (V7): The cramped sit-start is rumored to have been climbed…

THE GAMECUBE

The Gamecube (not pictured on the map) is a tiny boulder up and slightly right of the campground entrance, essentially one drainage to the right of Green Lung and the trail to the JY Boulders.

24. Sega V3 ★
Hug the off-vertical face on the down canyon side of the lumpy boulder with your right hand on a sloper in the cleft and your left hand on the arête. Slap up to slopers and mantle. Short, but great texture.

25. Wario V0
Climb the dirty uphill face from the flat top of the right-facing 'ear' feature. If the sit-down interests you, go for it.

26. Bowser V3 ★
Climb the right-leaning rail to a surprisingly tall-feeling finish up the arête near the tree.

UPPER JY BOULDERS

To find the Upper JY Boulders, follow the faint trail up and left from Nosebleed, trending at essentially a 45 degree angle across the hillside. The Upper JYs are roughly 100 yards below the Small World Crag, which marks the uphill end of the steep meadow; King Kong is the lowest large boulder in the cluster, roughly 50 yards below its neighbors.

27. Project
Climb the steep, blank dihedral roughly halfway between Nosebleed and King Kong from a small platform of boulders. Looks wicked, if you're into that sort of thing.

28. Donkey Kong V4 ★★
Start standing on the uphill side of the King Kong boulder with a right-hand crimp/pinch on the vertical rib and a good right foothold. High step and stretch for a small edge in the notch, finishing straight up the juggy arête.

29. Ex-Pat Scotsman V0 ★
Climb the uphill face of the boulder, staying right of the verti-cal rib to top out on good but crumbly crimps.

30. Hong Kong a.k.a. Johnny Appleseed V10
★★★
Start standing on the steep uphill arête of the King Kong boulder with your left hand on the arête and a tiny right-hand crimp on the face. Make a huge move up and right to a good sloper, then compress and slap up the arête to top out. Morpho (read: probably not possible for shorter climbers!). F.A. Johnny Goicoechea.

31. King Kong V6
★★★
Climb the tall left-leaning arête/lip on neat sloping crimps and heel hooks. Finish directly up the corner on the left arête as for Johnny Apple-seed. Starting from the small boulder eases the challenge, but won't make the top any less scary. Thumbs up!

32. Project?
Start on slopers on the right end of the suspended shelf. Climb across the lip and mantle, topping out the dirty dihedral above.

33. Unknown V3 ★
Start with a high incut edge on the left side of the tall face and layback up the tall arête. Amazing, though it will probably need some cleaning…

34. Unknown V4 ★★
Climb the left side of the tall, overhanging face from a bizarre basketball-hoop edge.

35. Unknown V5 ★★
Climb the center of the tall overhanging face, following calcium-streaked slopers to the lip, moving slightly right to top out.

36. Unknown V1 ★
Climb the fist-sized crack.

37. Unknown V3 ★
Climb the shortish, quartzy arête left of the tree.

38. Unknown V0
Several fun variations climb the salt-and-pepper slab above #s 34-37.

Cortney Cusack soaks up the October sun on *King Kong* (V6).

UPPER JY BOULDERS   KING KONG

BRIAN DOYLE

I have a couple requests for the future generations of Leavenworth climbers that will be using this guidebook.

Please don't fuck this up.

The cat's out of the bag. It's no longer a secret: Leavenworth is awesome. Anyone can pull out their smart phone and watch footage of Leavenworth climbing. People now travel from all over the place to experience our PNW granite! I couldn't have imagined this 20 years ago. Please keep in mind that you are one of many, and each individual can have a lasting impact on Leavenworth.

You are a part of Leavenworth's history.

This guide book and others like it are only possible because of the efforts of previous generations' hard work and sense of adventure. It takes a lot of time, money, sweat, blood, frustration, and grit to make first ascents. Most climbers never understand or appreciate this. I'm not implying that a climbing experience is diminished by not making first ascents, my point is simply that your experiences are borne on the efforts of those who've come before you, and all that effort can be erased instantly by abuse of these areas. Don't be the generation of Leavenworth's climbers that impact climbing access, trash the place, and ruin it for future generations. Be the generation that builds better trails, pushes difficulty standards, and is the acting steward of a very special place.

Be aware of your impact.

Keep in mind that you're not in the local climbing gym. Your trash will not be picked up by a friendly staff member. Just because your banana peel will biodegrade doesn't mean you should leave it in the boulders. Your music is not always appreciated. Other people may be climbing on your project. Other people may end up climbing above your pads. You are not escaping to solitude. You are just another climber attempting to enjoy the boulders that are owned by all of us and by none of us. Please behave in a manner that ensures the generation after yours has the opportunity to experience this amazing place. Be a positive part of our community.

An enormous amount of research goes into writing a guidebook. After years of effort, there is no guarantee of making any kind of profit from your work. Take a moment to appreciate what Kelly has done here. He has provided you with a road map to years of amazing experiences, and access to the fruits of a lot of effort. Kelly would not have put the time and effort into writing this book if he didn't trust the next generation of climbers to use it wisely. So, I'll ask again: Please don't fuck this up.

THE WASHOUT

Though this guidebook includes many areas that have not previously been published, the Washout is the only truly "new" area. The two large boulders that comprise the Washout were only several feet tall until April 2011, when a huge mudslide tore down the hillside above Eightmile Campground, gouging a deep cleft through the rocky earth and depositing several hundred cubic yards of debris on Icicle Road in the process. Though it took longer than a month for USFS-funded work crews to clear the road and re-store access to the upper half of Icicle Canyon, Leavenworth locals John and Andrew Deliduka, Scott Mitchell, and others went straight to work on the newly-exposed boulders, using a gravity-fed hose system to slough off the millennia of mud and dirt and get the boulders into climbing shape. Their efforts were well worth it! The Washout boulders sport a handful of unique problems on a smooth white granite that is more reminiscent of the Index River Boulders than most anything else in Leavenworth. Between the quality of the climbing, the short approach, and the experience of climb-ing on boulders that were part of the earth until a few short years ago, The Washout is well worth a visit.

To get to the Washout, park in one of the small pullouts on either side of the short stretch of brand-new asphalt 7.3 miles from Icicle Junction, roughly 0.15 miles after Eightmile Campground and the parking for the JY Boulders. Follow a faint trail up the left side of the still-fresh wash for about 150 yards to the two obvious boulders.

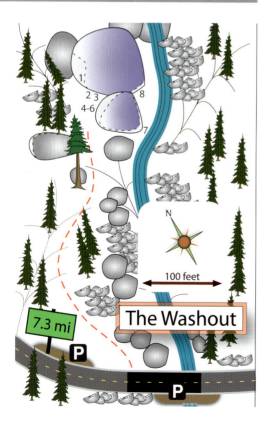

❏ 1. The Lion's Den V8 ★★★

Sit start at the edge of the narrow cave with your right hand on a sloper and your left on the lowest sidepull. Slap through a few compression moves on slopers and sidepulls to match on a good sloper at the nine-foot level. From the sloper, either make a big move up and left to an incut crimp, topping out straight up, or traverse right on slopers and smears to top out as for Dirty Dancing (the left finish being a bit more 'full value').

❏ 2. Dirty Dancing V4 ★★★

Climb the tall, clean slab from a good foot in the center of the rock scar, trending slightly left toward the top. Thankfully, it gets easier as you go!

❏ 3. Unknown V1

Climb the short slab right of Dirty Dancing to an early mantle. Top-out optional, but getting more fun every year as the boulder gets cleaner...

❏ 4. Unearthed V5/6 ★★

Start crouched with a flat triangle hold and a small sloper. Climb up and right on edges to a surprisingly involved top-out. Very unique!
Variation (V6): Start crouched down and left with opposing sidepulls, making two steep moves into the stand start.
Variation (V6ish): Start as for Unearthed and make a big move right into # 5.

❏ 5. Unknown V2 ★★

From a high start on a flat jug, stretch to a good edge below the lip, match up, and make an awkward mantle.
Variation (V3): Start with a small left-hand crimp and a sharp crimp on the right face and make one punchy move to the jug. The sit start could just maybe go on a cold day?

❏ 6. Unknown V2

Climb the short slab next to the downclimb from a high slop-ing edge.

❏ 7. Unknown V6 ★

Start squeezing two head-high sloping crimps on the blunt arête. Slap up to slopers and mantle.

❏ 8. Unknown V5 ★

Start at the edge of the stream with your right hand in the low right-facing feature and your left on a chunky sidepull on the face. Climb up and right to unique holds on the corner, then follow the arête back and left to top out.

AREA

Kelly Sheridan gets the sloper just right on *The Lion's Den* (V8). **[PHOTO]** Cortney Cusack.

The mudslide that unearthed the Washout area in April 2011, as viewed from the enterance to Eightmile Campground.

THE CARNIVAL BOULDERS

The Carnival Boulders are a dense cluster of blocks on a flat, sunny shoulder just above Icicle Road. An eponym of *Carnival Crack*, the "locally notorious" 5.11 offwidth uphill, the Carnivals have begun to see more traffic in recent years due to their deserved reputation as a great warm-up spot and an oasis of sunshine in the early spring and fall evenings. Though the area is probably best known for old-school classics like *Giant Man* (V3/4), *The Rib* (V4), and the four moderates on the Ferret boulder, Johnny Goicoechea has recently added two of Leavenworth's best problems that should attract any visiting crusher: the *Tornado Arete* (V12), a dramatic power problem up a steeply overhanging knife-edge that is one of Leavenworth's hardest problems, and *Big Happy or Legs Go Snappy* (V9), a *very* serious highball that climbs the prominent steep face that nearly overhangs half the boulders in the area. Most of the problems at the Carnival Boulders have friendly landings, and as mentioned, the Carnivals are one of the first Icicle areas to thaw in the spring and one of the last to catch the sunset in the fall.

The Carnival Boulders lie 7.4 miles from Icicle junction on the hillside above Icicle Road. Park in one of several lefthand pullouts just before an obvious roadcut (the crumbling cap of Eightmile Buttress). Walk back along the road for roughly 30 yards, then follow the faint trail up the short, steep incline to the obvious boulders. The Carnival Boulders are visible from the road, the most notable landmark being the huge "Big Happy" roof on the western edge of the cluster.

❒ 1. Heeler V2 ★
Traverse right along the lip of the overhang from an overhead jug on the left end. Finish in the notch with a strenuous mantle.

❒ 2. The Nike Dyno V8
Start in the steepest part of the quartz overhang with opposing sidepulls. Dyno to the lip and top out.

❒ 3. Mine V2/3 ★
Start with a weird square pinch in the center of the overhang, following painful holds up the seam to an awkward mantle. Better than it looks.

❒ 4. Butt Surfing V1
Start sitting with a low flake on the right end of the overhang, climbing straight up on grainy holds to the low lip.

AREA

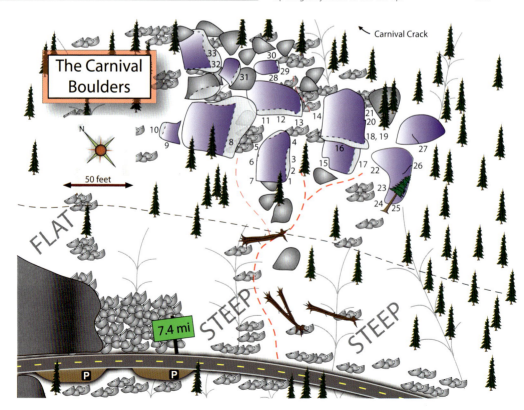

The Carnival Boulders

Johnny Goicoechea climbing confidently on the first ascent of *Big Happy or Legs Go Snappy* (V9).

5. Crispy Duck V7 ★
Start just right of the adjacent rock with a poor chest-high undercling. Work your feet up and lunge for the edge up and right. Very rarely done.

6. Against The Wall V1+ ★★
Climb the flake up the center of the face from a tricky start with left-facing edges and a good foothold.

7. The Campus Problem V0+ ★
Starting from a high jug on the downhill arête, climb the arête on large holds using Sly Stallone campusing or tricky heel hooks.

8. Big Happy or Legs Go Snappy V9 ★★★
Start matched on a right-facing incut in the deepest part of the prominent overhang. Make a big move to the featured rail, traverse left to the arête, and follow the sloping crack on the left face to the lip. Match on the hanging 'blob' feature on the corner and mantle with a good heel hook out right. Top out up the slab. Extremely proud.

9. Unknown V2
On a smallish boulder just above the Big Happy boulder, climb the slab from a stand start with a sloping right-hand sidepull on the left side of the face.

10. Unknown V0
Start on the calcium-deposit jug in the short overhang, move to the lip, and mantle.

11. The Ferret V3 ★★
From a chest-high edge in an alcove on the left side of the face, move up and right to a strangely-solid bar hold – the Ferret. Finish straight up and slightly left on the right-facing rail.
Variation (V3): From the Ferret hold, dyno up and right for the block on the lip.

12. Fen Fin V0+ ★★
Climb the featured intrusion just left of the arête, enjoying big holds as you head to a cruxy mantle up and left.

13. Grain Brain V3 ★★
Starting matched on a chest-high edge on the right arête, climb big moves between jugs to a crux mantle. Intimidating but well worth the mental effort.
Variation (V3): Start as for Grain Brain but move right to a big (and loose) flake, then crimp straight up the right face.

14. Giant Man V3/4 ★★★
Climb the center of the tall face, moving delicately up and left through sidepulls and edges. Height-dependent. A few pads are in order for this one…

15. The Stem V0 ★
Climb the stem corner on the small boulder right of Giant Man, pinching both arêtes as you go. Great fun. Can you do it in sneakers? Facing outwards? No hands??

16. Mr. Joel's Wild Ride V9 ★
This problems starts on the slab above The Stem. Start sitting matched on a low left-facing incut, then move up to crimps in the seam and grab the lip. You may want to get creative with the padding and spotting on this one to avoid rolling backwards down the slab… F.A. Joel Campbell

17. Feelin' Sappy V2
Start with a low left-facing jug in the tiny overhang. Move to the sappy lip, traversing left to a crux mantle. Kind of fun, but also kind of embarrassing.

18. The Tornado Arête V12 ★★★
Start on the flat edge on the right side of the dihedral and climb left to the steepest part of the arête, then crimp and slap up the arête feature. Top out. Very beta-intensive and exceptionally powerful. F.A. Johnny Goicoechea

Cortney Cusack stretches out on *Giant Man* (V3/4).

❐ 19. **The Dihedral V5** ★★

Start with a good blocky crimp on the right side of the dihedral. Use the bulgy sloper to the left to rock into the corner and reach for high edges. Excellent.

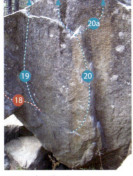

❐ 20. **The Rib V4** ★★★

In the secluded corridor, climb the tall rail feature from a stand start with a good detached foothold. At the top of the rib, make a committing move left to the shelf and finish with an easy mantle. Classic.

Variation (V4): From the sloping pinch at the top of the rail, dyno up and right to the lip and top out.

❐ 21. **Baby Back V2**

Start on the adjacent boulder with a good shelf. Follow the left-trending rail to the top.

❐ 22. **Dan Akroyd VB** ★

Climb the slabby arête on the left side of the face.

❐ 23. **Rick Moranis VB** ★

Climb the low-angle scoop on the right side of the face.

❐ 24. **The Brawl V1** ★★

On the downhill side of the tall boulder, climb the tall double arêtes from a head-high jug. Scurry left to top out as for Rick Moranis. Easy, but pretty high…

❐ 25. **Half Man Half Marathon V4** ★★

Climb the face right of the arête on small crimps. This climb was likely first bouldered in the fall of 2014, though the 1/4"

bolts betray a more storied history…

❐ 26. **Dutty Rock V1**

Climb the left-leaning crack to a dirty finish in the corner. Walk up and left on the vegetated ramp to top out.

❐ 27. **Over Myself V1** ★

Climb the 'semi-clean' slab at the eastern edge of the cluster. An adventure in modesty.

❐ 28. **Solar Powered V4** ★

Start in the narrow hole to the left of The Pickle with under-clings below the chest-high bulge. Slap to crimps over the bulge, high step, and finish up the tall off-vertical face.

❐ 29. **The Pickle V3** ★

Start sitting on the small boulder with a low left crimp on the arete. Slap up both sides of the arête to a committing move for the lip. Good fun.

❐ 30. **The Gherkin V3**

Start sitting around the corner from The Pickle with a left-hand sloper on the arête and a high right-hand sidepull. Climb to the lip and top out.

❐ 31. **Project**

Start sitting on the slab with the right arête and a good left-hand crimp.

❐ 32. **Project**

Anyone? Bueller??

❐ 33. **Drew's Problem V6** ★

From a broken crimp in the center of the overhang, climb up and left to a cramped top-out. Grade unconfirmed.

LEFT Jeanna Perotta on *The Rib* (V4).
BELOW Johnny Goicoechea sticks the lip on the first ascent of *The Tornado Arête* (V12).
[PHOTO] Max Hasson.

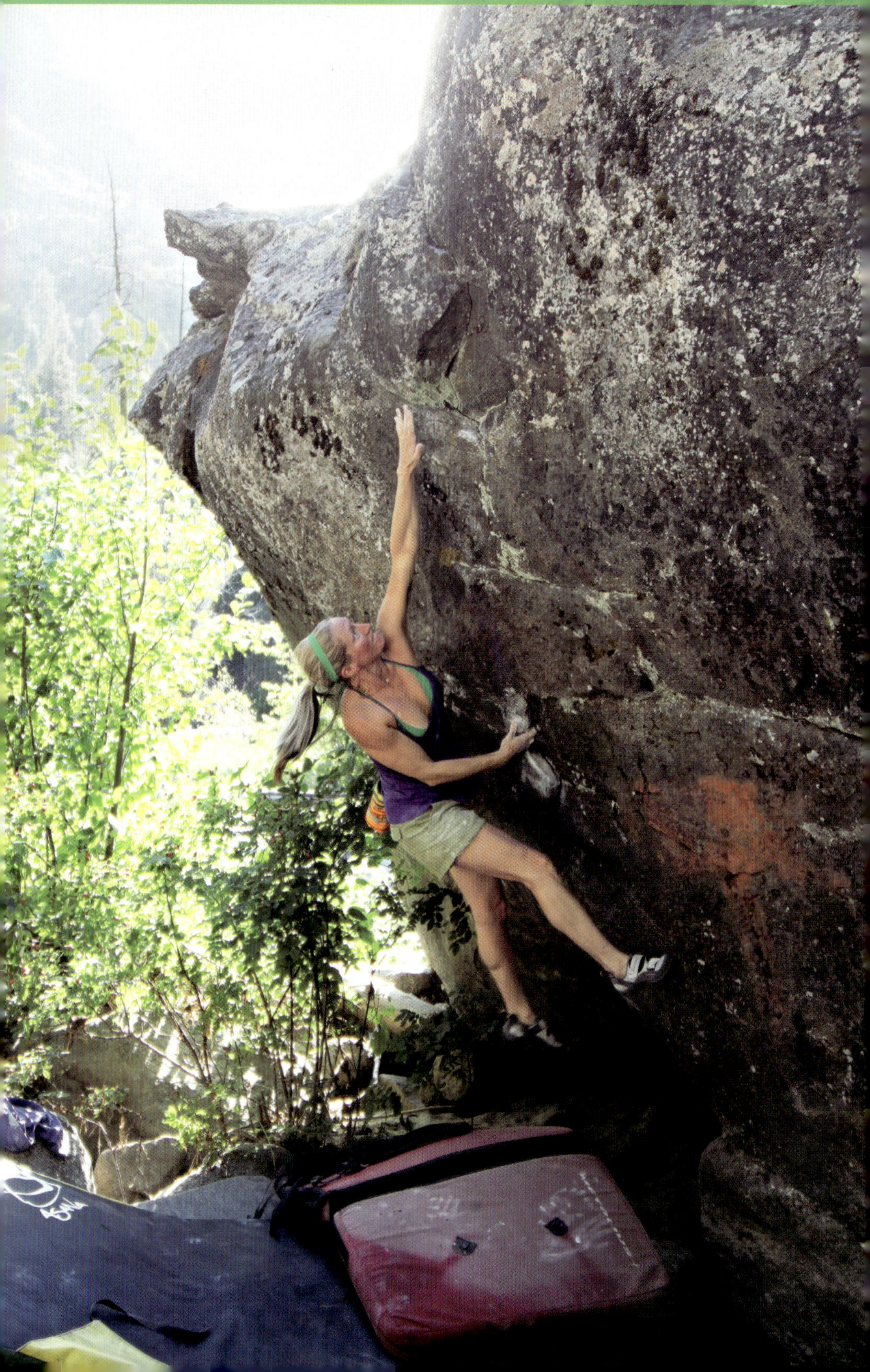

THE JESSICA CAMPBELL MEMORIAL BOULDER

You know you've reached legend status when you get your own memorial boulder. Visit this riverside block on a warm fall afternoon, as it its landing is submerged during the spring floods…

Park 7.5 miles up the Icicle for the JCMB, roughly halfway between the Carnival Boulders and the Pretty Boulders parking areas, in the lefthand pullout next to the granite dome that is the backside of Eightmile Rock. Hike down the steep trail on the east side of the cliff to the flat, open area below the quintessential Classic Crack (5.8). From the base of the cliff, walk east roughly 25 yards along the decommissioned dirt road, then follow the faint trail to the wide, squat boulder at the water's edge. Please be respectful of the property owners in the area, and don't drive or walk down the private drive to the west of Eightmile Rock.

❐ 1. Jessica Campbell Memorial Boulder

Problem V5 ★★

Start next to the water on the far left end of the overhang with a sloping shelf at chest height. Slap up incuts, using the left arête, to a confusing top-out.

❐ 2. Unknown V3 ★

Start with a sidepull jug next to some orange graffiti in the middle of the face. Make a big move to a sloping jug, then top out straight up on flat ledges.

❐ 3. Unknown V1

Begin with an overhead jug 10 feet right of #2. Move right to the jagged flake, then top out up and right around the small corner.

❐ 4. Unknown V1

Start (carefully) with a detached flake on the right side of the face. Top out straight up.

❐ 5. Unknown V1

Climb the dirty face over a seasonally-wet landing.

AREA

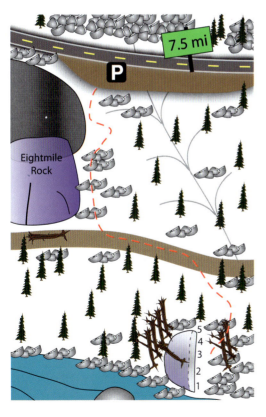

Cortney Cusack sticks the lunge on problem #2 at the Jessica Campbell Memorial Boulder.

THE PRETTY BOULDERS

The Pretty Boulders is a secluded off-the-beaten-path area that is home to a small collection of exceptional problems. The technical fin of *Pretty Girl* (V3) is one of the best moderates in the entire canyon, and the tall, clean slab of *Alexis C. Jolly* (V1) is a beginner climb to match. More aggressive boulderers can test themselves on the sequential slopers of *Pretty Woman* (V5) and the powerful "span moves" of *Pretty Hate Machine* (V8), a "timeless" arête that graced the cover of the *Central Washington Bouldering* guide. In addition to Cole Allen's new addition *The Last of A Dying Breed* (V8), the Pretty Boulders have a few other projects that will one day attract attention when Leavenworth's lower-hanging and better-looking fruit have all been picked. Hit the Pretty Boulders when you need some late-day sun, and enjoy the middle-of-nowhere atmosphere and the views of Mount Stewart up the Mountaineer Creek valley. The land downhill and up canyon from Pretty Girl is private property; please respect the landowner's privacy by keeping noise and exploration to a minimum.

The Pretty Boulders are supposedly hard to find. Park on either side of the road 7.6 miles from Icicle Junction, just after the roadcut that is the top of Eightmile Rock, home to the aptly-named Classic Crack (5.8+). The parking area is roughly 100 yards past the obvious parking for the Carnival Boulders. Pretty Boy is about a one-minute walk past the pullout, roughly 20 yards above an orange telephone cable marker; approach via a faint climbers' trail along the gentle roadside ridge. To find Pac-Man and the Pretty Boulders proper, start up the short slope directly above the parking. After cresting the small roadcut, meander straight up for a minute or two before cutting left and following the climbers' trail along the right side of the shallow gully. Walk directly away from the road. The trail to Pac-Man cuts sharply off the main trail roughly one-third of the way up the hillside. For the Pretty Boulders, continue up a few switchbacks until you reach a small shoulder at the top. Walk left for 20 yards, then straight uphill over a small rise, toward the small cluster of boulders. The entire hike to the Pretty Boulders should take between five and ten minutes from the car.

⌐ 1. Pretty Boy V7 ★★
A little harder than it looks… Start with your left hand in the sloping hueco and your feet on the large flake. Pop to a small crimp just below the lip and finish straight up.

⌐ 2. Pizzaface V1
Climb the left side of the downhill face from a high start with the calcium-coated jug. A bit loose but still fun.

⌐ 3. Ms. Pac-Man V2 ★
Press awkwardly onto the tallish face just right of the slight rib feature. Follow sloping crimps to a dirty mantle on the slab.

⌐ 4. Pac-Man V3 ★
Start sitting on the east corner of the large boulder. Slap up to a pinch on the corner, then mantle on the mini-bulge and stand up using grainy slopers.

AREA

⌐ 5. Pretty Girl V3 ★★★
Start with a good right-hand sidepull and a low left-hand sloper on the right side of the curved fin. Move left to good sidepulls on the face, then slap and stem up the perfect corner. An instant classic when found in 2006.

Cortney Cusack uses good techkneeque on the low crux of *Pac Man* (V3).

Joe Kerr on *Pretty Hate Machine* (V8).
[PHOTO] Max Hasson

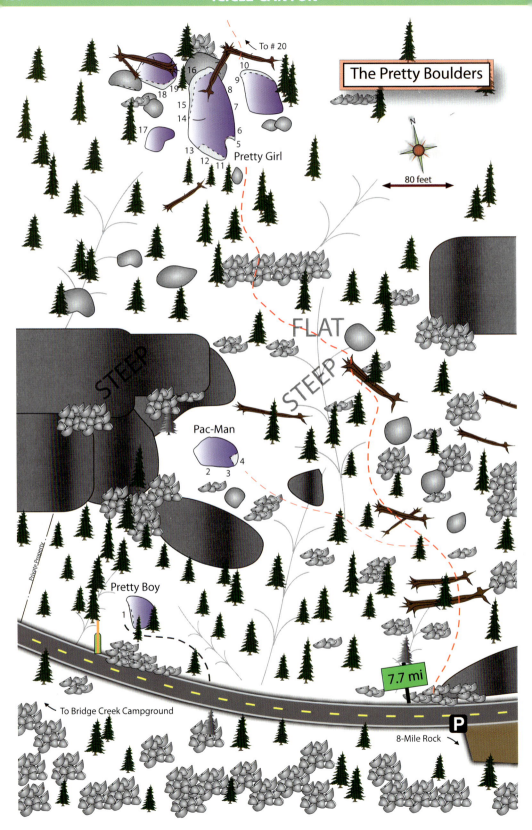

To # 20

The Pretty Boulders

16
10
9
8
18
19
15
7
14
6
17
5
13
12 11
Pretty Girl

N

80 feet

FLAT

STEEP

STEEP

Pac-Man
4
2 3

Private Property

Pretty Boy
1

7.7 mi

To Bridge Creek Campground

P

8-Mile Rock

6. Pretty Woman V5 ★★
Start as for Pretty Girl, but climb straight up sloping edges right of the fin to a jug on the lip. Grainy and technical.

7. Pretty Easy V0 ★
Climb the loose left-leaning rail in the middle of the face to an easy-as-pie mantle.

8. Pretty Stupid V0
Climb the right side of the face.

9. Pretty Hard Project
Climb the blunt corner from two fat crimpers. Will go, but is crumbly and sharp…

10. Project
Climb the face from crimps on the right side of the steeper face. Move to the shallow dish and bust to the lip.

11. Noland V1
Climb the arête on the downhill corner of the Pretty Girl boulder. Fun from either side.

12. John He-Man V2 ★
Start sitting with the flat edge in front of the tree. Climb up and right on flat edges to a fun finish right of the overlap.

13. Miller V1
Climb the undercut face from a left-facing edge at head height.

14. Cracked Out V1 ★
Start on juggy underclings in the seam at waist height. Move to a sloper, then finish up the juggy right-facing crack above.

15. Pretty Burly V4 ★★
Start with small underclings in the overlap on the rear of the Pretty Girl boulder. Slap up to the sloping edge on the lip, match, and lunge to a fat pinch at the apex. Awesome.

16. Pretty Silly V3 ★
Up and over the boulder left of Pretty Burly, start this short arête on a flat shelf, using a small crimp in the seam to reach the lip. Top out straight over the right side of the corner.

17. Alexis C. Jolly V0 ★★
Climb the hidden slab on the west side of the smallish boulder, squeezing between the arête and good rails on the face. An awesome slickfoot.

18. Pretty Hate Machine V8 ★★★
Pretty Hate Machine sits in a small alcove behind the rear side of the Pretty Girl boulder. Start from an undercling below the chest-high bulge and climb up and right to the corner. Reach high to a poor pinch on the arête with your right hand, set your feet up, and dyno to the juggy lip. A beautiful testpiece on impeccable rock. F.A. Kyle O'Meara.

19. Pretty Crimpy V4 ★
Start sitting right of Pretty Hate Machine with a low, flat left-hand crimp, move up to the sharp crimp on the face, then bust to the lip and top out straight over.
Variation (project): Start on sidepulls down and left. Hard!

20. Last of a Dying Breed V8 ★★

This problem climbs the uphill right arête of the long, low boulder visible 50 yards above the Pretty Boulder. Start crouched under the roof with a sharp right-hand sidepull and a left-hand sloper on the arête. Climb a few moves on crimps to a big dyno for a flat shelf several feet over the lip. Top out either by rocking straight over onto the jug, or traverse right through sequential slopers in the fold for full value. One of the latest, but not the last! F.A. Cole Allen.

Cole Allen on the first ascent of *Last of A Dying Breed* (V8).

Joel Campbell on the low start to *Pretty Crimpy* (project).

THE ORANGE WALL

The Orange Wall is an obvious mini-cliff just above Icicle Road, at a relatively sharp lefthand turn just before the parking lot for Angelina Jolie and the 420 Boulders. Longtime Leavenworth local and prolific climber Joe Treftz describes this as "the scariest boulder problem I've ever done." Not too many have followed in his footsteps!

The Orange Wall is visible to the right of Icicle Road 8.0 miles from Icicle Junction, 0.1 miles before the parking for the Angelina Jolie and 420 Boulders, and roughly 0.5 miles before the left turn for Mountaineers Creek Road and Bridge Creek Campground. Park as for the Ice Cube and walk roughly 50 yards back down the road to a faint trail on the down canyon side of the road-cut. Hike up and left to the tall scooped face with obvious orange and white streaks.

❒ 1. Unknown V5

The left side of the face is "short and hard." Your guess is as good as mine…

❒ 2. The Orange Wall V5

★★

Start standing in the dihedral on the right end of the tall scooped face with a left-hand sidepull crimp and your right hand on a sloping pinch on the arête. Climb a few moves on slopers to a very tall top-out in the left-trending crack.

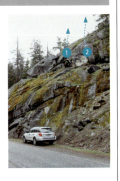

TWISTED TREE

The Upper Icicle's Twisted Tree boulder vies with Clamshell Cave's Fist Boulder for the "most obvious boulder in the Icicle" award. A stone's throw from the road, the Twisted Tree boulder is easily identifiable by the ancient ponderosa pine wrapped around its left arête. In addition to the roadside classics *Twisted Tree* (V4) and *Twister* (V7), this area is also home to the Angelina Jolie boulder and the difficult classics *Angelina Jolie* (V10) and *Scrambled Eggs* (V8). The Twisted Tree area is good most of the year, though some may want to save the challenging slopers of Twister and Angelina Jolie for a crisp fall afternoon!

The Twisted Tree area is pretty darn easy to find. Park adjacent to this roadside boulder, 8.2 miles from Icicle Junction, roughly 0.3 miles before Mountaineers Creek Road and the entrance to Bridge Creek Campground. Please park completely off the road and avoid the usual tailgate parties; with five more campgrounds up canyon, this wide curve can be busier than it might seem at first. To find the Angelina Jolie boulder, it's easiest to walk back along the road for 50 yards or so, re-entering the thin forest after a short rise just down canyon of a small seasonal stream; alternatively, park roughly 0.1 miles before the Twisted Tree and hike directly into the woods. Scrambled Eggs is roughly twice as far above the road as the Twisted Tree. The Ice Cube is a little closer to town, just below the road roughly 40 yards east of the trail to Angelina Jolie, on the edge of the Bridge Creek Campground group site. Please limit your exploration in this area, avoiding the private property boundary just uphill from problems seven through nine.

❒ 1. Twisted Tree V4 ★★★

Start sitting matched on the incut jug just left of the tree. Climb the steep corner to a tricky mantle and top out straight up the slab. Short and stout, an area classic.

❒ 2. Mr. Leftist V6 ★

Start as for Twisted Tree but climb left past a sloper on the lip to a sidepull flake and mantle.

❒ 3. Twisted Tree Dyno V7 ★

Start with crimps a couple feet right of the tree, pull on, and dyno to the bucket over the lip.

❒ 4. 101 Ways to Fling Poo V10/11 ★

Start sitting just right of the tree, matched on a low incut rail. Climb up and right on small, gritty crimps, making a hard move (which can be done with either hand) to gain the sloping crimps of Twister. Named for a uniquely Freudian scatological theory of human nature… F.A. Dave Thompson.

❒ 5. Twister V7 ★★★

Start on the chest-high flat edge in the small corner. Climb left to two nice round slopers at head height and continue left past sloping crimps to better holds and a tall-feeling finish. "Quit reading and do it."

AREA

LEFT PAGE Cortney Cusack on *Twisted Tree* (V4).
BELOW Right hand sloper, left hand to crimp... Herman Feissner playing *Twister* (V7).
[PHOTO] Jackie Hueftle.

❒ 6. With A Twist V1 ★
Start for Twister, but climb straight up to better holds, then finish up and left with a large, rounded gaston in the crack.

❒ 7. Straight Shot V0+ ★
Start as for With a Twist but finish slightly right on dirty buckets.

❒ 8. Little One V2 ★
Climb the mini overhanging prow from a crouch start. Sharp but pretty fun.
Variation (V2): Start on the good edge three feet left of the prow and finish as above.

❒ 9. Nuthin' V3
Climb the short arête from a crouch start. The sit is inviting but awkward…

❒ 10. Sumthin' V0
Start with the big sidepull on the uphill face of the boulder. Climb to the lip and mantle.

❒ 11. Scrambled Eggs V8 ★★
Start on two small crimps on the road-facing corner of the Angelina Jolie boulder. Climb straight up the blunt arête to a good high crimp and top out up the dirty slab. A typical Joel Campbell problem; finger and core strength a must.
Variation (V2/3): Start standing.

❒ 12. Angelina Jolie V10 ★★★
See Description on next page.

❒ 13. Twisted Stone V3 ★★
Start on the right corner of the tall face with a flexing jug and muscle up either side of the arête. Great fun.

❒ 14. Unknown V0
The boulder's downclimb also makes for a pleasant warm-up.

❒ 15. Over Easy V0 ★
Climb the textured slab from the small boulder in front of it. Head straight up using the left-facing sidepull, or step right to the good edges near the arête.

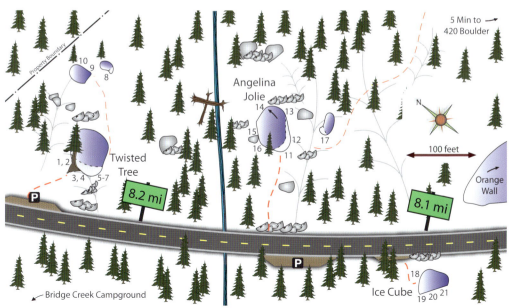

□ 12. Angelina Jolie V10 ★★★
Climb the obvious sloping rail up the center of the tall face
from a high start with the decent sloper on the far left
end of the rail. Much tougher than it looks, this line was a
longstanding project until Joel Campbell first deciphered
the sequence in 2008. Named for the problem's vague
resemblance to the famous Peak District problem Brad Pitt.
Variation (V11): Start standing with poor opposing
sidepulls and make one move to gain the sloper. F.A. Tim
Doyle.

Kyle O'Meara on *Angelina Jolie* (V10).
[PHOTO] Max Hasson.

❑ 16. **Deviled V2** ★

Start from the rocking boulder with an incut waist-high sidepull at the edge of the small dihedral, climbing straight up the arête with cool slopers to an insecure finish. Better than it looks!

❑ 17. **The Dildo V3** ★★

Climb the short arête on gritty holds from the big low rail. A lot of climbing for such a tiny boulder...

❑ 18. **Raptorman V3**

The uphill arête of the Ice Cube boulder. Grab high crimps on both sides of the arête, pull on, and shoot for the lip. Formerly climbed as a sit-start until several holds broke…

❑ 19. **Gatorade Bowling Balls V4** ★

Start on low opposing sidepulls, stab into the incut pinch on the arête, and top out straight up the right side of the dirty corner.

❑ 20. **Etna Mantle V3** ★★

Begin with both hands on the good head-high incut in the middle of the face. Climb to sloping holds on the lip and thrutch over to small crimps. Classy.

❑ 21. **Ben Carney's Bowling Balls V5** ★

Start sitting with your left hand in the obvious low slot. Pull on and stand to the sloping lip, finishing with a short mantle into the scoop on the slab. Very odd indeed.

"It's hard, but it's not that hard…" – *Ben Moon*. Joel Zerr bears down on the beguiling slopers of *Angelina Jolie* (V10).
[PHOTO] Max Hasson

THE 420 BOULDERS

The 420 Boulder and the small cluster of the Upper 420 Boulders lie on a small plateau directly above the roadside Orange Wall. Just a few minutes up and right from the Angelina Jolie boulder, the 420s offer a small circuit in a pretty meadow setting. In addition to the tall, thin *420 Slab* (V1), the technical compression climbing of *Shaniqua* (V5) should not be missed. Those who are interested in a less mellow experience should pit themselves against the funky, powerful body-tension climbing of *Emu Butter* (V8/9) and Kyle O'Meara's highball masterpiece *Reflection of Perfection* (V6). The 420s get plenty of sun in the winter and on late summer evenings, but can feel a bit burnt out in warmer months. Please take special care to stick to trails when visiting the 420 Boulders in order to help preserve the fragile vegetation and the area's natural beauty.

The 420s are a 5-7 minute walk above the Angelina Jolie boulder. Follow the obvious trail past The Dildo (V3) and over a small ridge, then turn left and head up the gentle valley. After passing a tallish, dirty slab (V2), turn slightly right and head straight up the narrowing valley to the flat plateau. To reach the Upper 420 Boulders, follow a faint trail sharply to the left a few yards before reaching the 420 Boulder. Pick your way up the right side of the steep gully to the obvious cluster a hundred yards or so above the 420 Boulder.

❒ 1. Unknown V2 ★

This rarely-climbed problem is on the largeish hillside boulder halfway between Angelina Jolie and the 420 Boulders. Start on the left (uphill) side of the west-facing slab, climbing up and right to follow the shallow crack to the top.

❒ 2. Unknown V1

Climb the tall, calcium-streaked face in the small cluster of boulders directly above #1.

❒ 3. Mr. Yuk V11/12 ★

Start sitting right of #2 matched on a low crimp rail. Move up to two miserable crimps at the lip, then slap up more terrible slimpers to finish straight up. One of the last-established problems to be included in this guide, the grade is unconfirmed but the grips are baaad! F.A. Ben Herrington.

❒ 4. Unknown V3 ★

Climb the blunt arête from a stand start with a high right-hand sidepull pinch and a low left sloper. Avoid the drilled pocket – one of only two or three in the entire Leavenworth area – for full value. This is also the boulder's downclimb/jump.

❒ 5. 420 Slab V1 ★★

Climb the center of the tall slab on unobvious edges. Finish slightly right on better holds. This climb unfortunately has a toprope anchor, likely put in by the same gutless wanker who drilled the pocket on #4.

❒ 6. Unknown V1 ★

Climb the left side of the slab.

❒ 7. Unknown V2 ★

Start underclinging the crack with your left hand and squeezing the arête with your right hand. Climb up and left, topping out in the groove. Good fun.

Cortney Cusack takes a stroll up the *420 Slab* (V1).

❒ 8. **Shaniqua V5** ★★★

Climb the clean double arête feature from a stand start squeezing slopers above your head. Heel hook and slap straight up to the thank-god jug on the lip. Excellent climbing. **Variation (V7/8):** Start underclinging the triangular flake at waist height.

❒ 9. **Project**

Climb the hanging slab.

❒ 10. **Unknown V6** ★

Start with a high crimp on the left side of the overhanging arête. Move up and left through crimps and rock straight over the lip.

❒ 11. **Unknown V4** ★★★

Climb the tall stepped arête from a stand start with a good right-hand sidepull and a high, quartzy left-hand sloper. Tic-tac up sidepull edges on the right face to an exciting finish. Awesome.

❒ 12. **Team Turquoise V2** ★

Climb the center of the slab from a stand start with two gastons in parallel seams.

❒ 13. **Unknown V0**

Climb up and left along the sloping arête.

❒ 14. **John's Problem V6** ★

Climb the deceptively hard overhanging arête from a sit start with a chunky right-hand crimp. Top out up and left using the dirty seam.

❒ 15. **Emu Butter V8/9** ★★

Start crouched with a good crimp rail on the left edge of the undercut feature and climb straight up the left side of the arête. Morpho; taller climbers can make use of the low left foot on the attached block for longer than shorter climbers can…

UPPER 420

❒ 16. **Unknown V3**

Start matched on a good sloper on the right side of the bulge. Climb up and left on slopers until you can rock over. Usually dirty.

REFLECTION OF PERFECTION

From the upper 420 Boulders, hike straight uphill on the faint trail up the left aspect of the very steep gully. Crest a ridge after 2-3 minutes, then hike another 1-2 minutes up a gentler hillside to a nice plateau and the obvious huge boulder. This cluster is also home to a number of unlisted moderates and a few projects, including the tall bulgy crack to the left of Reflection of Perfection…

❒ 17. **Project**

Climb the tall overhanging crack left of Reflection of Perfection.

❒ 18. **Reflection of Perfection V6** ★★★

Climb the right side of the obvious 20-foot overhanging arête from a stand start with opposing sidepulls. Move into the big, chunky underling then tech your way up the flared crack to an airy top-out. So classic it gets three stars despite the crumbly feet.

❒ 19. **Unknown V4** *

Start with high sidepulls on the end of the face right of Reflection of Perfection and climb straight up.

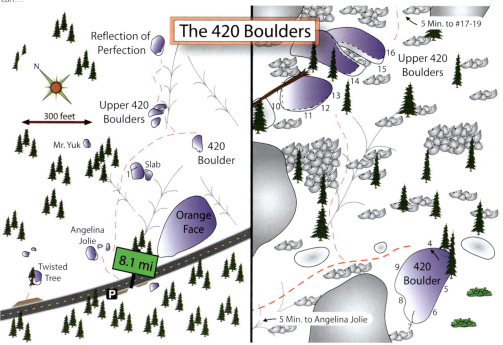

The 420 Boulders

← 5 Min. to #17-19

Reflection of Perfection

N

Upper 420 Boulders

Upper 420 Boulders

300 feet

Mr. Yuk

Slab

420 Boulder

Angelina Jolie

Orange Face

8.1 mi

Twisted Tree

P

← 5 Min. to Angelina Jolie

420 Boulder

LITTLE BRIDGE CREEK WALL

Little Bridge Creek Wall is hidden in the woods just past, and across from, the start of Mountaineer's Creek Road and the entrance to Bridge Creek Campground. This diminutive crag is home to several bolted and mixed climbs as well as Dick Cilley's burly toprope *Gutbuster* (5.12+), which has not been bouldered (and probably shouldn't be!). The cliff doesn't offer too much unroped entertainment, with the exception of the two striking hit-the-jug-and-drop problems *The Lefty* (V7) and *The Bazooka* (V8). Check this area out when you're looking for an obscure challenge, or if you've just got to climb in a light rain; the overhanging wall shields this section of the cliff, and the boulder problems will stay dry for several hours even in a light drizzle.

Park 8.5 miles from Icicle Junction for Little Bridge Creek Wall, in the small pullout on the left at the beginning of Eightmile Road. Walk into the woods a few feet left of the driveway across the street, then turn left onto the worn trail, following it west and slightly uphill to the base of the 50 ft. crag. Find The Lefty on the right end of the crag, easily spotted by the prominent quartz vein running across the face. There are a handful of boulders in the talus up and right of the crag, but they are very close to private property and have not been included in his guide out of respect for the landowner. Please take care when visiting this area to avoid the private driveway and keep a low profile.

Joel Zerr sticks the massive dyno on *The Bazooka* (V8).

☐ 1. The Bazooka V8 ★★

Start in the dark black water streak about 10 feet right of Gutbuster with a small left-hand crimp and a good right-hand sidepull. Dyno to the bucket in the horizontal seam above and drop. Boom!

☐ 2. The Lefty V7 ★★★

Start hanging from the sloping shelf at chest height, working up the clean face via three left-facing sidepulls in and around the quartz dyke. Slap to the juggy horizontal crack, hang out, and drop. Beautiful and technical.

Drew Schick spooks his way through the redpoint crux of *The Munsters* (V11), in the talus up and right from Little Bridge Creek Wall.

AREA

COLE ALLEN

I did my first lead climb in Leavenworth when I was in fourth grade. I've been climbing and bouldering in the area for 21 years, but my second ascent of Mount Stuart's complete *North Ridge* with Jens Holsten in 2010 still remains my favorite trip in the Leavenworth area. I had never climbed Mount Stuart before, but at the time Jens and I were doing a ton of climbing in the range, and a week before, we had just climbed a sweet ice flow up Colchuck Peak at WI4 5.7. Who knows if it had been done before; high up the route, Jens gazed off in the distance and his eyes lit up: "Look Cole, Mount Stuart looks like a go!" 3:00 a.m. a week later, we started off. As Jens broke trail through the snow once again, a flash of light lit up the sky. "What was that?!" I looked up. Glowing in glimmering dust in the sky, close overhead, was one of the most magical things I have ever seen as a meteor entered the atmosphere, leaving a trail of glowing debris in its wake. The climb took Jens and I 42 hours car to car. Later we learned that it was the first continuous winter ascent of Mount Stuart – F.C.W.A.! I've spent a lot of time in the Stuart Range bouldering and climbing mountains, including a winter ascent of the *Gerber-Sink Route* on Dragontail with no névé ice (during which we succeeded at our objective but I suffered serious frostbite on six toes), but that trip to Mount Stuart with Jens is my most memorable trip in Leavenworth.

Leavenworth is truly a special place on this earth. Imagine Fred Beckey pioneering through the mountains sixty years ago, with no trails and nothing but a dream to guide him. In perspective, times have changed dramatically, and Leavenworth's vast growth throughout the years means we are all responsible for our actions. It is very important that we as boulderers focus on the future of the area's bouldering development. In recent years, the Forest Service has given the area great attention, and has received grants to put climbing rangers on duty to regulate the laws and keep the area clean; this attention reflects boulderers' increased presence in the area, but it also requires us to be on our best behavior at all times. Please respect. In the midst of all this reflection, my thoughts go to Damian Potts, the author of the original Leavenworth bouldering guidebook. Though Damian died at an early age due to cancer, his passion and vision live on. I first met Damian on a trip to Leavenworth with my homie Brian Doyle, and though I was just a young teenager, he was welcoming and friendly to me and took me on a tour of the recently-discovered Mountain Home Road boulders. Thank you Damian. We will always miss you. Rest in peace.

Leavenworth defines beauty. Ruminating on all of this, I am lost in a sea of granite. First ascents seem to just pop up like seeds; just when you think the area is tapped, another boulder appears. Infinite exploration and reflective memories all combine. It's hard to put words to feelings. Every day is a new day in Leavenworth. I hope you lace your shoes up tight, and get ready for a long hike to find some new boulders. "So you guys are all probably wondering why I brought you here…"

BRIDGE CREEK
FREE SITE BOULDERS

There are a few dispersed blocks scattered along the south side of Icicle Creek across from Bridge Creek Campground, downhill from a popular free bivy site off of the Mountaineers Creek road. The Outhouse boulder sports several tall old-school moderates, as well as Drew Schick's highball arête *Members Only* (V8). The Best Day Ever boulder offers a handful of committing riverside challenges, and doesn't have a bad problem on it. The gems of the area, however, are likely Joe Treftz's incredible *Tigerlily Left* (V5) and *Right* (V4), sister climbs that ascend a smooth 20-foot overhang on a perfect series of evenly-spaced horizontal edges. The Bridge Creek Free Site Boulders are spread out, and can take a bit of luck to find, but they make for a great way to get off the beaten path and explore the quiet south side of the Icicle. Enjoy, but please respect your surroundings and minimize your impact by sticking to the trails and leaving no trace...

THE OUTHOUSE BOULDER

The Outhouse Boulder is just below the Bridge Creek Free Site. Turn left off of Icicle Creek 8.5 miles from Icicle Junction onto the Mountaineers Creek road (NF-7601) and drive past Bridge Creek Campground and across the river. Ascend the short, steep hill and turn left onto the steep, unmarked dirt drive, which is 0.4 miles from Icicle Creek and 0.2 miles from the bridge. Park among the ever-present kayakers, mountain bikers, and lurkers and follow the well-worn trail straight downhill, staying to the right of the obvious rock formation. The Outhouse Boulder is roughly one minute below the parking.

❑ 1. Unknown 5.8-10
There are one or two random topropes on this tall, slabby face. If you're lucky, you might see a drunken Russian wedding party giving each other hand belays up this side of the boulder. It's happened before…

❑ 2. Unknown V2 ★
Climb the bulge to a high crack, reaching right to the arête to top out.

❑ 3. Unknown V1 ★
Traverse up and right on jugs to the narrow corner.

❑ 4. Unknown V1 ★
Climb through clean quartz holds on the dirty face.

❑ 5. Members Only V8 ★★
Climb the tall arête over a stepped landing from a stand start matched on head-high sidepulls. Make a hard move to a prominent right-hand rail then top out straight up with a tough mantle. Morpho. F.A. Drew Schick.

❑ 6. Project
Start matched on the undercling and climb the blank face.

❑ 7. Unknown V1
Start on the shelf and climb the arête of the short, lumpy boulder.

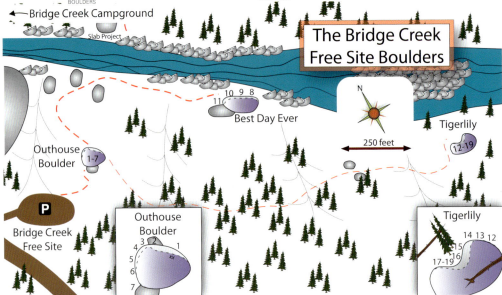

← Bridge Creek Campground

Slab Project

BOULDERS

The Bridge Creek Free Site Boulders

10 9 8
11
Best Day Ever

N

Tigerlily

250 feet

12-19

Outhouse Boulder

1-7

🅿

Bridge Creek Free Site

Outhouse Boulder

3 2
4　　　1
5　　xx
6
7

Tigerlily

14 13 12
15
16
17-19

Drew Schick crimps through the blank face of *Dusk* (V6)

BEST DAY EVER BOULDER

The Best Day Ever Boulder is on Icicle Creek, several hundred yards below and downstream from the Outhouse Boulder. Follow the well-worn trail straight down from The Outhouse to the water's edge, then traverse roughly 100 yards downstream along the edge of the river to this obvious whitish face with a flat slab landing.

❒ 8. Dusk V6 ★★
Start crouched with an incut left hand and a flat right-hand crimp on the left side of the face. Move up to crimps in the angled seam, then climb up and left to the lip.

❒ 9. Mercenary V6 ★★
Start crouched with a sloping crimp in the center of the face and climb straight up the prominent quartz streak to a high finish. Proud!

❒ 10. Best Day Ever V6 ★★
This problem begins in the chunky rock on the right side of the face with a good left-facing sidepull. Climb straight up and right along the arête to a dynamic move for an incut crimp and a high, technical finish. A rough-cut version of the perfect boulder problem...

❒ 11. May the Quartz Be With You V9 ★★
Start in the cave to the right of Best Day Ever and squeeze up the arête to a big move for the obvious sloper on the left arête. F.A. Kyle O'Meara.

TIGERLILY

The Tigerlily Boulder is the hardest of the BCFS trio to find, as it lies at the end of a long, faint traverse trail and is physically hidden, tucked into the hillside roughly 50 yards above the creek. From the parking lot or the Outhouse Boulder, follow the well-worn trail network directly downstream for a few minutes (maintaining roughly the same elevation) until you hit a shady, wooded gully. Cut straight downhill for roughly 50 yards, then continue trending directly downstream on a faint trail until the forest opens up and the river becomes visible. Pass a couple of low, round boulders, then an obvious huge fallen tree, and about one minute later the low, rounded top of the Tigerlily boulder will become visible below the path. The entire hike should take roughly 10 minutes from the parking lot.

❒ 12. Unknown V2
Climb the left side of the tall face on neat triangular edges. Needs cleaning...

❒ 13. Unknown V3 ★
Climb up and right on cool sloping pods in the middle of the face.

❒ 14. Unknown V2 ★
On the right side of the tall slab, climb the series of neat incut pockets a few feet left of the arête.

❒ 15. Tigerlily Left V5 ★★
See description, next page.

❒ 16. Tigerlily Right V4 ★★★
This climb ascends the right side of the overhanging face from a stand start with a good undercling pinch in the dihedral. Climb straight up Gold-Bar-esque horizontal edges to a high mantle right of the tree. Discovered in 2009 by Joe Treftz, the incredibly unique stone on this climb opened people's eyes to the potential on the south side of Icicle Creek.

❒ 17. Unknown V3 ★★
Climb the tall dihedral, topping out to the left as for Tigerlily Right.

❒ 18. Unknown V4 ★
Climb the center of the tall face.

❒ 19. Unknown V2
Climb the blunt arête on slopers. This climb is inaccessible at the time of writing due to a large fallen tree.

TIGERLILY

ABOVE Cortney Cusack on *Best Day Ever* (V6).
RIGHT Reaching for a nice seam on *Tigerlily Left* (V5).

□ **15. Tigerlily Left V5** ★★
Scale the left side of the tall face from a crouch start on two pods in the horizontal seam. Climb straight up a cryptic series of edges to a high mantle top-out.

THE NURSE BOULDERS

The Nurse Boulders are a small cluster of grainy, flaky boulders nestled below the small crags across Icicle Creek from the Carnival and Pretty Boulders. For their "freshness," the Nurse boulders are home to some of the best crimp lines in the canyon, and intermediate climbers will have a heyday on the chunky, gritty grips. Few problems here have been named, let alone graded, so I have not included specific problem beta, but believe me when I say the adventure is well worth it...

To access the Nurse Boulders, park off Mountaineer's Creek Road roughly 0.6 miles from Icicle Road (0.4 miles from the bridge, and 0.2 miles from the Bridge Creek Free Site) near the start of a short drive marked by a gate with a "road closed" sign. Follow the old road/trail down the steep hill, cross the creek on a log, and traverse the hillside to the obvious white boulders below the short, clean crags. You may want to make use of the GPS coordinates for this spot. The bridge that crosses the Icicle near Eightmile Rock, and the land below the Nurse Boulders, are private property and may not be crossed to access the Nurse Boulders.

ABOVE Cortney Cusack puts her medical training to good use on *Night Nurse* (V9).

BELOW Dimitry Kalashnikov on a nice V4 at the *Nurse Boulders*.

LOWER

UPPER

The Nurse Boulders as viewed from across Icicle Creek.

THE SABER

The Saber stands alone as one of the only established problems along Mountaineer's Creek, a hint of more things to come up the most easily-accessible of the Icicle Creek drainages. Established by Johnny Goicoechea in the spring of 2013, The Saber climbs an incredible 20-foot overhang on perfect crimps above a stepped landing.

To reach The Saber, park 1.2 miles up Mountaineers Creek Road in a tiny pullout on the left, roughly 100 yards before a low, brown stump to the right of the road with a diamond-shaped silver marker nailed into it. The pullout is 0.8 miles past the drive to the Bridge Creek Free Site. Hike straight up the faint, rocky gully across from the downhill end of the pullout, trending very slightly right as you follow game trails up the steep hillside. The Saber climbs the right side of the center-most gully in the jumble of low-angle cliffs roughly 150 yards above the road.

❏ 1. The Saber V11 ★★★

Start crouched with a low, flat jug on the left (uphill) end of the wide overhanging wall. Move through amazing flat crimps up the orange-streaked wall to a iron cross move to a right-hand gaston jug. Finish with a sequential and techy sequence up and left from the jug on poor crimps. F.A. Johnny Goicoechea.

CHOSS WALL

Though it is not at The Saber proper, this seems like the best spot to note that there is a semi-chossy schist wall visible to the right of the road roughly 2.7 miles up Mountaineers Creek road (1.5 miles past the Saber and 0.3 miles before the Eightmile Lake trailhead). A few easy highballs have been climbed on this wall, though it rarely sees attention.

PARKING

THE SABER

Johnny Goicoechea powering through the iron cross crux of *The Saber* (V11).
[PHOTO] Lauren Yang.

THE MACHINE GUN

Just past Bridge Creek Campground, the Upper Icicle's solitary Machine Gun boulder makes for a fun, quick warm up stop. This modestly-sized granite boxcar is home to some quality vertical warm-ups and the fun and punchy *Machine Gun Funk* (V2), and is well worth the one-minute walk for its fun, inviting climbs.

The Machine Gun is 8.7 miles from Icicle Junction, 0.2 miles past the junction with Bridge Creek Campground and Eight-mile Road. Look for a short, wide boulder on the right about 50 yards from the road, and park in the small pullout on the left. Follow the faint trail through the trees on the left.

1. Cougar Magnum V2 ★
Start on the flat inset ledge and climb straight to the lip between two sharp cracks. Finish with an awkward mantle.

2. Fight Like A Farmer V2 ★
Start with a low left-hand sloper and a right-hand sidepull. Move up and right through the horizontal seam to a big right-facing flake and rock over. Recently excavated.

3. Band of Gypsies V0+ ★
Climb through ledges a few feet left of the tree to an engaging mantle. The crouch start on the flat ledge trades a star for a grade.

4. Dirty Harry V1+ ★★
Start just right of the tree with hands matched on two high rounded scoops. Move straight to a hard-to-see edge on the stepped lip and rock over.
Variation (V2): Start sitting on the flat shelf down and right of the scoops, and climb through edges to the scoops to finish as above. A little footwork goes a long way.

5. Machine Gun Funk V2 ★★
Start sitting on the corner with good opposing sidepulls. Climb to the rounded jug halfway up the arête and make a big move to the incut edge high on the left face. Finish straight over the bulge with a hidden jug. Fun, dynamic movement.
Variation (V3): From the rounded jug, move right through slopers to finish as for Buddy Miles.

AREA

6. Buddy Miles V3 ★
Start sitting a few feet right of the corner with a low left-hand undercling and a big right sidepull. Climb straight up to a sidepull jug and finish on the slopers above. An extreme drop-knee earns you extra style points...

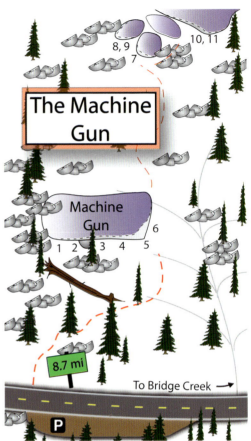

Problems 7–11 are roughly 30 yards above the Machine Gun in a small cluster just below the crest of the hillside.

7. Unknown V0
Start sitting with a low horizontal crack. Slap up the slabby arête feature.

8. Maniacal Moray V2 ★
Start sitting matched on a low seam on the eel-shaped boulder. Use heel hooks to slap to a higher rail, then traverse right and top out straight up with a big horn.

9. Eelin' Groovy V2
Start as for Maniacal Moray but climb straight up the arête, staying left to top out.

10. Hired Goons V0 ★
Start sitting in the slightly overhanging white scoop, climbing the obvious seam up and left to walk off onto the slab left of the tree.

11. Kingpin V3 ★
Start as for Hired Goons but top out straight up with a techy mantle onto the slab.

Scott Mitchell, spotted by his wife Susan, tops out Machine Gun Funk (V2).

9. The Prism V9 ★★★
Climb the steep arête from a stand start. "Too classic and too cryptic!" This problem broke after the publication of *Central Washington Bouldering*, becoming slightly more reachy and committing. The boulder below has claimed numerous ankles.
Variation: *The Prism Low* (V10): Start as for Bowled Over and make wide moves right to finish on The Prism. F.A. Cole Allen.

Tyler Weiss sticks the dyno on *The Prism* (V9).
[PHOTO] Aaron Matheson

THE SWORD BOULDERS

The Sword Boulders are one of the best areas in Icicle Canyon, offering quiet and shade in the busy summer months. For a relatively small group of boulders, The Sword sports a wide array of classic problems including *The Classic* (V2), *The Sword* (V3), *The Hourglass* (V7), *Resurrection* (V8), and *The Prism* (V9). Underwear Rock, the roadside landmark for this area, is a great sport to get a quick warm-up or show some non-climbers around. The Sword is an especially nice summer area, as many problems stay shaded among the upper Icicle's open forests. If you enjoyed the rock quality at the Swiftwater north boulders, you will be pleasantly surprised by the tall, clean, and nicely textured lines at The Sword.

Finding the Sword area is easy. Look for the round, flat face of Underwear Rock on the right, and park on the left in a riverside pullout 8.8 miles from Icicle Junction, 0.4 miles past Mountaineers Creek Road. Walk roughly forty yards back down canyon and follow the well-worn trail past Underwear Rock. To reach the Sword proper, follow the trail up a slight hill to the small cluster. Please do not camp in the small clearing above Underwear Rock.

PARKING

❒ 1. **Boxers V0** ★
Start on a chunky edge, climb right to better holds, and finish straight over crimps on the bulge.
Variation (V0): Climb up and left from the chunky edge, finish by stepping left onto dirty shelf.
Variation (V1): Start as for Boxers and continue up and right finishing on Briefs.

UNDERWEAR ROCK

❒ 2. **Briefs V3** ★
Begin on small edges in the middle of the face. Make crimpy slab moves up and left to a tall-feeling finish.

❒ 3. **The Crack V0-** ★★★
Climb the well-featured crack to a nice top-out ledge.

❒ 4. **The Taint V0** ★
Climb the featured face right of The Crack, finishing up and left via the dirty foot ledge.

❒ 5. **Dingleberry Junction V0**
Climb the dirty face right of the corner.

❒ 6. **Unkonwn V0**
Climb the left side of the short slab on a small plateau above Underwear Rock.

❒ 7. **Unknown V0**
Climb the faint crack on the right side of the short slab.

❒ 8. **Bowled Over V3** ★
Start in the corner with the small boulder at your back and climb straight up on interesting holds. A bit cramped, but climbs well.

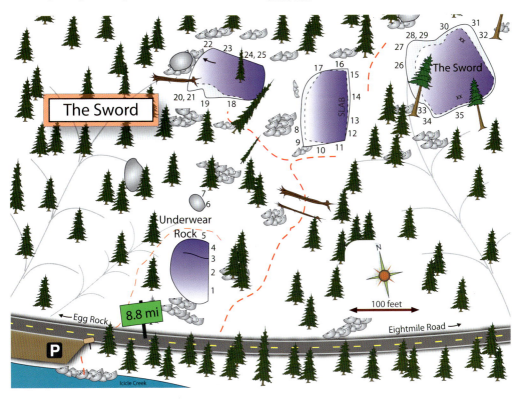

The Sword

The Sword

Underwear Rock

8.8 mi

← Egg Rock

Eightmile Road →

100 feet

N

P

Icicle Creek

9. The Prism V9 ★★★
See description on previous page.

10. The Hourglass V7 ★★
Climb the center of the slabby face to an akward stance with high crimps in the corner. When you're about to teeter off, leap to the good knobs over the lip and top out on flat ledges. Perfect.

11. White Sands V4 ★★
Climb the right side of the tall face, stemming between sloping shelves to a long reach for a hidden edge above the lip. Very good, and committing.

12. X1 V1 ★★★
On the left end of the large slab, follow blocky ledges to a thinner finish on the face to the right.
Variation (V2): Top out straight up.

13. X2 V2 ★
Climb the line of small quartz edges just right of #10, finishing the same.

14. Cubicle Gangster V0 ★★★
Follow the quartz vein up the center of the tall slab to flat jug one move below the lip.

15. Played Like A Poop Butt V0+ ★★★
Climb the right side of the undercut slab from an awkward high-step start.
Variation (V6): Start sitting down and right from the start with a chunky right-hand crimp and a low left-hand sloper on the shelf. Slap to a good sloper on the arête with your left hand and ease onto the slab.

16. Cole's Corner V8/9 ★★
Climb the stout little arête. Start on a small lefthand sidepull and a low righthand crimp. Follow the natural tick marks up and right to a jug on the lip.

17. Plain V0 ★
Climb the arête right of Cole's Corner to an awkward mantle on the left side of the corner.

18. Off the Couch V7 ★★
Start matched on the low sloping rail in the middle of the face. Climb slightly left, then straight up on small gaston crimps, finishing up and right.

19. Sofa King V0 ★
Climb the juggy shelves up the corner to a dirty finish.

20. I ♥ Jugs V2 ★★★
Start on the blocky low jugs and make cool moves straight up the corner to a delicate top-out. Great fun.

21. The Wizard V3 ★
Start on the square ledge of I ♥ Jugs but climb left around the corner to a small sidepull. Bring your right hand in to the tiny pebble and slap to the lip.

22. The Standard V1 ★
Climb the crack on the low-angle face right of the arête.

23. The Classic V2 ★★★
Climb the right-facing rail on the right side of the tall face to a jug at the fifteen-foot level. Engaging top-out. Super-classic!

24. The Stairway V0+ ★
Start on the large shelves on the left side of the tall face and climb straight up to the lip. Top out on the slab and walk up and over the back to descend.

25. The Antagonist V6
Start as for The Stairway and traverse right on small edges. Top out up The Classic.

26. Go Baby! V6 ★
The trail leading to The Sword boulder arrives at a chest-high bulge several feet right of the prow of Resurrection. Start with a head-high right-hand pistol grip and a small left-hand crimp, paste your foot by your navel and chuck for the sloping edge above. Continue through the dirty top-out of Resurrection for full value.

27. Resurrection V8 ★★
This semi-old-school classic climbs the undercut prow seen when first arriving at the Sword boulder. Start standing on the corner, iron-crossed between a good left-hand sidepull and a bad right-hand sloper. Paste your left foot on a high knob, slap to the lip, and grapple around the right side of the corner to top out in the dihedral high above. Descend via the tree behind #33.

28. Resurrection Low V10 ★★★
Start sitting around the corner from Resurrection with one hand on a triangular sloper and the other on a low, blocky undercling. Climb up and right on slopers to the left-hand starting hold of Resurrection, then make a wide move to the sloper and finish up Resurrection. F.A. Johnny Goicoechea. Variation (project): A much harder variation, yet undone, begins directly below the start of Resurrection.

29. Zorro V8 ★★
See description on next page.

En garde! Johnny Goicoechea nails the drop-knee riposte on a post-break send of *Zorro* (V8).
[PHOTO] Matthew Hall

29. Zorro V8 ★★

Start crouched on the left side of the prow as for Resurrection Low, with a left-hand sloper and a good right-hand undercling. Make technical moves in the dihedral to a high left-hand crimp, then slap up sloping holds on the corner until you can rock onto the ramp. Top out around the corner as for Resurrection. Wild! This problem broke in 2008 or '09, becoming much more technical and difficult.

❐ 30. Seam of Pain V5 ★

Start standing in front of the small tree with crimps in and around the nebulous seam. Climb straight up on edges to inobvious holds below the ramp. Top out either up and right with a delicate traverse along the high dirty ramp, or move up left to finish as for The Sword.

❐ 31. The Dagger V3 ★★

Start just left of the corner with two crimps at head height. Climb directly up through two sloping ledges, then move directly left into the finishing holds of The Sword. Can also be topped up the slab.

❐ 32. The Sword V3 ★★★

An old-school 5.11 toprope climb that is now a classic highball. Start on a head-high jug and climb powerful face moves to a heady finish on jugs. Top out by rocking onto the slab right of the corner. A must-do for any up-and-coming boulderer.

Variation (V3): Start sitting on a crimp rail down and right of the start jug. Adds a bit of pump, but not much in terms of quality.

❐ 33. The Tree Problem V7 ★★

Climb the bulge in front of the descent tree, starting matched on two small right-facing sidepulls in the corner. Move left to the sloper, pinch the sideways credit card, and slap for better holds up and right. It is legit to drop once you've mantled onto the jug in the corner, but the climb has been topped out by stepping right to the ledge and climbing straight up the arête.

Variation (V6): Skip the bulge and the business by moving straight left to the micro gaston and rocking directly up to the jug.

❐ 34. The Sheath V4 ★

Climb straight up the tall corner right of The Tree Problem from decent holds at head-height. Delicate reaches between sloping holds lead to a good crimp halfway up. For those less inclined to air it out over the uneven landing, a toprope can be rigged from The Sword anchor with a long sling on The Sword Toprope anchor as a directional guide.

❐ 35. The Sword Toprope Project

The tall downhill face of the Sword boulder sports an extremely thin toprope route that has broken significantly since it was first climbed, and has not been climbed since. Start on the left arête, climb up and right to incut holds in the center of the face, then move straight up through very small crimps to the crux move just below the lip. Dead-vertical 5.13+? A ropeless ascent of this climb is almost inconceivable…

Jens Holsten sharpens his skills on *The Sword* (V3).

THE SWORD

CORTNEY CUSACK

I want to enjoy the experience. I want to be present in the moment and live every minute. I want there to be space and time for the freedom of thought and movement. I want to feel what is happening right now.

Beyond the incredible and exquisite quality of the climbing, all of this occurs for me in Leavenworth. Whether I am gazing at the mountains, contemplating a boulder problem, soaking my feet in the river, or working with a unique individual to take a step towards obtaining their optimal health and zest for life – it is all about living and being with this present experience.

Leavenworth is a special place that gives me this feeling, this groundedness, that I can tuck inside me and always come back to. I let go of any worldly troubles and in a certain sense, slow down. I breathe and sweat, laugh and do handstands with friends. I experience the moment. In the beauty that is Leavenworth I sit and reflect about life as it unfolds. I find peace in the grandness of the valley. Being there I feel inspired and free. As the seasons change, I can feel my growth and watch that of those around me. With each experience, I observe different levels of excitement, wonder, and ability. It's also my place for

being physically challenged and learning to be patient and gentle with the process of gaining strength and courage.

I carry all of this back to my life outside of Leavenworth. It reminds me to be conscious of my intensions on a daily basis. I can be present wherever I am, and when necessary, close my eyes and immerse myself in the essence that is Leavenworth — feel the river, feel the sun, feel the earth, feel the rock. It rejuvenates me even when I am away and drives me to go back… And I can be present here in the next breath.

May you be in the moment, and enjoy the experience. I sincerely hope you enjoy it.

THE SCAT BOULDERS

The Scat Boulders are an obscure collection of boulders in an open talus field roughly 15 minutes above The Sword. The area retains a very wild and "raw" feeling, and no map or beta is provided. Enjoy!

Drew Schick climbs an Unknown highball at the Scat Boulders in the spring of 2010.

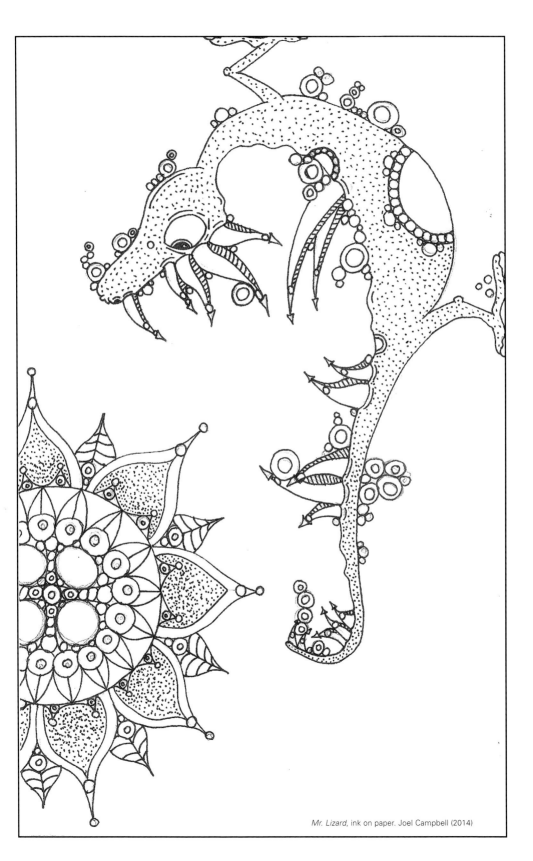

Mr. Lizard, ink on paper. Joel Campbell (2014)

EGG ROCK
A.K.A. THE JERRY GARCIA BOULDERS

Egg Rock is another small but concentrated area in the "Upper Icicle" zone past Bridge Creek Campground. Despite being next to the road, Egg Rock has a quiet and secluded feel, with superb stone to match. The granite at Egg Rock is subtly different from the neighboring Sword area, whiter and with a slightly larger grain. Don't miss classic moderates such as *Smokestack Lightnin'* (V2), *Weather Report* (V3), and *Dark Hollow* (V6). If you're looking to test yourself, the powerful slopers of *Musashi* (V9) are a perfect complement to the tall, crimpy face of *I ♥ Jerry Garcia* (V8). Egg Rock sees a good deal of shade, and is pleasant most times of the year – though in winter it's a half-mile trudge from the nearest dry pavement. Keep an eye out for poison ivy lining the edges of the trail and some landings.

Egg Rock is 9.0 miles from Icicle Junction in Icicle Canyon. Park in the narrow pullout on the left-hand side of the road directly across from the nine mile marker. The "I ♥ Jerry Garcia" graffiti on the first large boulder is vaguely visible from the road, as is the small, round egg rock itself.

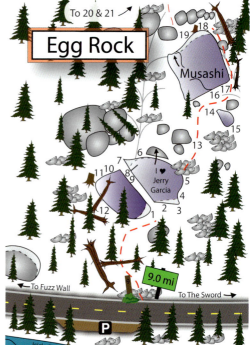

□ 1. Sunshine Daydream V4 ★★
Climb the bulgy arête from a low right-hand sidepull and a large flake foothold. Finish on the left side of the arête.

□ 2. I ♥ Jerry Garcia V8 ★★★
Climb the tall painted face from a stand start with two high slimpers. Climb straight up using either a micro crimp on the face or a sloping right-hand gaston. This problem was listed as a project in *Central Washington Bouldering*.

□ 3. Ace V4 ★
Climb the right arête of the Jerry Garcia face, finishing straight up to the left of the notch. May be a bit dirty.
Variation (V8): Start on sloping crimps on the face and dyno up and right to finish as for Ace.

□ 4. Funiculi Funicula VB ★★
Start on a big sidepull, climb to the obvious shelf, mantle, and top out. Very pleasant indeed.

□ 5. Carlisle V1 ★
Begin sitting with a decent undercling on the left side of the face. Move to a good flat hold, and again to the large jug. Fun, strange stone.

□ 6. Hell In A Bucket V8 ★
Climb the short face from a stand start with a tiny left-hand undercling and an even smaller right-hand crimp. Set your feet up, move to a silly right-hand sidepull, and top out up and left. "At least I'm enjoyin' the ride!"

□ 7. Weather Report V3 ★★
Start crouched with your left hand on the fin and your right on a good sidepull. Smear your feet and lunge to the rounded jug, finishing straight up the arête.
Variation (V7): Start matched on the fin and climb straight up.

□ 8. Dark Hollow V6 ★★
Climb the shallow finger crack on the left side of the corridor, trending slightly left to edges at the top.

□ 9. Terrapin Station V0+ ★
Climb the chimney in between the boulders. Won't learn this kind of climbing in the gym…

John Stordahl on / ♥ *Jerry Garcia* (V8).

10. China Cat V2 ★
Climb the slab to the right of the corridor. A little footwork will go a long way…

11. I Know You Rider V0 ★★
Climb the small bulge just left of the tree trunk with sidepulls in the crack.

12. Dark Star V6 ★
Climb the back side of the boulder from a stand start matched on a strange squarish ledge. Make one hard lunge and finish straight up the face. Variations can be done to the left and right.

13. Deal V1+
Climb the low trailside arête from a sit start.

14. Bertha V0 ★
Start crouched and climb the small corner next to the trail on cool incuts. This climb has broken recently and is now somewhat questionable.

15. Estimated Prophet V1 ★★
Start sitting with a flat ledge in the center of the diminutive face. Maybe the best eight foot tall V1 you'll ever do…

16. Smokestack Lightnin' V2 ★★
Climb the left-leaning seam on the left side of the tall face to a jug at the nine-foot level. Make a big move to the lip, then gather your wits for the committing high-step finish. Sharp, but well worth the adventure.

17. Dire Wolf V5 ★★
Climb the balancey arête on small crimps to an incut jug and a committing mantle. This problem formerly began on a huge flake that appeared solid, and had been pulled on many times, but recently detached from the wall after about 10 seconds of wiggling. Yikes!

18. Musashi V9 ★★★
A.K.A. **The Egg Pt. 2**
One of Leavenworth's best. Start on the obvious jug rail, bear-hug the wide slopers, and chuck to the perfect brick-shaped pinch on the corner, finishing straight up. The "smiley face" start rail lost a tooth in 2011, making the start only slightly harder. If you supuinate, you'll levitate… F.A. Cole Allen.

19. Hara-Kiri V8 ★
Start with two low underclings and slap to sidepulls in the dirty seam. Top out straight up the tall, dirty face. Rarely done.

20. Ship of Fools V5 ★
From Musashi, scramble about 25 yards uphill to the obvious rounded boulder in the talus. Start sitting on the slab, matched on flat seam holds on the downhill arête. Move through two sharp crimps to squeeze flat holds on the double arête feature.

21. Touch of Grey V0 ★
Climb the clean uphill face of the rounded boulder from the obvious ledge.

FUZZ WALL

Fuzz Wall is a small roadside boulder that is among the furthest developed bouldering areas in Icicle Canyon. The air is generally noticeably crisper than in town, and the rock sees less traffic than most other Icicle spots. Formerly home to the now-defunct Epoxy Flake problem, Fuzz Wall is now only visited for the nice moderate arête of *Busted* (V3) and Kyle O'Meara's nearby compression problem *Span Man* (V10).

Fuzz Wall lies on the north side of the road 9.2 miles from Icicle Junction. Park 20 yards up canyon from the boulder, in the eastern end of the rocky cul de sac just before the road passes through an obvious roadcut. Fuzz Wall is the dark west-facing wall 10 yards above the road.

❒ 1. Peach Fuzz V0
Climb the short left arête of Fuzz Wall from a stand start. Dirty but solid.

❒ 2. Project
Start crouched with two sidepulls in the steepest part of the face, climbing up and slightly left on terrible holds.

❒ 3. Epoxy Flake V2/3
This oddity formerly climbed the center of the face from a left-hand sidepull in the seam and a very low right-hand undercling. The reinforced flake that gave this problem its name broke in 2010, however, and the problem is now only climbable from the high left-leaning crimp rail that used to mark the end of the hard climbing. Good riddance to Leavenworth's only known glued hold…
Variation (project): Could the low start still be done?

❒ 4. Pod Racer V1+
Climb the incut pods in the dirty crack a few feet right of center, finishing with a cruxy mantle.

❒ 5. Busted V3 ★★
Start in the crack as for Pod Racer and climb straight up until the distant right arête comes within reach. Hug the grainy crack and arête in opposition as you finish straight up the corner. Quite good.

❒ 6. Unknown V2
The boulder roughly 10 yards down canyon from Fuzz Wall has a few overlooked variations on its downhill face.

AREA

❒ 7. Haunted Shack V2 ★
Find this little gem some 100 yards east of Fuzz Wall on top of a short rise. From two head-high crimps, climb the series of smooth edges up the east face to the juggy lip. The sit start on low, small edges on the right side of the face is a fun V3.

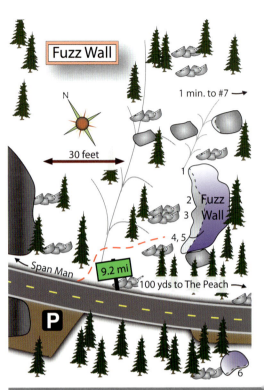

Fuzz Wall

1 min. to #7 →

30 feet

Fuzz Wall

9.2 mi

← Span Man

100 yds to The Peach →

THE PEACH

There is an obscure lumpy boulder directly below Haunted Shack, roughly 100 yards down canyon from the parking for Fuzz Wall. This boulder has a handful of easy to moderate climbs, with the stand-outs being the tall west-facing slab (V1) and the bulgy sit-start from a low, diagonal crimp on the downhill side (V6).

SPAN MAN

Span Man is a roadside boulder roughly 0.1 miles past Fuzz Wall, directly across the road from the dirt cul de sac. Hike up the short, steep hill to this streaked boulder and find Span Man in the steep roof on the west end.

❒ 8. Span Man V10 ★★
Start inside the small cave with a low left-hand hueco and the right arête. Climb directly out the tube feature, performing several 'span moves' to reach the triangular jug on the face. Swing your heel around and climb

up and right on grainy slopers to a cruxy finish. The left finish is about the same grade. Hard. F.A. Kyle O'Meara.
Variation (V5/6): Start matched on the triangular jug and top out either left or right.

Cortney Cusack stretching out in the summer haze on *Busted* (V3).

Kyle O'Meara swooping the first ascent of the rarely-repeated
Seams Dangerous (V6).

TIN MAN

The Tin Man boulder is a boxcar-sized fortress on a flat
plateau a few minutes' walk above Icicle Road at the upper
reaches of the canyon's bouldering. The delicate, reachy *Tin
Man* (V7) alone is worth the visit, as is the pure movement
of the *Slot Problem* (V4). On the way up, you'll pass Kyle
O'Meara's *Seams Dangerous* (V6), a highball masterpiece
that has still only seen a few ascents almost 10 years after
its first ascent. Save this area for a lazy afternoon when you
think you've seen it all – you won't be disappointed.

*The approach for Tin Man begins 9.4 miles from Icicle
Junction, roughly 0.1 miles down the road from the end of
the Fuzz Wall-Span Man pullout. Park in a small righthand
pullout just after a small stream runs under the road and
just before the hillside becomes steep and rocky. Walk up
and right through lush foliage past a short wall, then past
a helpful log to the steep, sandy Pen 15 wall and Seams
Dangerous. For Tin Man, follow the steep, sandy slope
around the right side of this wall, eventually topping out
onto the flat plateau above. Tin Man lies straight ahead in
the clearing, the big, square boulder lurking at the base of a
steeper hillside.*

❒ **2. Seams Dangerous V6 ★★★**
Climb the tall, slightly overhanging face a few feet right of
the tree on cool edges to a high crux. Finish up the high slab
over the dangerously sloping landing. Most will opt to at least
preview the route on rappel… F.A. Kyle O'Meara.

❒ **3. Spanish Traverse V2**
Start on big, sharp edges in the middle of the rail, climbing up
and left to a balancey reach for the lip and an easy mantle.

❒ **4. The Slot Problem V4 ★**
Start on two sharp edges on the right end of the crimp rail.
Work your feet up and stab for a gaston pocket left of the ancient tree, then climb through the huge slot to an easy mantle
finish. Very good.

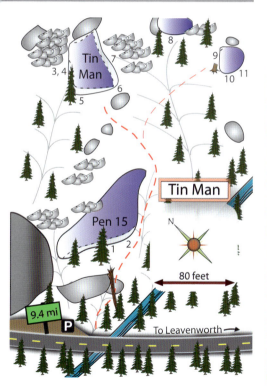

❒ **1. Tonya Harding V5 ★**
Start on the big flake jug in front of the
tree. Climb up and left to the incut pod,
then traverse left on slopers to a high
jug in the dark rock above and drop.
Morpho.

AREA

5. Tin Man V7 ★★★

Climb the tallish arête right of the partially-burnt tree from a crouch start with the triangular block in the low roof and a crimp one foot to the right. Move to the prominent right-hand sidepull rail, reach to the arête, then hit the odd sidepull flake high on the face, slap the jug around the corner, and top out. Strange and beautiful.

Variation (V6): Start standing with your left hand on the arête and your right on the sidepull rail.

6. Joe's Nose V5 ★

Start sitting on the low corner matched on the lip or with a low undercling jug. Slap up the blunt, low corner to a wide rock-over move for an edge on the face. Very silly, and pretty fun too.

7. Unknown V0

Several variations climb the dirty, featured face around the corner from Tin Man.

8. Ryan's Slab V3 ★★

This climb ascends the tallish slab roughly halfway between Tin Man and Divided Sky. Start with an incut right-hand sidepull and climb technical moves to a square jug in the center of the face. Finish straight up with big holds. A great recent addition to the area.

9. Divided Sky V3 ★

Start with a high edge just right of the arête on this short face. Stab straight up on cool edges and arête holds to the lip.

10. Antelope V1

On the downhill arête of the square boulder, start with slopers near the right arête and climb up and left to a flat jug.

11. Faht V0 ★

Climb the juggy flake on the rear of this little cube.

Sol Wertkin busts out his award face to send *Tin Man* (V7).
[PHOTO] Max Hasson

DAYDREAM

Daydream is one of the furthest developed climbs in Icicle Canyon, and is the last climb to be added to this book. Day-dream climbs the downstream side of an overlooked boulder next to Icicle Creek across the road from the Fourth of July trailhead. This climb is seasonally inaccessible, and tall – you may very well want to put a rope down it before throwing yourself at its high, difficult moves. Props to Cole Allen for adding yet another gem to Leavenworth's pantheon!

To find Daydream, park at the Fourth of July trailhead on the righthand side of Icicle Road, 9.4 miles from Icicle Junction, and follow the trail directly across the road. Daydream is at the downstream end of a steep mini-buttress about three minutes down the trail, at the bottom of a very steep hill that is best accessed from the downstream side. The hike is somewhat ambiguous, but head for the river and you'll know it when you find it…

❒ **1. Unkown V2** ★★★
Start in the crack on the right side of the face and follow the crack up and left to a high top-out. You will probably want to toprope this one before you boulder it…

❒ **2. Daydream V8** ★★
Start in the crack on the right side of the face, but roughly halfway up, make a big lock-off to a pair of small crimps high in the center of the face. Slightly contrived but good nonetheless.

❒ **3. Project**
Start on the left arête and climb into the top out of #1. V10ish?

AREA

MIGHTY MOUSE / THE SLOPING LADY

The Mighty Mouse / Sloping Lady / Grandview area is the furthest developed granite area up the Icicle Canyon at this time. Each of these three boulders is home to a unique and off-the-beaten-path Leavenworth classic that has been developed since *Central Washington Bouldering* was developed. Hopefully this offering of "Upper Upper Icicle" boulders will inspire others to pursue the presumably endless supply of boulders in the canyon's upper reaches, where the creek's flow eases and the hillsides spread apart…

MIGHTY MOUSE

Mighty Mouse is 10.5 miles from Icicle Junction, just below a gated dirt drive on the left similar to the drive near Fuzz Wall. Park near the gate and follow the faint trail just up the road towards, and over, a riverside dome of rock. Mighty Mouse climbs the upstream side of the overhanging dome.

1. Mighty Mouse V6 ★★★
Start sitting matched on an undercling in the right side of the low roof. Climb straight up to incut edges, then trend slightly left to a jug below the lip. Top out straight up. The stand start is an enjoyable V4. Five star location!

2. Unkown VB
Climb around the boulder from the upsteam side of Mighty Mouse. A good slickfoot.

3. Here I Come V2
Start on head-high edges and top out on dirty shelves.

MIGHTY MOUSE

Kelly Sheridan on the first ascent of *Mighty Mouse* (V6).

To find Grandview, hike until the pyramid-shaped peak across the valley is framed as in this photo. Photo, and ingenious beta, courtesy of Scott Mitchell.

THE SLOPING LADY

The Sloping Lady is just below the last pullout on the left before the large, round pullout with a "RV Camping Only – No Campfires" sign. Park in the shallow pullout and walk down the steep gully next to the Sloping Lady boulder.

4. The Sloping Lady V0

★★★

Start on horizontal ledges on the left side of the corner; after gaining the good foot ledge, traverse rightward to the creekside face. Follow horizontal jug ledges to a very tall finish. A true must-do for the obscurity aficionado.

Variation (V3): The direct start with a toothy pocket on the river face is just barely worth it.

GRANDVIEW

The Grandview Boulder is a rarely-visited gem roughly fifteen minutes above Icicle Road, more or less directly above Mighty Mouse. The trail is faint to nonexistent, and it is difficult to give precise directions... The best beta is to use the GPS coordinates given and hike until the pyramid-shaped peak across the valley is framed as pictured. The hike, to the extent it can be described, is as follows: Park at the Sloping Lady pullout, hike up the steep rise roughly 50 yards back toward town, and follow a game trail steadily up and right. Stay left of (above) the wooded gully to the right for about five minutes, then cut right at the first decent opportunity, cross the gully, and climb a steep hill to an open, rocky plateau. Cut right again, across a second wash, and top out at the bottom of a gently-sloped, open meadow. The Grandview boulder is nestled between two large, dark trees roughly five minutes uphill, at the top right side of this meadow. Grandview was discovered by Scott Mitchell in the spring of 2009, and is a good example of what you find when you venture way off the beaten path in the upper Icicle...

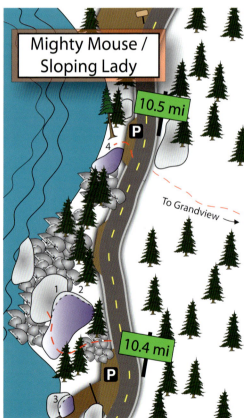

Mighty Mouse / Sloping Lady

10.5 mi

To Grandview →

10.4 mi

SLOPING LADY

5. Buena Vista V5 ★

Start in the center of the boulder's south face with a juggy left-hand undercling sidepull and a good right-hand crimp. Climb powerful moves straight up the good chunky crimps to a big lunge for the flat ledge below the lip.

6. Grandview V5 ★★

Start crouched with opposing sidepulls at the base of the orange arete. Climb left on good crimps and pinches to reach out for a tiny right-hand crimp, then make delicate moves up slopers to top out slightly left.

7. Unknown V1?

Climb the featured face to the right of Grandview.

JACK CREEK BOULDER

The Jack Creek Boulder is a true oddity, a random metamorphic boulder several miles past the next-furthest established bouldering in the Icicle. Developed by Leavenworth locals Shaun Johnson and Aaron Scott in 2013, this fun 'power band' features a series of overhanging arêtes with funky and unique holds. The leftmost of the three arêtes is *RJD2* (V4), the center is *Johnny 5* (V3) and the right is *Terminator* (V5). Numerous variations can also be done, especially with some cleaning. It's exciting to see steep, solid rock this far up the Icicle – especially an odd schist blend that is unlike the area's granite and the Swiftwater schist – a hint of things to come?!

Find the Jack Creek Boulder by driving 16.5 miles from Icicle Junction and turning left toward Rock Island Campground at the fork and crossing the bridge through the middle of the campground. Turn left at the sign for "Jack/Trout" at 16.7 miles and park at the trailhead (a day pass or Northwest Forest Pass is required). Follow signs for the Jack Creek trail, staying left at the fork a few yards into the woods. The trail reaches Jack Creek after just a couple of minutes; the top of the boulder will be directly below the trail.

AREA

Untitled, linocut. Karlyn Koughan (2012).

DAVE THOMPSON

Since my first visits to Leavenworth as a teenager, it has metamorphosed from a little-known climbing area to an international bouldering destination. As the popularity of bouldering has increased, so too has its environmental impacts: crowded boulders, vegetation loss expanding around landing areas, trails going every which way, garbage, erosion... to name a few. This story is not unique to Leavenworth and has provided me one of the most important lessons that I've learned in my climbing career: the sum of our actions as a user group can harm the land and reduce biodiversity in much the same way as other more large scale forms of land development. On reflection I feel that the scale of these impacts result from the dangerous and often unconscious attitude that Nature's primary function is to provide resources and entertainment to the burgeoning human population. It's my hope that we rethink this attitude.

As boulderers, we have the opportunity to halt the trend of growth for the sake of growth – the root cause of many of the environmental problems present in the world today – by a reorientation of how bouldering is practiced and the way boulder problems are established. Among other things, this means we make a distinction between bouldering in the gym and the practice of bouldering outside. Each boulder that we climb on is a unique expression of its surroundings, and is so much more than the name or number associated with it. If we look at the landscape with the same affinity as we do the boulder problems themselves it will only enrich our experience. For those who wish to establish new boulder problems this means that not every boulder with a climbable surface should be: scrubbed; a "safe" landing made under it; sent; rated; a short video made and uploaded to YouTube or Vimeo; a trail to its base established, then printed and published so it may be viewed as some sort of abstract form of consumer commodity or souvenir for the ever-growing population of boulderers.

If bouldering is the first activity that brings you to North America's wild and undeveloped areas, know that it is an opportunity to connect with a world that you are a part of on a deeper level than your career, social status, possessions, or any other abstraction of western culture. For many, this is the reason to visit the outdoors in the first place: the essential awareness of the sublime experienced in the remaining wild places of Earth. These boulders are part of ancient biological communities that have existed, uninterrupted, for unfathomable amounts of time. As such, they command our respect. Who are we as a user group to trample them, cut them back, and otherwise impair them? The loss of a few plants and lichens seems harmless enough, but only if you know what you are stepping on and scrubbing off. Let's look at areas not solely as collections of boulder problems but as ecological communities in which we have the fortune of existing with, not as invaders, subduers, or occupiers, but as members.

Under these circumstances, the art of bouldering takes form, and with it the opportunity to connect with some of the more primal and essential elements of the human psyche, largely repressed in contemporary urban existence. To this end, bouldering is: to get dusty and dirty, cold and wet; to get bloody finger tips, bloody ankles and arms; to learn the plants, the animals, the rocks; to get poison ivy, or stung by a bee; to rouse a rattlesnake; or to smell a flower; an opportunity to connect with the earth on a level that is devoid of most human-constructed filters, to meet the landscape on its own terms, and respect its ability to exist without human input or presence; to experience the rapture of executing unique movement over a surface that exists as a unique expression of the landscape that formed it; to venerate and leave unimpaired what is left of places not altered specifically for the safe and timely travel and entertainment of humans; to make the impacts associated with our presence slight.

Bouldering in Leavenworth is at a fork in the road. To one side, there is a multi-lane super highway: A mundane theme park-like experience ready to be consumed by the masses, where Nature's beautiful randomness is subdued so that the modern comforts and conveniences of western culture can be dutifully applied to the activity of bouldering. On this fork the presence of boulderers as a user group would equal the loss of an art, the demise of the land, and a missed opportunity to understand our place as humans on it. To the other side is a bumpy one-lane road where the tire treads quickly disappear, where we are left walking in a wild and untamed landscape. On this fork there is the potential for something more subtle and infinitely more valuable to occur: we may realize that all is kindred; that instead of being invaders and consumers, going bouldering provides the potential for us to understand that Wild Nature is the source of our existence.

DICK CILLEY

Dick Cilley is a living legend, an elusive stonemaster who's left his mark on nearly every major bouldering area in the United States. In addition to many highball masterpieces, cracks, and still-notorious topropes, Cilley is given attribution for several world-class quotes like "The beauty of climbing is searching for the limit and finding there is none" and "I became the best climber in Washington when I drove across the Oregon border." Cilley is still traveling the United States, and I tried to pin him down when he ended up in Washington in 2014. The closest I came was an email exchange in which he told me he had been crashing at the Torture Chamber. I asked him whether the recent graffiti and vandalism in the cave bummed him out, and his response was classic:

It didn't bother me too much. I've renamed it the Beer Cave. I'm more bothered by Leavenworth itself. It sure was fun in the 70s...

PART 2
TUMWATER CANYON

Hatchery Creek Road

Wenatchee River

Tumwater Cg. 10.0

2

Swiftwater 6.9

Tumwater Canyon
Overview Map

N

1 Mile

That Demon 5.5

2

King Size 4.6

Jolanda
Lake

Alps Candy
Store

Drip Wall Boulder 3.7

Jenny Craig 3.3

Driftwood 2.9

The Beach (1.6)

Castle Rock 2.6

Pitless Avocado 2.3

Labyrinth

Leavenworth

Beach Parking 1.6

TC

0.5

0.0

Grandmother's
House

Range
Boulders

0.9

Icicle Road

TUMWATER CANYON

Many visitors to Leavenworth first experience the grandeur of the Wenatchee Mountains as they wind their way through the narrow valley of Tumwater Canyon on Highway 2. Fittingly, many boulderers have their first experiences in Leavenworth at popular Tumwater venues like the Swiftwater Picnic Area and The Beach. While these two major spots get all the traffic, the Tumwater is also home to a handful of other areas that offer small concentrations of superb problems. Dubbed "The Canyon of Granite" by Fred Becky in *Challenge of the North Cascades*, Tumwater Canyon's dramatic slopes are generously sprinkled with rocks of all shapes and sizes, from gigantic monoliths like Castle Rock to the top-heavy blobs that get us so psyched. Though the bouldering options on the steep hillsides and narrow floor of the Tumwater may be somewhat lacking in quantity compared to Icicle Canyon, the rock quality certainly makes up for it. Diversity is the theme here, from the Squamish-like stone of The Labyrinth area to the fine-grained slopers of Swiftwater north, the schist at Swiftwater south, and the river-polished cave at Jenny Craig. The sheer slopes of the Tumwater Canyon keep it somewhat shadier than the Icicle during the summer months, and areas like The Beach remain tolerable on the warmest days even despite the canyon's low elevation – a worthwhile trade-off for the steady hum of vehicles along Highway 2, the Tumwater's only major drawback. Though Tumwater Canyon has very little private property, the volume of traffic through the canyon can make parking cruxy in some areas. Always park with all four tires off of the roadway, and respect the private property around The Alps candy store. Keep an eye out for rattlesnakes on warmer days, and make plenty noise around sunrise and sunset to avoid startling the occasional bear. For camping, hit up the Tumwater Campground on the west end of the canyon, or head up the Icicle for some peace and quiet. Finally, it ought to be mentioned that the Tumwater is home to several fine swimming holes, popular among locals for their mild temperatures, easy access, and relative quiet compared to the Waterfront Park beach in downtown Leavenworth.

Tumwater Canyon stretches some ten miles north of the town of Leavenworth before Highway 2 breaks west. For purposes of this guide, the bouldering areas in the Tumwater have been arranged from south to north, ones closest to town first. As with Icicle Canyon, all mileages are given from the junction with Icicle Road just east of Leavenworth's famous "Willkommen" sign. Directions are given from Leavenworth, so a 'left-hand pullout' will be on the right if you're coming from the west. Those traveling from the west should reset their odometers at Swiftwater and use the between-area mileages for navigation. For map-reading clarity, it should be noted that the Tumwater Canyon actually runs north-south after the Beach area parking; thus, the Wenatchee River is to the west of Highway 2 at most areas.

Even more so than the Icicle, Tumwater Canyon is a misunderstood place. Most boulderers climb at one or two areas here, and write off the rest of the canyon. If they only knew! For a good first day's orientation, park 2.6 miles from Icicle Junction in the large pullout across the road from the Wenatchee River. You might notice the huge granite monolith rising straight above the highway. This is Castle Rock, a popular climbing spot best known for the 1948 Fred Beckey route Midway (5.5). The climber's trail leaving the north side of the parking lot heads to Logger's Ledge and the summit, a short and steep hike to a gorgeous vista. Directly across the road are the scenic riverside blocks of the Beach Boulders. Catch the trail to this area on the other side of the rusting red bridge about a mile downstream, and don't miss the sweet Forest Area about five minutes before the Beach proper.

On this side of the road, the less-traveled Pitless Avocado area is 0.3 miles away, adjacent to the next big pullout towards town. In the next pullout away from town (0.3 miles away again), the lone Driftwood Boulder offers a couple of off-the-beaten-path easier climbs. There are also a handful of smaller areas at the mouth of the canyon, including The Last Unicorn (0.1 miles from town), The Labyrinth (0.5 miles), and the Range Boulders (0.9 miles).

When you're done taking in the view, head 4.3 miles north from the Castle Rock pullout to Swiftwater Picnic Area, a great place to start your Tumwater Canyon climbing adventures. There are a handful of boulders scattered around the picnic area, as well as a nicely-textured cluster sprinkled throughout the woods across the road. Once you've warmed up and sampled some of the classic problems at Swiftwater, you can head to The Beach for a similar circuit, The Pitless Avocado or Beach Parking for quality intermediates, or Jenny Craig (seasonally) for some difficult challenges. If you're feeling more adventurous, drive most of the way back to town and start the hike to the Labyrinth for an abundance of fresh rock. The Tumwater's got it all – you've just got to take the first step!

TUMWATER CANYON MILEAGE TABLE

TUMWATER CANYON	Mileage from Icicle Junction	Mileage from Previous Area
The Last Unicorn	0.10	
Exit Drop	0.40	0.30
The Canal Boulders	0.40	
The Torture Chamber	0.50	0.10
The Labyrinth	0.60	0.10
The Range Boulders	0.90	0.30
Beach Parking / Trail	1.60	0.70
Grandmother's House	2.30	0.70
The Beach	2.30	
The Pitless Avocado	2.30	
Driftwood	2.90	0.60
Jenny Craig	3.30	0.40
Drip Wall Boulder	3.70	0.40
King Size	4.60	0.90
That Demon	5.70	1.10
Swiftwater	6.90	1.20

Isaac Howard on
Claim Jumper (V4).

Cortney Cusack homes in on the pristine texture of *The Last Unicorn* (V5).

THE LAST UNICORN

The Last Unicorn area is the closest bouldering area to town, a lonely couple of boulders perched on a narrow shelf above the Exit Drop rapid at the mouth of the Tumwater Canyon. This area is only home to a handful of established problems, and on weekends, any serenity that might be had is drowned out by the din of Route 2. Still, the granite is as fresh as any other, and you're very unlikely to see any other pad people here…

Park for The Last Unicorn near the Wilkommen sign on the south side of Route 2 just before Icicle Junction. Park well off the roadway and walk back along the edge of the road for roughly 100 yards until you reach the start of the guardrail. Follow the obvious trail downhill to a small clearing, then take the faint trail west for roughly 50 yards to the obvious round boulder.

AREA

WARM UPS

❑ 1. **The Last Unicorn V5** ★

Start matched on head-high crimps on the east face of the obvious short, round boulder. Slap up edges and top out straight up.
Variation (V6): Start on two slopers on the right arête and climb into the start crimps.

Roughly 100 yards west of The Last Unicorn, there is a squat boulder with two moderate climbs on its south and west sides. A Cole Allen V10 named Rough Rider is also rumored to lurk in these woods…

EXIT DROP

Yet another roadside Tumwater Canyon gem, Exit Drop is one of the closest climbs to town, but it still feels wild. Nestled into the rocky talus between Highway 2 and the Wenatchee River, the Exit Drop boulder is named for the eponymous Class V rapid it overlooks. Check out Exit Drop on a nice early morning or late afternoon in the end of the summer, as it will feel objectively moist at times of high water – and subjectively moist when in the sun.

Exit Drop is 0.4 miles from Leavenworth, just below the pull-out on the left (river) side of Highway 2. Park well off of the highway and hike down the super-steep slab on the downstream side of the pullout. Exit Drop ascends the river side of a medium-sized whitish overhang that is hard to miss.

AREA

❑ 1. **Exit Drop V8** ★★

Start crouched with decent crimps on the steep arête. Gain the sidepull on the face, then make a big move to the jug on the arête. Quite good! F.A. Drew Schick.

❑ 2. **Project**

Climb the steep face to the left of Exit Drop.

THE CANAL BOULDERS

The Canal Boulders are a small cluster of boulders located at the end of a now-defunct irrigation tunnel on the south side of the Wenatchee River, visible across the river and slightly downstream from the Exit Drop parking for the Torture Chamber and Labyrinth areas. This area was developed in 2007 and 2008 by a group of local climbers, but access has since been cut off, and this area is included for historical purposes only.

The Canal Boulders are not currently accessible. The trail to the boulders, which is itself posted "No Trespassing," begins at the end of a private drive just past the Wenatchee River bridge that is posted with a not-so-subtle sign reading "No Bouldering." Besides organizing a river crossing, the only alternative access to the Canal Boulders is via the red bridge at the Beach Parking area, a roughly 1.5 mile bushwhack. Godspeed.

AREA

Kyle O'Meara tops out a crimpy V8 on the smooth, wide face of the Canal Boulder, visible from Highway 2.
[PHOTO] Max Hasson

THE TORTURE CHAMBER

The Torture Chamber is a jumbled mass of boulders just inside the mouth of Tumwater Canyon. Visible above the road at the western end of Route 2's last big curve, the Torture Chamber is bound to catch your eye as you zip in to Leavenworth for the first time. Though there are only a few established problems here, the Torture Chamber is home to two proud Joel Campbell problems, *David and Goliath* (V8) and *Chalksucker* (V8) that are well worth the short walk. Unfortunately, the Torture Chamber has become a party spot for high-schoolers and river guides in recent years, and has been plagued by the graffiti, trash, and grime they bring. Please do your part to prevent further impact to this area by removing any trash you find – people are much less likely to desecrate an area when it doesn't already look like a hobo's been living there…

To reach the Torture Chamber from Leavenworth, drive 0.5 miles west from Icicle Junction on Rt. 2 and park in the small paved "Exit Drop" pullout on the left (river) side. Walk roughly 10 yards back toward town, cross with care, and follow the well-trod path 20 yards uphill to the obvious cluster. The trail to the Labyrinth area departs from the west end of this pullout.

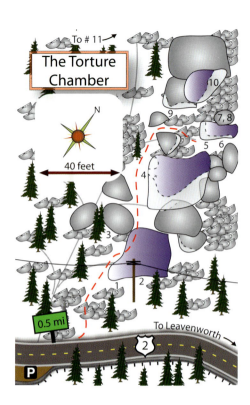

The Torture Chamber

To # 11

N

40 feet

0.5 mi

To Leavenworth

2

P

❏ 1. Project?
Traverse along the huge lip of the first boulder you reach. Definitely needs some cleaning.

❏ 2. Project
Climb the tall, thin face by the telephone pole wire.

❏ 3. Water Torture V4 ★
This clean, whitish boulder is home to a fine problem that has almost been reclaimed by the trees in recent years. If you can get in there, start standing with the right-facing rail and slap up to better holds to finish.

Jump!

❏ 4. David and Goliath V8 ★★
"Improbable" doesn't quite describe this problem. Start uphill of the mouth of the Torture Chamber cave, facing the road. Make a short sprint, launch off the boulders, and hop onto the edge of the steep slab. Finish straight up past an oddly-placed bolt with V2ish climbing. Committing and futuristic, even if it's more parkour than climbing. F.A. Joel Campbell.

❏ 5. The Lobster V4 ★
Start standing matched on the flat shelf in the corridor. Climb left around the bulge on cool pinches to a powerful move for the lip and top out.
Variation (V2): Lunge straight up from the rounded jug, finishing with a nice press on the flat ledges above.

AREA

❏ 6. Chalksucker V8 ★★
Start in the dark corner with a good flat hold at head height. Climb straight left to finish as for The Lobster. This line originally climbed slightly lower than the easier current beta, using a miserable left-hand pinky lock under the bulge (V10). F.A. Joel Campbell.

❏ 7-8. Unknown
There are reportedly two problems directly adjacent to the top-out of the Chalksucker boulder that are brand-new at time of press. Check 'em out!

❏ 9. Drawn and Quartered V13 ★★★
Formerly a longstanding project, this problem was established by Jimmy Webb in the fall of 2014, as this book was being sent to press. Climb the blank overhanging arête from a square-cut right-facing rail. Very hard, and reachy!

❏ 10. Project
Climb the overhanging corner inside the cave. Reachy—there's a reason this one is a project.

❏ 11. Pick Your Poison V9 ★★
From the Torture Chamber, follow the faint trail uphill from the top left side of the cluster. Hike straight up to the left side of the open talus area to find this gorgeous compression problem hidden in a cluster to the right of a large obvious boulder. Start sitting on the pointy adjacent boulder with your left hand on a low sidepull and your right on the lip, climbing up and left between sidepulls on the green streaked face and slopers on the right arête. An awesome addition to the area that was discovered by Drew Schick in the spring of 2014.

PICK YOUR POISON

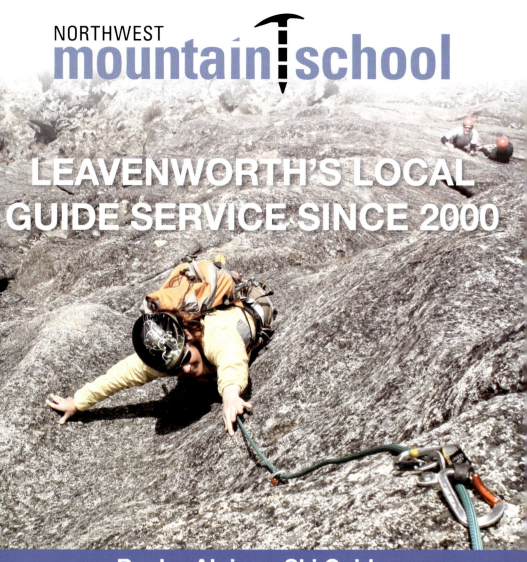

THE LABYRINTH

Just a half-mile from Leavenworth, the steep hillside below the Clem's Holler crag is home to a bewildering mass of boulders, Leavenworth's mini-Squamish. The Labyrinth lies within a denser, steeper forest than found in other Leavenworth areas, and offers a bounty of quality problems for those willing to tackle the sustained approach. There are a handful of quality moderates at the Warm-up boulder and the area around *Beckey's Problem* (V6), while the talus to the east is home to a trifecta of near-perfect testpieces: *Ivy* (V8), *Double My Dosage* (V9), and *The Nine Iron* (V10). Further uphill, the exotic *Girlfunk* (V8) and the striking *Gracious Mama Africa* (V9) lurk around the back of a huge boulder to the left of the trail. A few established problems, as well as some potential, can also be found in the talus below the crag further uphill. Slow to dry out in the spring, the Labyrinth is a good shady option on warm summer days, though you'll be sweating on the hike!

The Labyrinth is near the mouth of Tumwater Canyon, on the hillside just west of the obvious Torture Chamber boulders. Park in the second paved pullout on the left-hand side of the road, about 0.5 miles from Icicle Junction on Rt. 2. Walk to the west end of the pullout, then cross the road and head up the well-worn climbers' trail to Clem's Holler. The trail climbs straight up the hillside, staying atop a gentle ridge with a gully to the left. Roughly five minutes from the road, the trail makes a natural switchback formed by a trailside boulder, which marks the side trail to the Squamish Problem (V5). A few minutes later, the trail to Candyman (V6) leaves just above an obvious bomb-bay overhang 40 feet right of the trail. The Warm-up boulder is right next to the trail roughly 10 minutes from the parking area. To find the Girlfunk area, hike a few more minutes up the trail, then cut left below a tall vertical face just after you pass the trailside Stinkfoot (V2). The Labyrinth area is quite confusing and more intricate than the map indicates; prepare for an adventure!

1. Project
I couldn't find any holds in this steep roof – can you??

2. The Squamish Problem V5 ★
Start with a head high crimp rail, move to the next rail, then press out the mantle. Good movement.

3. Crayola Crack V2 ★
Traverse up and right along the dirty crack. Watch for poison ivy in the landing zone.

4. Crayola Dyno V5? ★
Start on low jugs on the right side of the face and dyno to the wide sloper above.

5. Project
Jump start to a high jug just above a prominent right-facing corner on the left side of the face, then climb up and left with the boulder at your back. This climb has been done via stacked pads on toprope at roughly V7, but has not been done clean from the ground.

6. Unkown V6
Climb the obscure slab roughly halfway between #5 and Candyman.

7. Candyman V6 ★★
Start on the downhill arête of this

hidden boulder with a right-hand sidepull at chest height and your left hand on the high sloper. Move up and right along the arête. Harder than it looks!

8. Nightmare on Elm Street V8 ★★
Start with opposing sidepulls under the mini-corner, stab to a sharp crimp on the corner, then bust left to an incut sidepull just under the lip. Top out up and left with a small horn.

9. Chucky V6 ★
Start as for Nightmare on Elm Street but traverse right along the obvious seam. One of every kind of hold imaginable!

10. Unkown V6 ★
Start with a head-high horizontal crimp and a good foot. Move left to a gaston flake, then top out straight up jugs.

11. Ryan's Problem V3+ ★★
Start in the center of the tall face with the guano-coated jug, stretch high for the prominent horizontal, then reach even higher for the lip and top out. Reachy and scary!

12. Black Roses V9 ★★★
From a huge start jug on the downhill corner, climb up and left through the "worm" hold, then straight out the left side of the prow. Gain a good crimp around the left side of the lip, then kick your left foot out to a flat ledge and mantle to a high flat hold on the lip. Very hard and committing. F.A. Drew Schick.
Variation (V10): "Mo' Roses." Start as for Black Roses, but grab the incut crimp in the center of the prow with your left hand. Top out on slopers up and right (i.e. on the downhill side of the boulder). Even more committing!

13. Ditch Witch V0 ★
Follow the mossy, juggy crack up and right, making a final tricky traverse to the right to top out.

14. Gymania V1 ★★
Climb the classy line of crimps straight up the shallow scoop in the face to a nice mantle finish.

15. The Method Left V2 ★★
Starting from two good head-high crimps, climb up and left on sharp crimpers into the finish of Gymania.

16. The Method Right V2 ★
Climb straight up and right from the head-high crimps to a tenuous rock-over.

17. GZA V6 ★
This tiny nugget climbs the far side of the short, steep boulder across the trail from the Warm-up boulder. Start matched on the good shelf next to the tree, move left to a small crimp, and punch for the stepped crimper above to gain the lip. Climbs better than it looks.

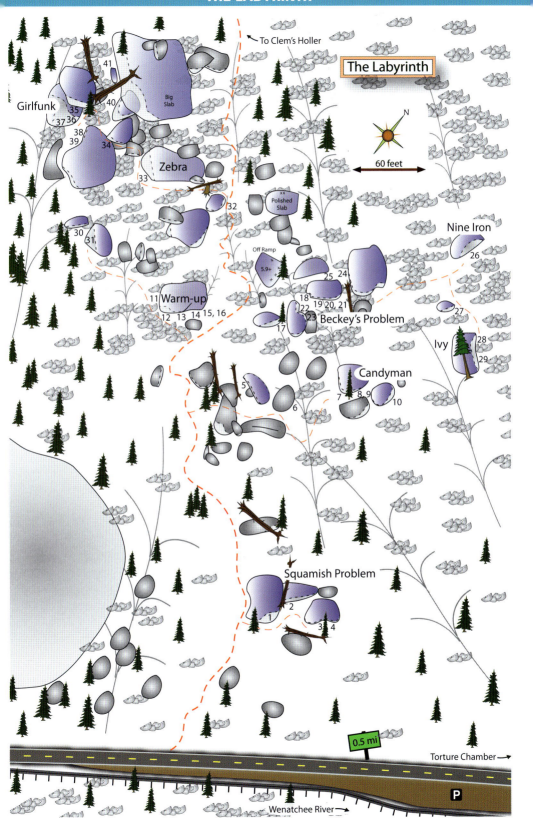

To Clem's Holler

The Labyrinth

N

60 feet

Girlfunk
41
35
37 36
40
38
39 34
Big Slab

Zebra
33

32

Polished Slab
xx

Nine Iron
26

Off Ramp
5.9+

30
31

25 24

27

Warm-up
11
12 13 14 15, 16

18
19 20, 21
22
23
17

Ivy
28
29

Beckey's Problem

Candyman
7
8 9
10

5

6

Squamish Problem
2
1
3 4

Torture Chamber →

0.5 mi

P

Wenatchee River →

Joe Treftz contemplates the last reach on *Ryan's Problem* (V3+). **[PHOTO]** Max Hasson.

18. Jazzercise V8 ★★
Start standing on the left arête with a good right-hand sidepull and an incut left-hand crimp. Climb to the jug on the lip using either funky high feet or the age-old dyno-to-the-lip technique. This problem was formerly known as the "Jazz Arête Project" until Issac Howard first climbed it in 2009.

19. The Bone Collector V6 ★★
Start in front of the pointed rock with two tiny crimpers and a good foothold. Climb straight up through perfect crimps to a big move for the lip and a real-deal mantle. It might help to be fearless for this one – or to have a boatload of pads.

20. Beckey's Problem V6 ★★★
See description in next page

21. 5.9+ V8 ★★
Start as for Beckey's Problem, but grab the right-hand gaston with your left hand and make a wide move to a right-hand sidepull on the arête. Finish straight up the right side of the face with cool opposing slopers.

22. Jennifer Connelly V3 ★
From a low incut slot, twist and stretch up the overhung corner to a neat square jug and top out.
Variation (V3): Start as above and climb left into David Bowie.

23. David Bowie V3 ★
Climb the white overhanging face from a left-hand sidepull and right-hand arête hold. Move to a cool pinch, then crimps, finishing straight up with a cruxy press into the notch.

24. Green Eggs and Ham V0 ★
On the uphill end of the huge boulder right of Beckey's Problem, climb the slight scoop from a good edge and neat-o pocket. Finish up and left of the prominent sidepull, away from the scary gully.

25. Seussology V3 ★
Start on slopers on the right arête, climbing up and left on sweet holds to finish at the top of the corner.

26. The Nine Iron V10 ★★★
Start crouched in the center of the scooped overhanging face, matched on the prominent sloping rail. Climb up and left to a hard move for a unique juggy pinch at the nine-foot level. Top out up and left. Amazingly good. F.A. Joel Campbell and Cole Allen.

27. Unkown V4 ★
Roughly halfway between The Nine Iron and the Ivy boulder, this problem climbs a short overhang perched above a small platform. Start with a high left-hand crimp and a sharp right-hand sidepull and climb straight up the dirty arête.

28. Double My Dosage V9 ★★
Start standing on the uphill side of the tall overhanging face, matched on a gritty chest-high sloper. Climb twisty moves up sharp crimps to a high left-hand gaston sloper, then top out up and right. Funky! F.A. Johnny Goicoechea.

20. Beckey's Problem V6 ★★★
From good head-high edges, climb the right side of the tall overhanging face over bushes using a left heel hook and a fair bit of technique. Very popular, and with good reason!
Variation (V7): Start sitting, crimping on the footholds for the start of Beckey's Problem. Trades a grade for a star.

Jens Holsten bears down on *Beckey's Problem* (V6).
[PHOTO] Max Hasson.

□ 37. Girlfunk V8 ★★

Start standing at the mouth of the cave with your right hand on the small incut edge in the roof. Jump to the tough-to-latch 'ear' hold, campus to the lip, and climb out right along the lip to mantle as for Relentless. Strange and beautiful.

Variation (V5): Use the big rock to the left to get up to the lip, finishing out right with the mantle, and you've conquered "Girlfunk Light."

Variation (V9): Start as for Girlfunk, but finish directly over the bulge.

Ryan Paulness tops out *Girlfunk* (V8).

Joe Treftz on *Ivy* (V8).

29. Ivy V8 ★★★

Start standing on the left (downhill) side of the tall overhang with two square-cut jugs. Make a big move up and right to a wide, flat rail, then make a huge move to a prominent right-facing sloper above. Finish straight up with a technical mantle. Proud! F.A. Johnny Goicoechea.

30. Green Tea V4 ★

This hidden problem climbs the left side of a secluded alcove up and left from the Warm-up boulder. Climb the center of the face from an obvious rail. The landing is a seasonal streambed.

31. Project

Climb the tall overhanging spur to the right of Green Tea from the head-high shelf in the center of the face. Climb up and left to a triangular pinch, then make a hard move to the juggy lip. The Tumwater Canyon's version of The Penrose Step, a.k.a. The Ladder Project.

32. Stinkfoot V2 ★

Climb the very low trailside bulge from a sit start with a flat knee-high ledge and your feet down and left, climbing up and right to finish with a dodgy high-step. Pretty silly, but pretty fun.

33. The Zebra V4 ★★

This beautiful streaked overhang used to have a perfect starting hold in the center of the roof – until we tried pulling on it. Now, try the stand start with the sloping rail at head height. Pull on and bust for the lip, then mantle into the scoop just right of the tree.
Variation (project): There are two potential Zazen-style projects on either side of The Zebra. Are they possible?

34. Cinderella Boy V4 ★

Start sitting at the edge of the steep arête with opposing crimp slots. Fire to the incut crimp on the corner, then hit the sidepull jugs above to press it out and stand for the lip.

35. Sine of the Times V5 ★★

Start matched on the left-leaning rail below the nicely curved lip. Climb up and left along the sloping shelf to the small fin on the left corner and press it out.

36. Relentless V7 ★★

Climb the steep lip right of Girlfunk on sloping pinches to a hard mantle on crimps in the shallow dihedral.

37. Girlfunk V8 ★★

See description on opposite page.

38. Tap V2 ★

Paw up the nice zig-zag slopers on the short left end of the face, finishing up and left with the flat shelf on the slab. Might need some brushing…

39. Ballet V3 ★★

Climb the center of the wide wall from a big low rail at the edge of the stepped landing. Head up through jugs to a slopey sidepull under the lip, finishing straight up with a perfect hidden crimp on the slab above.

40. Gracious Mama Africa V9 ★★★

Nestled inside the huge overhung 'room,' climb heinous slopers up the left arête of this gorgeous streaked prow. This problem was listed as the "Africa Project" in *Central Washington Bouldering*. F.A. Joel Campbell.

41. The Tube V0 ★

Climb the left arête of the small detached block on fat brick pinches to mantle on the sharp lip. If only it were three times as tall…

THE RANGE BOULDERS

The Range Boulders are a small, lesser-known area in the Tumwater Canyon. These few boulders can be found on a small island in the Wenatchee River, and are only accessible in the late summer and fall. Though you won't find any killer desperates here, a couple of fun climbs make a visit to the Range Boulders a nice once-a-year treat. *Washed Up* (V0+) and *The Scorpion* (V2) make for classic warm-ups, complemented by a few moderate challenges like *Vaseline* (V4). The Range Boulders do get a bit of sun, but during the heat of summer, chances are you won't be able to get across the river anyway. The landings here are fine with just one pad, but bring a brush along as the Range doesn't see too much traffic.

The Range Boulders are 0.9 miles from Icicle Junction in the Tumwater Canyon. Park in the small lefthand pullout easily identified by the small white sign reading "Range Area Watch Out for Livestock." Approaching from the west, a similar sign reading "Leaving Range Area" indicates the pullout. Follow the redneck party trail down the short, steep incline to the obvious Washed Up boulder on a narrow rocky shoal. The Scorpion boulder lies just beyond, on the larger, forested island. Getting across the river can be a bit cruxy even at its lowest, but this section can be easily waded during much of the fall season.

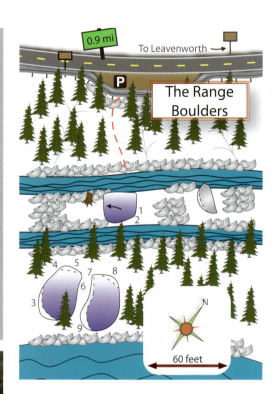

❒ **1. Washed Up V0+ ★★**
From the curved flat hold just overhead, climb the tall east face through a vertical gaston rail to the high lip. Mantle using the rounded bucket up and right. Classic!

❒ **2. The Soap Dish V1 ★**
From a perfect head-high sidepull on the boulder's far corner, climb straight up the blunt arête to finish on the better holds around to the right.

❒ **3. The RZA V7 ★**
Start sitting, matched on the far right end of the sloping shelf. Climb the short corner on tiny crimpers to the blunt lip and finish up the arête.

❒ **4. Stinger V2 ★**
From a high edge on the corner left of RZA, climb up and left to a good sidepull under the point and mantle on the juggy lip.

❒ **5. The Scorpion V2 ★★★**
The area classic. From head-high edges on the left face, climb up and right using the arête and the good pinch under the point. Chuck to the juggy lip right off the apex and top out.

❒ **6. Pokin' The Pope V0 ★**
Climb the dirty slab on the right side of the corridor on right-facing sidepulls and a funky pocket. Might need some brushwork…

❒ **7. Vaseline V5 ★★**
Hop to the high incut on the left side of the corridor, working up and right on the blunt lip to an insecure mantle. Great moves, if not a bit dirty.

AREA

❒ **8. The Mole V4 ★**
Start crouched in the sandy hole with a low sidepull rail and a cool knob on the lip. A few awkward bumps on small lefthand edges lead to the huge jug on the corner and a thrutchy mantle. The sit-start might go; bring a shovel.

❒ **9. Open Range V8 ★★**
Added in the late summer of 2014, Open Range is one of the last problems to be included in this guide. Walk through the corridor between Pokin' the Pop and Vaseline, turn around, and climb the right arête from a stand start with opposing sidepulls. Tall and proud! Bring plenty of pads for the rocky landing.

S|M|C

Quality Gear for Life

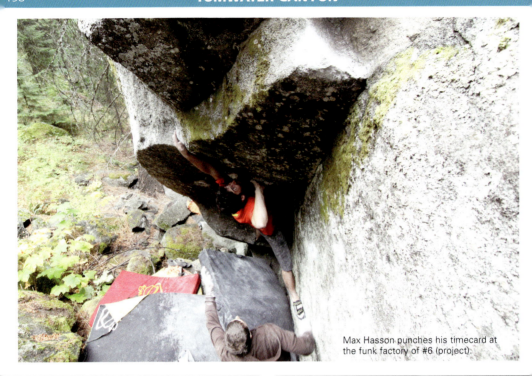

Max Hasson punches his timecard at the funk factory of #6 (project).

THE BEACH PARKING BOULDERS

With boulders scattered along most roads and approaches in Leavenworth's canyons, sometimes you don't even end up at the area you meant to visit. The Beach is one of those areas, as there are several boulders in the vicinity of its trailhead that are just as enticing as the problems at the Beach proper. The Grasshopper Boulder offers a few shady climbs on nice Squamish-esque rails, the H.S.L.T. boulder boasts the all-out sports-action dyno of *Han Solo's Lightsaber Tournament* (V6), and the River Boulder offers a handful of enjoyable moderates at the water's edge. The Beach Parking Boulders are a good option for easy-access shady climbing in the summer, but watch out for poison ivy around the Parking Lot Boulder and the H.S.L.T. Boulder.

The Beach parking area is a popular swimming hole next to the Wenatchee River in Tumwater canyon, 1.6 miles from Icicle Junction. At the break in the guardrail, turn downhill and follow the short dirt driveway to the parking area. Though not signed, the Beach parking is the only large parking area with an outhouse between Leavenworth and the Swiftwater picnic area, and is easily identifiable from the west by the large red bridge that marks the beginning of the approach to the Beach Boulders.

GRASSHOPPER

HSLT

THE GRASSHOPPER

The Grasshopper Boulder is directly across the road from the Parking Lot Boulder. Cross the road carefully and follow the fail trail up and left along the faint ridge to the obvious overhang roughly 50 yards above the road in a thin forest.

❑ 1. **Project**
If the sheer, steep downhill face of this boulder is too blank, there is at least a right-to-left lip traverse to be done…

❑ 2. **Unknown V7** ★
Start standing on the right side of the bulge with your right hand on a small triangular crimp at the bottom of the diagonal rail and your left on a low sloping sidepull. Slap up the bulge and top out up and right.

❑ 3. **Unknown V3**
Start matched on the far left end of the sloping rail, move straight up to the higher incut rail and follow it up and right to top out.

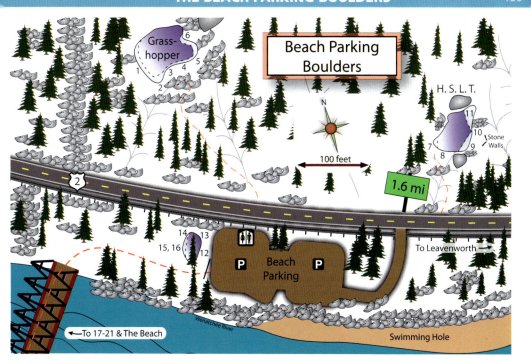

4. Three-Armed Baby V4 ★

Start matched on the better (right) sloping rail in the middle of the face. Throw your heel up and reach to an incut edge, then the lip, pressing out a tough mantle onto the dirty slab above.

5. Gaze of the Grasshopper V4 ★★★

Start matched on the rounded sloper at head height on the prominent blunt arête. Move right to a good sidepull, then climb the increasingly positive rails above to an eye-opening mantle. Beautiful!

Variation (V7): Start on the far left end of the sloping rail, heel hooking through the start of Three-Armed Baby to finish up the arête. Feel like you're in Squamish yet?

6. Project

Start low in the dihedral and climb up and right over the jumbled landing. Will be difficult and proud.

H.S.L.T.

The trail to the Han Solo's Lightsaber Tournament boulder starts a few yards back towards town from the entrance to the Beach Parking lot. Cross the road carefully and follow the faint trail straight uphill, just before the small cluster of trees.

7. The Executioner V6 ★★

Climb up to two underclings on the tall west face of the boulder, finishing via crimpers on the left side of the mini-prow. Sees surprisingly little traffic for how good – and close to the road – it is.

8. The Hobo V0

Climb the featured face on the downhill side of the boulder. This climb has some neat holds, but could (still) use some traffic.

9. Unknown V3

Start matched on the chest-high triangular feature just in front of the small hobo-wall. After an awkward first move with cramped feet, climb up and right on positive edges to a dirty top-out. Could also use some traffic…

10. Unknown V2

Climb up and right on the dirty lip. Rock over on the left side of the corner.

11. Han Solo's Light-saber Tournament V6 ★★

Start with your right hand on a head-high incut sidepull in the middle of the steep overhang, pull on, and dyno to the lip. The vertically-challenged can start left hand on the edge and make a series of crunchy bumps to grab the lip in the notch. A very unique granite problem.

Variation (V8): Start crouched down and left from the start of H.S.L.T. with an incut left-hand edge and a sloping right-hand sidepull. Slap to the start edge of H.S.L.T. and bust for the lip. Powerful!

Erik Lambert sticks the dyno on the first ascent of *Han Solo's Lightsaber Tournament* (V6).

Max Hasson on #18 (V3).

THE PARKING LOT BOULDER

The Parking Lot Boulder is just to the right as you begin the walk to The Beach (just downwind of the outhouse…).

❒ 12. **V1-3** ★
Several variations climb the slab facing the outhouse.

❒ 13. **Yeti V5** ★
Climb the slopey bulge from a crouch start matched on a flat ledge on the left. Throw your heel up and rock straight up to slopers, then top out up the low-angle arête.
Variation (V5): Start spread between the left-hand sloper and a wide right-hand crimp.

❒ 14. **One Stupid Problem V6** ★
Climb poor sloping ledges up the faintly overhanging arête from a left-hand sloper and a small right-hand crimp. Puzzling.

❒ 15. **Unknown V7** ★
Start crouched on a far side of the boulder with an incut right-hand gaston and climb up through an incut undercling to a jug on the lip. Grade unconfirmed.

❒ 16. **D'Anjou V9** ★
Start as above but finish by traversing up and left along the sloping lip. Powerful! F.A. Cole Allen.

THE RIVER BOULDER

The River Boulder is just across the red bridge from the Beach Parking area. Turn right down a well-worn trail immediately after the bridge, and traverse upstream along the water's edge to the obvious riverside boulder with a tall, smooth side facing away from Highway 2. This boulder is only accessible from June-September when the Wenatchee River is low enough.

❒ 17. **Unknown V0** ★
Climb the tall slab on suspect flakes. Down climb on the left side of the slab, heading down and right as you go.

❒ 18. **Unknown V3** ★★
Climb the angled arête to an airy finish reaching right for the lip.

❒ 19. **Unknown V6** ★
Climb straight up the center of the face on crimps and finish straight up, mantling with your right foot in the notch.

❒ 20. **Unknown V4** ★★
Start with a high left-hand undercling and a right-hand sloper on the arête. Slap between the arête and underclings on the face to a big left-hand lunge for the lip. Really good.

❒ 21. **Rusty V6** ★
Rusty is hidden in a small cluster of trees roughly 20 yards to the left when looking at the face of the River Boulder. Climb the blunt left arête just right of a large tree from a rust-colored left-hand sloper and a tiny right-hand crimp, moving through good crimps below the lip to top out at the boulder's apex. A hidden beaut'.

Cortney Cusack slaps the arête on #20 (V4)

RIVER BOULDER

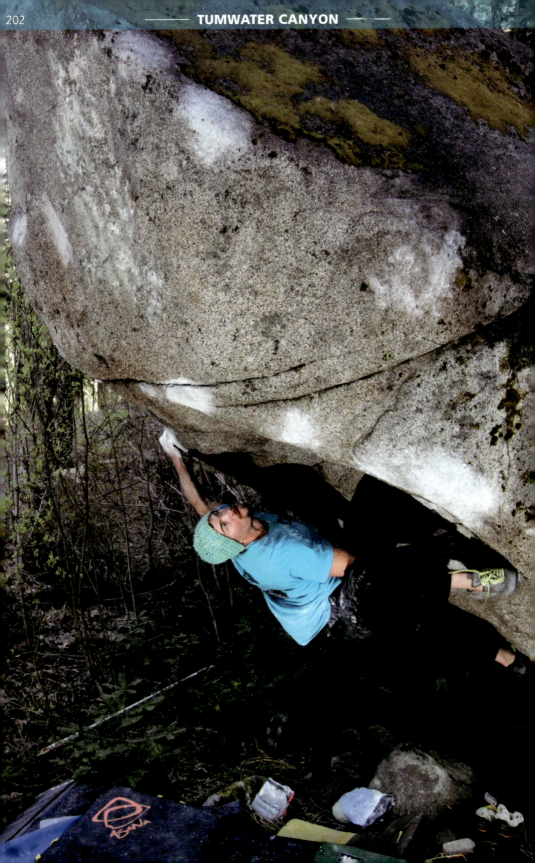

GRANDMOTHER'S HOUSE

"Over the river and through the woods…" This obscure boulder was discovered by Scott Mitchell in 2006, tried by the author several times, and then abandoned until the spring of 2014, when it began to generate interest again. The Grandmother's House boulder is home to two established climbs and, at time of writing, two very proud projects. Get after them!

Grandmother's House is across the Wenatchee River from Highway 2, roughly one half mile east of the Beach Parking area. Cross the river on the red bridge, then immediately turn left and walk down the short steep trail to the water's edge. Traverse downstream, passing a dense, rocky section to reach an open beach area. Pass a cluster of small boulders after about 10 minutes, then three minutes later, cut up the hill between two prominent trees that are about 20 feet apart. Continue downstream, but trend uphill on the game trail toward a dense forested area. Once in the woods, hike up the rocky streambed past a big, round boulder to find Grandmother's House, about 20 yards to the east of the stream. The hike should take 20-25 minutes total, depending on how high the river is.

GRANDPA'S HOUSE

There is another boulder a few hundred yards above Grandmother's House that has two or three established lines.

GRANDMOTHER'S

❏ **1. Unknown V3**
Climb the short face left of the roof.

❏ **2. Project**
Climb the steep overhanging dihedral from a good incut jug. Top out either directly left or up and slightly right.

❏ **3. Unknown V5** ★
Start matched in the high seam, campus to the lip, and mantle straight over.

❏ **4. Grandmother's House Project**
Start with a small incut right-hand crimp and a left-hand sidepull on the grainy shelf at chest height. Climb straight out the steep prow on poor slopers and crimps, finishing straight up with the double arêtes. At time of writing, this problem has not even been done from the crimps in the high seam.

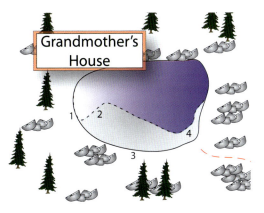

Cole Allen on the Grandmother's House project.

THE BEACH

For seclusion and a nice variety of moderate problems on quality rock, the Beach can't be beat. Uniquely located across the river from Rt. 2 in Tumwater Canyon, the Beach is in fact two areas: one in the forest, and one actually on the beach. The rock at the beach is a finely textured granite similar to the Swiftwater north boulders, home to nearly as many slopers as crimps. In addition to classic three-star moderates like *Brickwork* (V0), *The Fin* (V2), and *U2* (V3), the forest area is home to two old-school testpieces: the crimpy and powerful *Aggressive Reject* (V9) and the super-steep seam of *Goicoechea* (V9), both of which are must-ticks for any aspiring Leavenworth hard-man or –woman. Five minutes down the trail from the Forest area are the true Beach boulders, home to a small circuit of easier problems on a gorgeous sandy beach next to the Wenatchee River. Located directly across from the monolithic Castle Rock, the daunting *Beach Slab* (V1) is not to be missed, as is the enjoyable *The Wave* (V1) and, if you're feeling bold, the classic sploosh climb *Beach Arête* (V2). While the Forest stays relatively well-shaded throughout the day, the Beach area is a great place for catching some rays and mixing your climbing with some swimming…

Park for the Beach in the Beach Parking area, 1.6 miles from Icicle Junction in the Tumwater Canyon (see previous chapter). Turn left down a short, steep hill toward the river as you head away from Leavenworth; the pullout is unmarked and easy to miss until you're driving past it, but it is the only pullout besides Swiftwater with an outhouse, and the large, rusting red bridge is easily visible from the west. Park and follow the trail from the end of the parking lot west and across the bridge. Follow the pipeline trail north along the south side of the river, crossing a small stream after roughly 10 minutes. After a few more minutes, stay left at the fork and enter the forest 10 yards further, among the remnants of a small stone wall.

THE BEACH – FOREST AREA

❐ 1. Evil Petting Zoo V4 ★
A funky classic. Start standing on the corner adjacent to the trail with a decent right hand sidepull, mantle, and top out. Way harder than it looks!

❐ 2. Rocky V2
Climb the short face around the corner left of Evil Petting Zoo using the arête and poor holds on the slab.

❐ 3. Bullwinkle V0
Climb the mossy finger crack and/or the face around it. Pretty dirty.

❐ 4. Ledges V0 ★★
Climb the short face around the corner from the large tree using edges and ledges. This is also the boulder's downclimb – might want to climb up it first.

❐ 5. Aggressive Reject V9 ★★
Start sitting matched on the small, incut crimper two feet left of the tree and make two savage moves up the short arête. Sadly, this problem's aura was greatly tarnished as a result of graffiti that occurred in 2008. Oh to catch the vandals in the act… F.A. Leif Palmer.
Variation (V2): Stand start on head-high crimps and deadpoint for the lip. Good fun.

FOREST AREA

❐ 6. Tweaker V4
Climb the center of the face on small, tweaky crimps. Could still use some cleaning.

❐ 7. Veltex V6 ★
Start standing on the left side of the face with a small right-hand sidepull and a high lefthand sloper on the blunt arête feature. Climb up and right on the sloping lip to an awkward mantle. Years of neglect have made this problem quite hard for the grade.

❐ 8. Walk the Line V4 ★
Climb the tallish corner on flat, flexing holds from head-high slopers down and left. A bit inobvious and dirty, but good climbing still.

❐ 9. Mossline V1 ★
Climb the left-facing rail on the right side of the face. Will likely need some cleaning.

❐ 10. Swamp Thing V0+
Climb the left side of the face on small edges. Will probably need even more cleaning.

❐ 11. Alpine Cow V0- ★
Start on a sloper on the left arête of the smallish boulder. Mantle, walk up the slab, and finish on better holds up and a little right. A great beginner's climb.

❐ 12. Off-Kilter V0 ★
Climb the off-vertical face from cool left-facing sidepulls. Top out straight up with a nice high-step.

❐ 13. Fountain Blues V0 ★★
Start crouched on the corner with chest-high slopers and slap up and right to incuts. Very groovy.

❐ 14. Get Shorty V0- ★
Climb the short face on good holds. Lots of fun variations.

❐ 15. The Backstroke V1 ★
Climb the short slab around the back of the boulder. Try avoiding either arête for a bit of contrived fun.

❐ 16. Bofunk V2 ★
Strange is as strange does. Lie down between two trees on the back of the short boulder and mantle on the sloping shelf to top out.

❐ 17. Nosy V1 ★
Mantle the small 'nose' feature on the right side of this squat boulder and finish up the low-angle arête.

❐ 18. Presto Change-O V2 ★
Mantle on small edges on the undercut lip of the smallish boulder, finishing up the short slab.

❐ 19. The Hardest Problem in the Universe V0-
Climb the rear arête of this boulder on nice big holds.

❐ 20. The Fin V2 ★★★
Climb the obvious short fin from a sit start, finishing straight up on blocky jugs. Great moves. A nice introduction to the world of steep bouldering.

❐ 21. The Savage Act V5 ★
Start as for #20 but climb the face on the right side of the fin using a small righthand sidepull. Just one hard move, but pretty darn cool.

❐ 22. Spooner V0 ★
Climb the scoop left of the fin from a stand start.

Flashback! Johnny Goicoechea making the first ascent of *Goicoechea* (V9) circa 2000. **[PHOTO]** Ryan Paulsness.

23. Jumper V3 ★★
Start in the dirty crack on the right end of the wide face, reach to a flat edge just overhead, and lunge to a perfect sloper on the lip. Very good.

24. The Terrible V7 ★★
From the low flake on the left arête, climb up and right to the sloper and lunge to the terrible sloping edge out right. Rock to a crimp below the lip, and finish nearly straight up from the start.

25. U2 V3 ★★★
Climb the arête from the same start as The Terrible. A strenuous undercling move near the start leads to sloping crimps below the lip. Classic!

26. The Crystal Method V3 ★
Start as for U2, but climb up and left left to the right side of the white crystal plate. Finish straight up on painful sidepulls at the edge of the dyke. Sharp.

27. F*ck The Crystal V3 ★★
Start on blocky jugs near the left end of the face and climb up

and right to a flexing flake on the left side of the sharp crystal dyke. Note: this problem is given two stars solely for sadistic purposes.
Variation (V5): Start from two sharp underclings at the bottom of the dyke. Ouch!

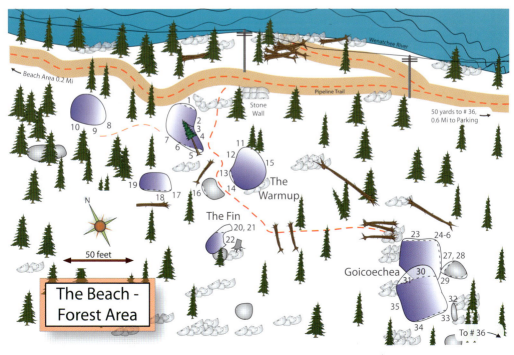

The Beach - Forest Area

Drew Schick on the steep beginning to
his riverside gem *U-Boat* (V8).

28. Brickwork V0 ★★★
Start on the blocky jugs on the left end of the face, climbing
up and left through inobvious incuts to top out to the right of
the log. One could not find better granite.

29. Get Up, Stand Up V6 ★★
Start sitting with a low jug around the corner and over the
boulder from Brickwork. Climb up and right with the slab at
your back to a tall move for a jug on the arête. Finish straight
up the corner. This problem is relatively committing and does
not see many ascents.

30. Goicoechea V9 ★★★
Head up the slab right of Get Up Stand Up to find one of
Leavenworth's most classic old-school lines. Start matched
on a rounded crimp rail at the bottom of the seam and climb
up and left on crimps to a lunge for better holds on the lip.
"About as mellow a landing as you could want, so go for it!"
F.A. Jonny Goicoechea.

31. Project
Start in the cave right of Goicoechea and top out, either joining Goicoechea or finishing straight up via the arête.

32. Flex V2 ★
Climb the tall face left of Get Up, Stand Up on sharp incut
flakes. Not the cleanest, but very good.

33. Top Foot on the Good Foot V2 ★
Climb the steep right arête of the friable uphill face from two
opposing crimpers at chest-height. Big moves on big holds
lead to a delicate high-step and top out. Scary! The face to
the left is equipped with toprope anchors but its history is
unknown.

34. Project?
Climb the tall arête on friable edges. There is a toprope anchor
above the face but its history is unknown.

35. Project?
It's unclear whether anyone has climbed these tall slabs…

36. Project
There is a nice 45-degree overhang roughly 75 yards above
the Goicoechea boulder that has likely not been climbed.

U-BOAT

*The U-Boat Boulder lies next to the river roughly 50 yards
before the entrance to the Forest Area, roughly halfway
between the Forest Area and the rocky wash / seasonal
stream one crosses a few minutes before. Turn right down a
well-worn trail next to a telephone pole with a large boulder
in front of it (two poles past the wash, two poles before the
Forest Area) and walk roughly 20 yards downstream to the
obvious suspended block.*

1. U-Boat V8 ★★
Start matched on a sidepull pinch/
jug under the hanging nose feature.
Smear your foot high and slap
out the right side of the bulge to
a good high edge. Make a 'techy
mantle' and top out in the right-
leaning corner feature above. F.A.
Drew Schick.

2. Project
Start as for U-Boat but finish up
and left on poor opposing slopers.
No joke.

3. Project
On the downstream side of the U-
Boat Boulder, start on the detached
block below, move to a high right-
hand pebble-edge, and slap up and
left to a high sloper. Only sort of
a joke!

U BOAT

Kyle O'Meara on *Beach Aréte* (V2).

THE BEACH – BEACH AREA

The Beach area is another 10 minutes down the trail from the Forest area. The boulders become apparent to the right of the trail a few minutes after passing a small black boulder on the right in a bit of talus. Several faint paths lead to the beach from the pipeline trail – it's easiest to keep going until The Beach Arête is visible from an open clearing at the north end of the cluster. If you pass a low spray painted boulder on the left, it's time to turn around. The beach boulders stay partially submerged until well after the spring thaw, but make a fantastic swimming hole in the late summer.

1. The Wave V1 ★★★
Climb the tall overhang over a sandy landing, exiting either straight up in the notch or slightly to the left for a bit more of a challenge. Great fun.

2. Beach Slab V1 ★★★
Follow the edges of least resistance up the left side of the tall slab, beginning either on the arête or slightly right on the face. Fantastic!

3. Beached Whale V3 ★★
Climb the middle of the big slab.

4. Unknown V3 ★★
Wander up the sea of small edges…

5. Flotsam V1
Climb the low arête from decent holds on either side, following the arête up and left to finish.

6. Jetsam V0 ★
Start standing with a high jug and small crimp, get your feet set and lunge to the top.

BEACH AREA

The Wave · Beach Slab · Dyno 101 · Beach Arête

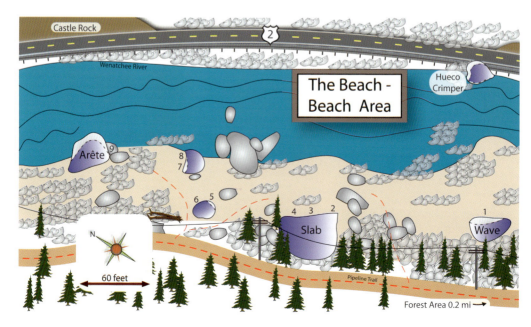

The Beach - Beach Area

⌐ 7. **Dyno 101 V3** ★★★
Climb the center of the uphill side of this squat, cube-shaped boulder. The beta? Grab the rail and jump for the top! A nice introduction to dynos.

⌐ 8. **Rocks for Jocks V1** ★
Climb the left side of the square boulder, slapping between the left arête and sidepulls on the face.

⌐ 9. **Beach Arête V2** ★★★
This super-cool problem climbs the big, blunt lip 15 yards upstream of Dyno 101. Lean out over the water to grab the starting hold, throw a heel up, and it's "summit or soak!" Not a spring problem – try this one when the current is too strong and you'll be joining the kyakers headed towards town!

Andrew Philbin wandering up the edges of *Beached Whale* (V3).

JOE'S CLUSTER

There is a small cluster of boulders roughly halfway between the Forest and the Beach Areas that is accessible during the warmest months of the year. When you're hiking from the Forest to the Beach, turn right down a short, steep path roughly 25 yards past the obvious boulder in the middle of the stream (i.e., just past the swimming hole below the parking for the Pitless Avocado). Cross a huge old log and walk to the cluster at the water's edge. There isn't much here besides one or two jump starts and a potential low project, but it's a fun place to chill out in the summer – swim over from the Pitless Avocado pullout for the quickest approach!

"**THE BEST CLIMBER IN THE WORLD IS THE ONE HAVING THE MOST FUN.**"
- Alex Lowe

Drew Schick sticks the first move of *Slingblade* (V6).

THE PITLESS AVOCADO

The Pitless Avocado is an awesome small area located right next to Highway 2 with a small collection of unique moderates on excellent stone similar to that of the Swiftwater North area. First developed in 2005, the Pitless Avocado area takes its name from a now-legendary story in which Leavenworth local Joe Trefz sliced open an avocado in the parking area, became distracted by a glimpse of the boulders, and walked up to discover the Pitlesss Avocado boulder, pitless avocado in hand. The area's eponym is a serious and committing roof-to-highball (V5), that was established in the dark by Kyle O'Meara and has unfortunately seen little traffic in recent years, save for the few visits it took Johnny Goicoechea to establish the low start (V11). *Slingblade* (V6) and *Between the Legs* (V6) are two exciting and challenging testpieces that can withstand comparison to any of Leavenworth's best moderates. The Pitless Avocado isn't a very good place to warm up, but it is a great spot for summer shade, as most of the problems are nestled among the pines, and the approach couldn't be shorter. If the thermometer is topping out the double digits, be sure to check out the swimming hole across the street and upstream for a midday cool-down and some fun mantles on the boulder in the middle of the river.

The Pitless Avocado is just over 2.3 miles from Icicle Junction in the Tumwater Canyon. Park on the north side of Highway 2 in a large pullout identifiable from either direction by a sign with an arrow indicating curves ahead. This is the last large pullout on the Leavenworth side of the Castle Rock pullout (the latter of which is identifiable by a forest service info board, and the giant rock looming overhead). From the pullout, walk north for 50 yards along the road to a faint trail up the short, steep hill toward the looming Slingblade boulder. Bring a few pads and an appreciation for the still-fresh stone.

❒ 1. Slingblade V6 ★★★
Start standing on the angled platform spread between a good right-hand sidepull and a sloping left-hand crimp. Pull on and 'sling' your left hand to the good jug at the eight foot level, holding it together for the committing finish up the tall corner. Classic!

❒ 2. Slingblade Low V9 ★★
Start down and right from the start of Slingblade, squeezing between a left-hand sloper in the shallow groove feature and a right-hand sloper on the blunt arête. Slap to the prominent sloping shelf, then finagle your way into the start of Slingblade. Makes the first move of Slingblade much, much harder! **Variation (V13):** Start crouched down and right and compress the faint "tube" feature into Slingblade Low. F.A. Jimmy Webb.

❒ 3. IHOP V1 ★
Climb the tall slab on the right side of the corner from a waist-high crimp. Finish left in the brush-filled notch from the jug, or proceed directly up the slab for bit more climbing.

PITLESS AVOCADO

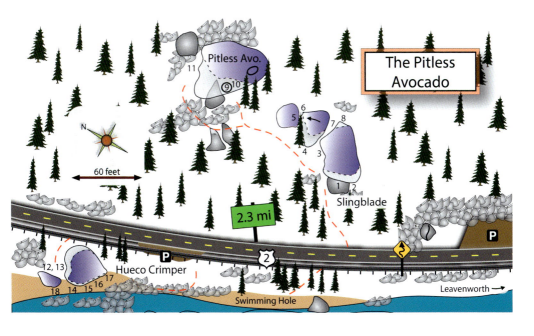

Now that's a pinch! Drew Schick on *The Layman* (V5).

4. **Between the Legs V6** ★★★
Climb the tall arête next to the tree from a high left-hand sloper. Squeeze and crimp up the right face to a direct finish high on the arête.

5. **Salem Slab V0**
Climb the tall, dirty slab from the top of the short boulder. To descend, downclimb this route or shuffle down the tree.

6. **Skittles V3**
Climb the dirty arête from high slopers. Needs some cleaning.

7. **Solar Arête V3**
Start crouched on slopers on the right arête, climbing up and left along the lip to the horn. Finish straight up.

8. **The Layman V5** ★★
Start on sloping edges at the bottom of the left-facing corner and climb straight up on slopers and sidepulls. Technical and very good.

9. **The Pitless Avocado V5** ★★★
Jump to the huge hueco in the middle of the roof and establish with hands and feet. Make committing moves over the lip and onto the featured face of the enormous boulder. Tops out up and right of the huecos on looser rock. Scared? The first ascent was done in the middle of the night!

10. **The Pitless Avocado Low V11** ★★
Start ten feet back in the deep cave with an obvious jug. Make a powerful six-foot dyno to the Pitless Avo hueco without dabbing, and top out as for that problem. Probably not accessible to anyone with a wingspan less than six feet or so…

11. **The Kiwi V5** ★★
Start on the unique wedge-shaped pinch in the middle of the overhanging scoop. Climb right, up, and back left on increasingly friendly holds.

THE HUECO CRIMPER

The Hueco Crimper is a large riverside boulder roughly 50 yards past the Pitless Avocado parking that has gone from overlooked obscurity to well-deserved acclaim in the past few years. Walk past a small pullout on the south side of the road and the boulder will be visible at the west edge of the forested patch; it is easier to descend the short hill straight to the boulder than to follow the faint trail through the patch of trees.

HUECO CRIMPER

12. **The Hueco Crimper Left V11** ★★
Start as for the Hueco Crimper, but move left to a good sloping horn in the middle of the face. Transition to leading with your heel and make a series of hard slaps up the left arête. Finish straight up the arête with a funky mantle. Drew Schick says "Don't show Tim Doyle your project!" F.A. Tim Doyle.

13. **The Hueco Crimper V6** ★★
Start crouched on the right side of the low overhang with a right hand-heel match and a good left-hand edge on the lip. Climb straight up the right side of the bulge using strange pinches and the "Hueco crimper" to a tenuous rock-over finish.
Variation (V8): A low start, beginning on an edge a few feet left in the roof, ups the grade a few notches.

14. **Missin' Nugget V2** ★
Begin on the left side of the tall wall with a good right-hand gaston and a high left pocket. Climb straight up through one small crimper to a juggy finish.

15. **Real Imagination V9/10** ★★
Start sitting down and left from Claim Jumper with a very low left-hand sloper and an incut right-hand sidepull/undercling at the three foot level. Climb wide, beta-intensive moves between opposing sidepulls to latch the right-hand start hold of Claim Jumper, then toss a harder version of the Claim Jumper dyno and finish straight up. Very good. F.A. Cole Allen

16. **Claim Jumper V4** ★★
Start in the middle of the face with a head-high right-hand sidepull and a high left-hand crimp. Pull on and lunge to the awesome brick-shaped pinch, then fight your way through a few seemingly-footless gaston moves to top out on good shelves.

17. **The Hueco Sloper V6** ★★
Start standing with a good flat shelf on the right arête. Climb left to good holds on the face, then use a poor sloper on the arête to slap for the lip.
Variation (V7): The Joe's Crimper: Start as for The Hueco Sloper but move left on the face, using the squiggly 'Joe's Crimper' to reach to a small incut jug a few feet left of the arête.

18. **Bad Karma V2**
Start matched on a right-facing sloping edge on the water's edge with a good foot edge. Move through two good sloping pods to a good triangular jug on the corner.

ABOVE Leavenworth locals Megan and Rob Lewis at the *Hueco Crimper* (V6). **[PHOTO]** Max Hasson BELOW Isaac Howard stakes a claim on *Claim Jumper* (V4).

THE DRIFTWOOD BOULDER

The Driftwood Boulder is a small riverside boulder just west of Castle Rock in Tumwater Canyon. A couple fun moderates make this a good place to break away from the typical areas and get some sun and solitude. The off-vertical *Bubbleslab* (V4) on the boulder's north side ascends a slicker, more polished stone, while the riverside *Driftwood* (V2) and projects are a bit rougher and steeper. Whatever your preference, be prepared to do a little brushing, as these climbs don't see much traffic.

The Driftwood Boulder is 2.9 miles from Icicle Junction in the Tumwater Canyon. Park in the large right-hand pullout (non-river side); it is the first pullout north of the Castle Rock pullout, and the second one past the Pitless Avocado area. This particular pullout is also marked on either side by a triangular sign reading "rocks." Thanks WSDOT! Cross the road and the guardrail, walking north along the road for roughly 20 yards before descending to the obvious boulder next to the Wenatchee River.

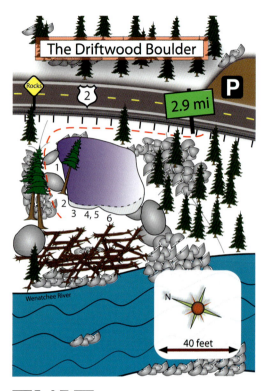

❒ 1. **Bubbleslab V4** ★★
Start standing in the hole made by two boulders, iron-crossed between two small edges. Climb the tall slab on bubbly crimp pockets, eventually heading slightly right to the lip. Scary!

❒ 2. **Gooseneck V1** ★
Start sitting just right of the tree with two really low sidepulls. Climb straight up on crimps and squeeze under the branches to finish. Will probably need some cleaning.

❒ 3. **Clipped Wings V0**
From questionable jugs on the upstream corner, climb up a few moves before mantling and finishing in the dirty corner among branches. Sound like fun? It actually kind of is.

❒ 4. **Driftwood V2** ★
Climb up and left from the low jug in the center of the overhang, moving through sharp crimps to better holds above. Top out up the dirty face.

❒ 5. **Project**
Start on jugs just right of Driftwood and climb straight up. Extremely thin.

❒ 6. **Project**
Start on jugs and move right through small sidepulls.

AREA

FRED BECKEY

I had the chance to meet the Master himself in late 2013 at the home of longtime Washington climbing steward Matt Perkins. Unable to help myself, I asked Fred if he had ever done much bouldering back in the day. His response was classic Beckey:

"Bouldering? No. Try to avoid it if I can. Too much hiking!"

Go figure!

[PHOTO] Ray Borbon, Wikipedia Commons.

Adam Healey demonstrating the post-break rose move on *The Whirlpool* (V10)
[PHOTO] Matthew Hall

"IT DOESN'T HAVE TO BE FUN TO BE FUN."

- Barry Blanchard

BELOW Joel Campbell stretching out on *Finished Product* (V9).
[PHOTO] Matthew Hall

JENNY CRAIG

Jenny Craig is a unique bouldering spot for the Leavenworth area. Two riverside boulders have settled against each other to form a small, sheltered corridor echoing the sounds of the Wenatchee River. The Jenny Craig cave is partially-submerged during the spring months, but a small selection of challenging boulder problems can be found here during the remainder of the year. Flooding in 2006 deposited several additional feet of driftwood on the upstream side of the boulders, burying a number of problems in the process and providing a tangible example of seasonal change acting upon a bouldering spot in the Leavenworth area. The area's eponym, the strange and bizarre Jenny Craig (VBlahblah-blah) requires the boulderer to top out through a narrow slot *a la* Hueco Tanks' *Birth Simulator*, while the recently-added *The Current* (V10) will test anyone's ability to climb spread-eagled. Jenny Craig is a miniature area without any warm-ups, but well worth a visit for its unique ambience and problems.

Jenny Craig is in Tumwater Canyon, located at the water's edge 3.3 miles from Icicle Junction. Park in the large lefthand pullout and follow one of several trails to the large boulders by the river. Access the cave from either side.

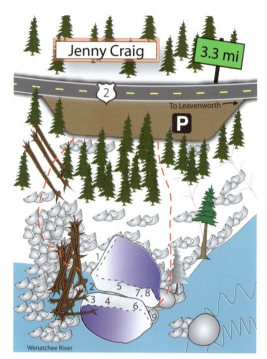

❐ 1. Kim + Randy (Project)
Climb the tall, slightly overhanging face on small edges over a number of small boulders. If you ever find yourself in Lincoln Woods, RI, check out the Egg Boulder's "Norma + Rico" project for some serious déjà vu…

❐ 2. The Logmonster V5 ★
This problem used to begin sitting on top of the logjam, but is now mostly buried. From a strangely solid incut sidepull at the (now) six inch level, make a hard move right to an incut gaston. Finish up and right as for The Current. F.A. Cole Allen.

❐ 3. White Fang V2
Start matched on a low sloping rail next to the logs on the river side block. Climb straight up, then right on crimps to finish on the arête. Currently inaccessible.

❐ 4. Jenny Craig VBlahblahblah ★★
Start next to the huge logjam with your left hand on a slick crimp and your right on the sloping rail of White Fang. Climb up and directly left past a flat jug at head level to slopers below the lip. Finish straight up through the hole, using anything you can grab. You may want to go on a diet for this one… F.A. Joel Campbell.

❐ 5. The Current V10 ★★★
Start at the low end of the curved, incut rail and traverse left to an incut crimp on the face. Heel hook and slap to set up for a big left-hand bump, then top out straight up. Reachy and powerful! F.A. Johnny Goicoechea.
Variation (V11): Start on the furthest right end of the rail as for The Whirlpool and traverse into the start of The Current.

❐ 6. Anorexia V4 ★
Begin matched on a good undercling on the left side of the face. Move up to crimps, then the lip. Drop from here or traverse either direction if you're dead-set on topping out.

❐ 7. Head and Shoulders V4 ★
Start on the right end of the juggy shelf, climbing up and left along the incut seam. When the holds run out, stab backwards to the jug on Jenny Craig, switching boulders and finishing through the narrow slot. A real oddity.

❐ 8. The Whirlpool V10 ★★★
Formerly the gem of the area at V9, this problem broke in 2010 and is now significantly more difficult. From the juggy shelf, climb right through the roof using a small, sharp crimp (formerly a good incut) to a chunky crimp rail. Match and move right to a cruxy lip encounter and finish on the slab high above the river. A fall past middle of the climb will send you tumbling backwards into the river. F.A. Kyle O'Meara, F.A. post-break Johnny Goicoechea.

❐ 9. Finished Product V9 ★★
Climb the dark face on perfect little crimpers from flat jugs at the water's edge. A nice sloper on the lip leads to an easier top-out in dodgy territory. The start hold of this beautiful testpiece has broken since it was first done, making it slightly more difficult. Landing seasonally wet. F.A. Joel Zerr.

THE DRIP WALL BOULDER

The Drip Wall Boulder sits alone next to the short but steep approach to the Drip Wall crag, home to one of Leavenworth's best sport climbs, *Roothless* (5.12d). Though the Drip Wall Boulder doesn't have any established problems, it's not for lack of trying. The line up the center of the face is an obvious future-classic, and there's potential on the large steep face to the right. Cole Allen's *Hophenge* (V9) is a recent addition that makes the area worth the stop for those who want to seek out all the off-the-beaten-path testpieces they can.

Park for the Drip Wall Boulder 3.6 miles from Icicle Junction, roughly 0.4 miles past the Jenny Craig area, in a small pullout on the river side of the road. When approaching from the west, the pullout is on the right 0.1 miles past the larger pullout next to the Lake Jolanda dam. Climb a bit of third class on the left side of the large low-angle slab across the road, then follow the trail roughly 50 yards uphill to the obvious overhanging face.

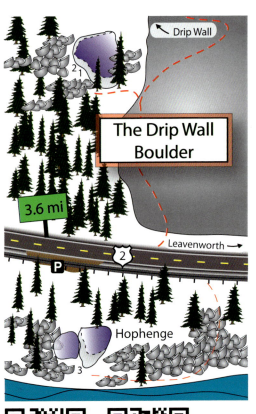

❒ 1. Project

Start on the low sloping shelf in the small alcove, make a big move to the good flat sidepull jug, then make one or two very difficult moves to gain the juggy lip. Will be proud!

❒ 2. Project

Start on the low sloping shelf but climb up and slightly left along the faint corner feature.

❒ 3. Hophenge V9 ★★

Walk roughly 50 yards south from the parking, descend the steep rocky slope to the river's edge, then walk 25 yards back north along the shore. Climb the river-side arête of the large boulder from a wide start with two opposing sidepulls. Make a big move to a positive hold on the right lip, match (creatively), and top out. F.A. Cole Allen.

DRIP WALL BOULDER   HOPHENGE

JASON MIKOS

When Kelly asked me to contribute to his new guidebook on Leavy Bouldering, I was pretty elated at the prospect of having an addition to a book that blew up the bouldering here. For the Leavenworth area, there is no other standard – he set it!

But as I thought more about it, the subject became more complex for me.

I'm 36 years old as I write this. Been climbing in Leavenworth for 24 years. If you've done your math right, I've been climbing here since 1992. Before crash pads and the 'acceptance' of bouldering as a mainstream style of climbing. A few of the problems that are now considered 'high ball' were topropes and the famous '*Bolt Rock*' (5.11b, now changed and off limits to climbers) was a proud bouldery send.

When I was in junior high, I (and Brian Doyle) met my mentor, Erik Mohler. Look him up in a previous guide – you'll see that he's put up some good stuff – like *Formunda Cheese*, 5.11c – bouldery, cruxy, and old school. But I digress.

In looking back at over 20 years of climbing in the Icicle and Tumwater canyons, it's amazing how many great memories I have and how spending time in Leavenworth has shaped who I am as a person, all for the better.

My favorite camping areas were right across the street from Alphabet Rock, and where the Forestland parking lot is now. Fifteen-plus years ago, you could drive up Icicle Canyon and pretty much plant a tent anywhere there wasn't a 'Private Property' sign. Our fires were small, using only existing pits, and we were very careful about the impact we had on the place; picking up after ourselves, leaving the space better than when we found it. We also didn't have to worry about finding a place to park or full campgrounds – we knew the gem that was Leavenworth and valued it greatly, hoping no one would find out about it and the masses would stay away. Every hidden gem is always found… Like I said, great memories.

But I won't continue to talk about the 'good ole days' and milk being $0.58 per gallon because it really doesn't do any good for the present or future of what will become of Leavenworth. If I've gained anything, it's perspective on what it means to hold onto a place that has value in it and why it impacts me.

For most of us, we have a place that feels like we belong there. Whether it is a place you grew up and want to grow old in, or some random spot you visited that stained you in some way, that place is there. I think that place becomes important to each us because of the profound, positive perspective it gives us and that draws us back – we are better people just for being in that environment. Leavenworth is mine.

The climbing community has always been one that I'm attracted to because, for the most part, each of us shares in something bigger than ourselves: community, nature, the struggles with gravity and the utterly speechless joy when we send a project!

But every community has its small band of rejects and detractors that don't 'get it.' They say they love the outdoors and love climbing, yet pay no attention to 'No Parking' signs, 'No Trespassing' signs, and 'No Camping' signs, toss pieces of tape or food on the ground, leave cigarette butts everywhere, and basically act like a bunch of assholes that ruin what myself and countless others try to enjoy and protect. There is nothing to be done about people who talk like they care, but act as if they don't give a shit and have a right to treat the outdoors as though it were their own house.

Like I said, if I've gained any perspective that I can share, it would be this: Don't talk like you care about Leavenworth (or any other place outside), *act* like you care. Do something about shit laying around – be the example. If not for anyone but yourself. Because you find value in going to these places. I don't rely on anyone to tell me to pick up someone else's trash – I make sure to do it because I love being outside and being a part of nature. Beyond that, my three kids are now growing up in Leavenworth and I want them to be able to enjoy this place long after I'm gone. Big things happen because of many small occurrences, and the impact each of us has on a daily basis really does matter.

You have this guidebook in your hands, hopefully because you want to climb and enjoy what this magical place has to offer – now pack an extra plastic bag from Safeway and get ready to clean up someone else's shit. Because if you don't, who will?

KING SIZE

Recently established in May of 2014, *King Size* (V9) is a truly amazing addition to the Tumwater Canyon in a number of respects. For one, the fact that a line of this quality, just several hundred yards away from (and visible from!) the road, was neither climbed nor even discovered until 2013 or 2014 is almost beyond belief. Next, the fact that this climb even exits is wild – a perfect 50-degree overhang on the downhill side of a massive 40-plus-foot boulder perched on a steep hillside, with just enough of a landing to be doable. Then there is the climb itself, a beautiful streaked wall that starts matched on an overhead jug and climbs powerful and dynamic moves up perfectly-formed holds to a tall, slabby, and scary top-out. It's simply amazing! Hit up King Size in the morning, however, as it gets late afternoon soon, and you will want good friction for this one…

King Size is on the hillside above the Tumwater Canyon. Park 4.6 miles from Icicle Junction in a large pullout on the right, 0.2 miles past The Alps candy store. When approaching from the West, the pullout for King Size is on the left 2.2 miles past Swiftwater, across from a west-facing "Left Turns Ahead" sign. From the far west end of the pullout, follow the faint trail straight uphill through the woods for roughly five minutes, then trend up and right into the steep open area toward the obvious huge boulder (yes, this one really is obvious!). The hike should take 10-15 minutes total, depending on the number of pads you bring.

⌐ 1. King Size V9 ★★★

Start standing on the left side of the clean overhanging face, matched on flat opposing sidepulls on the triangular rail. Move your right hand to the incut slot above, then make a hard move to the prominent sloping rail, match, and climb straight left to an incut mail-slot jug in front of the tree. Top out up and right in the shallow dihedral up the low-angle slab.
Variation (project): The low start matched on an under-cling down and left of the start hold is still a project.

Johnny Goicoechea in mid-flight as he sticks the crux move on King Size (V9).

THAT DEMON

That Demon is another seasonal riverside boulder in Tumwater Canyon. Easily visible on a large sandbar near the edge of the Wenatchee River, That Demon is typically only climbable in the late summer and fall. The small handful of problems to be found here are worth the mission, from the beautiful rail of *The Skuke* (V3) to the tendon-busting one-mover *The Virgin* (V8). The ambience of climbing in the middle of the river isn't bad either, that is, if you can ignore the gawking motorists and the perilous half-water landings. Bring a friend to spot and a sense of adventure, and you'll rest happily knowing you've put this eye-catching 'demon' to rest.

That Demon is 5.7 miles from Icicle Junction in a rocky side channel of the Wenatchee River. Park in the large lefthand pullout at 5.5 miles and descend to the riverbank. Walk north through bushes and small rocks on the wide sandbar to this round, dark boulder. That Demon is a highly seasonal area, and isn't worth visiting until the landing is at least partially dry. The upstream face of That Demon has been blocked by a huge log for the last several years; it will take a big spring flood to make problems 1-3 accessible again.

AREA

☐ 1. **The Skuke V3** ★★
Start crouched with the obvious square-cut jug on the right end of the face. Climb left through edges to the striking curved rail. Traverse up and left until you can rock up to the lip and top out.

☐ 2. **That Demon V5** ★★
From the flat jug of The Skuke, climb left to edges, then straight up on more edges. Finish in the flat, scooped ledge on the lip. Awesome!

☐ 3. **Damian's Thoughts V6** ★
From the same start as the previous two climbs, move straight up to a sloper and better holds below the lip.

☐ 4. **The Virgin V8** ★
Begin this heinous finger-wrencher on the boulder's less-steep south side with a high mono pocket and a poor undercling at head height. Pull on and bust for the lip. Yowie! F.A. Johnny Goicoechea.

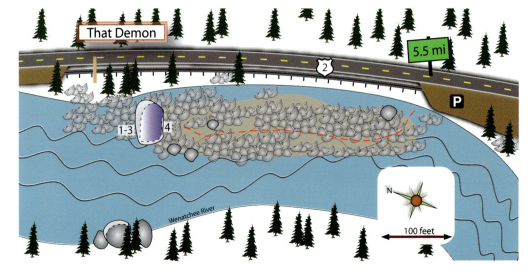

JOHNN GOICOECHEA

All I can say about Leavenworth is this: Love this place.
Be humble and respectful, because a part of you
never leaves. That is why it's so hard to leave on those
Sunday afternoons!

SWIFTWATER

The Tumwater Canyon's Swiftwater Picnic Area is home to one of Leavenworth's most varied and historic bouldering circuits, easily the most-visited bouldering area in the Tumwater. Swiftwater boasts a good variety of problems in all ranges of difficulty, with plenty to occupy the beginning boulderer. As with the difficulty, the rock quality is also quite varied, from schist, to the large-grain granite of Hate Rock, to the fine sandpaper texture on the north side of the highway. If this is one of your first stops, don't judge all of Leavenworth based on the Swiftwater south boulders, as many visitors do… Instead, catch a quick warm-up and venture across the road to the concentration of assorted intermediate challenges from the Fontainbleau-esque "grandstone" of *Sitting Bull* (V3), *Sleeve Ace* (V3), and *Premium Coffee* (V7) to the famous roof crack *Royal Flush* (ridiculous V2). Swiftwater is also home to two of Leavenworth's largest featured caves: the sustained and funky Schist Cave and the steep, three-dimensional climbing of the Footless Traverse boulder. Virtually all of the landings at Swiftwater are flat, and the area stays relatively shady during the summer.

Swiftwater is located on the south side of Rt. 2, 6.9 miles west of Icicle Junction in Tumwater Canyon. Park in the southern of the two well-signed parking areas, the second as you approach from Leavenworth. Hate Rock is located just south of the parking area; follow the trail on the north side of the lot to Heel Hook Rock, the tall schist overhang, and the steep Schist Cave. To reach the Swiftwater North boulders, walk north along Rt. 2 for roughly 40 yards, cross the road, and follow the short path to Premium Coffee. Continuing on, the trail runs parallel to the road through a vegetated burn area to the Royal Flush cluster and the west-facing Footless Traverse cave. Use the constant traffic noise from the highway as a reminder to walk well off the road, and please use extreme caution when crossing.

NORTH

Johnny Goicoechea on an early ascent of #30 (V9/10). **[PHOTO]** Max Hasson

☐ 1. **Cramps V2** ★
Start with head-high edges just right of the arête, crimping up and right to top out.

☐ 2. **Hate Monger V3** ★★
Start sitting, matched on the obvious flake jug on the left end of the boulder. Move your right hand to the grainy Vulcan grip, finishing up and left with grainy sidepulls. Good climbing on not-so-pleasant stone.

☐ 3. **Slap and Dangle V3** ★★
Jump start to a flat shelf at the nine foot level, roughly two feet right of the small left-facing corner. Campus up and left to press out an awkward mantle on slopers.

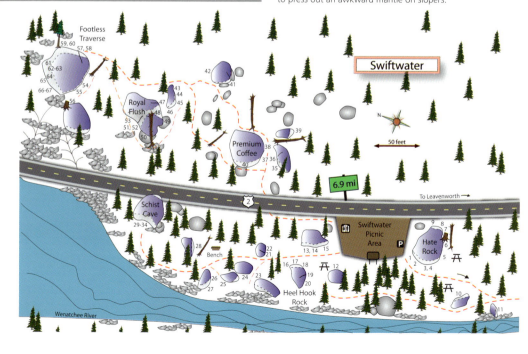

4. Shock and Awe V3+ ★★
Jump to the flat edge as for #3, but campus and heel hook rightwards to top out on better holds. Gritty but good.

5. Raven V9 ★★★
Somebody's climbed *that*??? Just right of the overhang, jump to a small crimp pocket at the 12 foot level above the "DJ Merced" graffiti. Climb up and left to a crimp and mantle onto the near-vertical wall to reach the lip. Feel free to stack a couple cheater stones if you need to – the first ascent was done using two crash pads and a spare tire! F.A. Joel Campbell.

6. Snake Eyes project
Starting from the tree stump, climb the tall slab to two identical pockets a few feet below the lip.

7. 14 Years V6 ★
Start sitting on the corner with a small righthand sidepull and a left sloper. Slap up to better holds on the arête, finishing slightly left on easier ground.

8. Lip Gloss V2 ★
Start standing with a good hold on the left arête of the short roadside face. Climb up and right on the arête to finish on the corner. Can also be done as a dynamic throw to the right arête.

9. The Transverse V1
Start crouched with slopers on the right arête and traverse up and left on better holds to top out on the point.

10. The Devonian Fish V0 ★
This baby boulder offers several variations, all of which are pretty darn easy. A nice option for those of us who prefer *really* easy warm-ups.

11. Caveman Cole V8 ★

This rarely-attempted one-mover lies roughly 20 yards past the Devonian, just below the trail that traverses above the river's edge. Start matched on the small crimper in the overhang, move to the sloper above, then wildly chuck for the jug on the lip. The second hold on this problem has unfortunately been chipped recently, making the problem significantly easier. F.A. Cole Allen.

12. Unknown VB
Several mellow variations climb the lumpy boulder near the southwest corner of the parking lot.

13. Unknown V3 ★
Start squeezing the gentle arête feature on the left side of the overhanging schist face. Climb up and right into Schisthead using a funky two-finger crimp.

14. Schisthead V2 ★★
Start in the center of the tall face and climb straight out the steepest part of the overhang to a big reach for a hard-to-spot jug.

15. The Prey V0 ★
Climb the shorter right side of the face on increasingly large holds. Variations abound.

16. Heel Hook Right V3 ★
From a low incut on the right end of the tiny overhang, move up to a flat sidepull and finish up and left on slippery slopers.

17. Heel Hook Center V2 ★
Start sitting under the overhang with a smallish crimp pocket and a decent low foot. Move up to the flat crimp, then the lip and top out. Good fun.

18. Heel Hook Left V2 ★
Start sitting on the left side of the small overhang with good slopers on the lip. Move up and right on slopers to top out by rocking over to the left.

19. Minnie V1
Climb the ultra-short finger crack from a sit start.

20. Mickey V0 ★
From a crouch start with both hands in the low seam, climb up and right to good holds on the lip and a beginner's mantle.

21. No Pitons Here V0 ★
Climb the widening crack on the miniature boulder. A good place to experiment with those bizarre crack climbing techniques… Hand jam? What's that???

22. Bubbles VB ★
Just right of No Pitons Here, climb the short face on super-cool bubbles and grooves. Fun for the whole family.

23. The Ripple Effect V1 ★
On the short uphill side of this large boulder, climb the wavy slab over a slanted landing. There are one or two fun lines on the downhill of this boulder as well.

24. Oceanfront V1
Traverse either direction along the riverside lip of this squat boulder.

25. Joel's Traverse V6 ★
On the boulder just below Oceanfront, traverse the low lip up and right on neat slopers.

26. Goat Boy V7 ★
Start matched on a small undercling and balancing on a big foot ledge right of Chicken Man. Your simple goal here is to reach the flat crimp just in sight above – alas, simple but for the effects of gravity…

27. Chicken Man V8 ★★
Jump from the edge of the flat rock to slap two high, opposing slopers on this semi-hidden boulder, finishing straight up via a small crimp and tenuous mantle. The difficulty can vary from year to year with the ground level. F.A. Cole Allen.

28. Bam V2 ★★
Hop to the good sloper just above head height, and finish straight up with a nice mantle. A nice short problem on fantastic rock.

29. Unknown V3 ★
Climb up and right on ledges on the far left side of the cave, rocking over whenever you can, then dropping off.

30. Unknown V9/10 ★
Start on a low horizontal jug as for the Schist Cave problem, climbing to the big depression halfway, then climb left out of the steep prow.

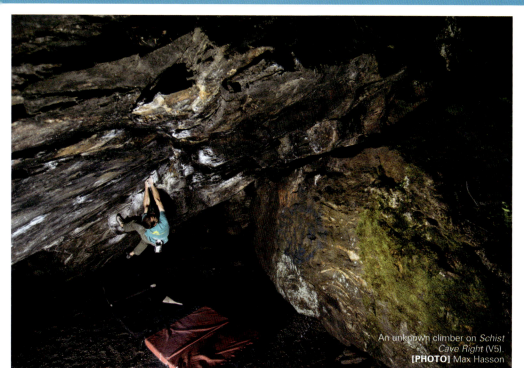

An unknown climber on *Schist Cave Right* (V5).
[PHOTO] Max Hasson

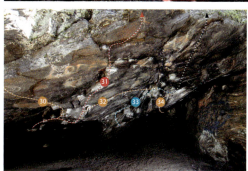

31. Schist Cave V10 ★★★

Start on a low horizontal jug in the center of the overhang, climbing out jugs to a semi-rest at the edge of a steep overlap. Use the prominent right-facing sidepull to gain the sloping edges above, then climb a few difficult moves to an obvious jug on the lip about four feet right of the Donnie Darko graffiti. Though the rock in this cave is not as pretty as Leavenworth's granite, it sure is unique, and this problem in particular climbs like a gem.

32. Unknown V7 ★★

Start as for Schist Cave, but climb directly right from the prominent right-facing sidepull on sloping edges along a straight seam. Climb to the finish jug of #33 and drop, for now.

33. Schist Cave Right V5 ★

Start on very low jugs 10 feet or so right of The Schist Cave. Climb up the obvious right-facing corner on good sloping holds to an awkward interchange to gain an obvious flat jug at the 7 foot level. This problem formerly topped out, but a crucial flake broke in 2013 and it has not been climbed since.

34. Unknown V9 ★

Start deep in the steepest part of the cave right of Schist Cave Right and climb hard moves to the jug. Grade unconfirmed.

35. The Barista V1 ★★

Climb the bulge just left of the tree to a good left-facing flake, then layback to the top and press the dirty mantle. Awesome!

36. Unobvious V2/3 ★

Follow weird sidepulls and finger locks up the obvious seam on the left side of the boulder facing Premium Coffee. The grade depends on whether you start from the rock or the ground.

37. Premium Coffee a.k.a. Heavy Petting Zoo V7 ★★★

Upon entering the woods on the east side of the road, your eyes may be immediately drawn to this obvious smooth bulb on the left. Start matched on the lowest sloper with a tricky square-cut foothold, slap up and left on fine-grained slopers, then rock up to the jug and drop or, for full value, climb up and right to top out. Extremely temperature-dependent, so prepare for a good sandbag in the summer. One of Leavenworth's most unique and beautiful problems, even if a bit short by modern standards.

Colorado legend Herman Feissner enjoys the espresso-grind texture of *Premium Coffee* (V7) during a short visit in 2006 that resulted in the first ascent of *The Practitioner* (V11).

38. Percolator V1
Climb the arête right of Premium Coffee from a bubbly head-high jug to a scary top-out.

39. The Squatter V3 ★★
Find this short, blunt arête behind the corner left of Unobvious. From the loaf hold at chest height, hug and slap your way to better holds in the vegetated seam.

40. French Press V7 ★
Start standing next to the dark, crumbly rock and jump to the diagonal sloping pod above. Top out straight up using a small nipple hold. Grade unconfirmed.
Variation (V5): Start grabbing the pod from the adjacent rock.

41. Lowe Rider V1
Climb the wide crack from a sitdown start in the small alcove, finishing on top of the detached flake.

42. Joel's Slab V3 ★
Climb the right side of the tall slab on the west face of the Lowe Rider boulder.

43. Pod Racer V1 ★
Start matched in the pod above the small boulder and traverse left to follow decent holds up the arête.
Variation (V0): Start standing at the arête and climb the finish of Pod Racer.

44. Tentacles V0 ★
Layback up the short flake to a jug and the strange fin feature above – but don't pull it off!

45. Bangladore Torpedo V6
On the left end of the face, find two right-facing sidepulls at waist height. Pull on with a crap low foot and stab up through crimps to finish slightly left. Formerly quite difficult, this climb was unfortunately chipped down to some idiot wanker's level sometime in 2013-14…

46. Lead Pants V3 ★★
Start sitting on the left corner of the small prow with a left-hand sloper and a poor right undercling. Move to the good sloper rail and finish straight up, or for an extra grade and unimaginable personal satisfaction, continue right on crimps to a more powerful finish.

47. Raging Cow V1
Climb the wideish crack on the right end of the short over-hang from a sitdown start. Truly terrible.

48. Sitting Bull V3 ★★
Start sitting in the mini-roof with good holds in the crack. Move right to jugs on the low lip, then face forward and climb sloping sidepulls to a cruxy slap for the lip. Very nice.

49. Hormonal Monkey V9
Start sitting on the rock a few feet left of Sitting Bull with two pinches near the edge of the roof. Pull on and slap the juggy lip above. Might be the hardest problem in Washington.

50. Jack of Spades V6 ★
A few feet right of the prominent Royal Flush crack, climb the undercut corner from a low right-hand crimp and the lowest sloper on the lip. Stuff your foot in the crack, slap your left hand to the pinch, and climb up and right on crimps to finish.

51. Royal Flush V2 ★★★
The famous roof crack. Start in the deepest part of the cave and climb the nearly-horizontal fist crack to finish up the slab above. Not your typical tick-marked gymbo crimpfest, and a huge sandbag for those of us who get confused when the back of our hands touch the rock… "It's so good that even French climbers have been known to look at it."

52. Full House V10 ★★★
Start as for Royal Flush and climb into Jack of Spades. Very spanny and very powerful. F.A. Ryan Paulsness.

53. Sleeve Ace V3 ★★★
From the lowest jug in the overhang left of Royal Flush, climb over the bulge on flat holds until you can get a foot up and rock over to a mellow top-out. Use that power!

54. The Witch's Titty V9 ★★
Climb the faint dihedral on the back (south) side of the Footless Traverse boulder using a small "nipple" hold.

55. Project
Climb the face left of The Witch's Titty.

56. Balance Slap V4 ★★
Climb the slabby face left of the stump to, well, a balancey slap for the top. Starting off of the stump and using the arête makes the climbing easier, but the landing sketchier.

57. Unknown V0 ★
On the furthest left end of the Footless Traverse boulder, layback the large-fists crack from a crouch start.

58. Total Domination V8 ★
Start with your feet on the good ledge, your left hand in the crack, and a tiny crimp for your right hand. Dyno straight up to two sloping horns on the lip. Powerful.

59. Dark Days V2
Starting from an incut crack jug behind the tree, traverse left along the sloping shelf to finish up the wide crack on the left end of the boulder.

60. The Backscratcher V6 ★
Start as for Dark Days but climb straight up from the incut jug to an edge just behind the tree, then lunge for the lip and top out. A fall will generally lead to a painful raspberry from the tree behind you…

61. Raging Bull V7 ★★
Start sitting under the low bulge with an angular left crimp and a sloping right-hand sidepull. Squeeze and heel hook to two good slopers on the lip, finishing up and slightly right with an easy mantle onto the shelf.

Cortney Cusack on the *Footless Traverse* (V5).

🔲 62. **Immortal Techniques a.k.a. Immoral Techniques V10** ★★

Start sitting in the deepest part of the cave with a comfortable incut right-hand sidepull. Climb intricate steep moves into the top-out of Raging Bull. F.A. Cole Allen.

🔲 63. **Projects**

Starting as for Immortal Techniques and climbing into *Big Booty Bitch Slap*, and vice versa, are both projects, a.k.a. *the "36 Chambers Project."*

🔲 64. **Big Booty Bitch Slap a.k.a. Heaviness of the Load V10** ★★

Start in the rightmost part of the roof, matched on a wide low sidepull/undercling with the bulge in your face. Kick your right foot on and slap around the corner to the crack, finishing left around the corner on the ramp.

Variation (V10): For full value, top out as for Shadowboxing.

🔲 65. **The Footless Traverse V5** ★★★

Start in the middle of the tall face with jugs on the right end of the obvious flake. Traverse left in the crack to the loaf hold at the edge of the steep roof, finishing up and left on the ramp with a casual drop-off. Can be topped out.

🔲 66. **Shadowboxing V6** ★★★

Climb straight up from sloping crack holds on the right side of the campus section of The Footless Traverse. Gain a good undercling on the bottom of a vague bulge, then move left and top out straight up the shallow left-facing corner. Quite possibly the best problem on the boulder.

Variation (V7): Take the undercling with your left hand, then stay just right of the bulge, eventually topping out as above.

🔲 67. **Lion of Judah V9** ★★★

Start six feet right of the Footless Traverse with a high double-crimp. Cross to a sloper, make a big move out right to a better sloper, then continue straight up to a high top-out. Impressive and oft-overlooked.

Variation (V7?): Climb the first few moves of the Footless Traverse, then traverse right into Lion of Judah.

SWEETWATER

There is one more climb at Swiftwater which is not indicated on the map. Park to the south of the southernmost parking area, at the far end of the paved pullout some 6.7 miles from Icicle Junction. Walk to the water's edge, then head west. Sweetwater is on the first overhanging boulder you come to.

🔲 68. **Sweetwater V2** ★

Traverse right to left along the lip/arête on the boulder's river side. Fun and funky.

Max Hasson demonstrates his crane technique on *Shadowboxing* (V6).

WE HAVE A LOT OF FUN TOGETHER, GOING OUT BOULDERING AND MONKEYING AROUND, AND WE ALWAYS HAVE... AND THAT'S THE IMPORTANT THING, YOU KNOW? IT DOESN'T MATTER HOW GOOD A CLIMBER IS, IF YOU CAN'T GO OUT AND HAVE FUN WITH HIM CLIMBING THEN IT'S NOT REALLY THAT MUCH USE, IS IT?

- Jerry Moffatt, The Real Thing

SOUTH

THE MARLEY BOULDER

The Marley Boulder is a lonely giant, isolated on the far side of the Wenatchee River past the remainder of the Tumwater's bouldering. A slightly different type of rock than the granite found in the steeper part of the canyon, the Marley Boulder has several highball lines, but it's not clear whether they've been done: history is lacking, and at time of writing it is unknown whether there are any established climbs on the boulder.

The Marley Boulder is the obvious brownish cube across the river from Route 2, roughly 0.8 equidistant from Swiftwater and the bridge that marks the western end of the Tumwater Canyon. Access the Marley Boulder by turning left (south) onto Hatchery Creek Road just west of the Tumwater bridge and across from the entrance to Tumwater Campground. Park roughly 0.5 miles up the road, just after passing a grouping of forest service buildings on the left, and follow a faint climber's trail downhill and downstream. Good luck!

AREA

THE EARTH DOES NOT WITHHOLD, IT IS GENEROUS ENOUGH,

THE TRUTHS OF THE EARTH CONTINUALLY WAIT, THEY ARE NOT SO CONCEAL'D EITHER,

THEY ARE CALM, SUBTLE, UNTRANSMISSIBLE BY PRINT,

THEY ARE IMBUED THROUGH ALL THINGS CONVEYING THEMSELVES WILLINGLY,

CONVEYING A SENTIMENT AND INVITATION, I UTTER AND UTTER,

I SPEAK NOT, YET IF YOU HEAR ME NOT OF WHAT AVAIL AM I TO YOU?

TO BEAR, TO BETTER, LACKING THESE OF WHAT AVAIL AM I?

-Walt Whitman, from *A Song of the Rolling Earth*

KYLE O'MEARA

December 1, 2009. High: 41 degrees. Mostly sunny, wind SW at 10 MPH.

I couldn't believe my eyes as I scoped the forecast for the day. I raced out the door and headed for the most beautiful place in the world! I thought about what I wanted to climb on that day throughout the two hour drive. The list of my projects flashed through my mind over and over again… Simply thinking about the movement, the holds, and the appeal of each problem made my fingertips sweat and my heart skip a beat.

Leavenworth means more to me as a climber than anywhere else in the world. These canyons taught me about patience, perseverance, the power of the psyche, the art of exploration, and the role creativity plays in the process of development. These canyons taught me how to be a climber and revealed to me the reasons why I love climbing so much. Beauty like this can only be found in a magical place. The canyon walls transform as the seasons shift. Every so often, the space between your body, your mind, and the environment all mesh together to form a perfect moment where you feel so connected to the rock and to the place where you're climbing that you become a part of it. Those are the moments I'm constantly searching for.

I was part of the Icicle canyon that perfect December day. Each boulder I attempted was a project of some significance to me. Every hold I grabbed felt like perfection, and the texture of each individual crystal under my fingertips was like a dream come true. I ticked one, then another, then another! My 'hot streak' had to come to an end… or did it? I set up shop under my most coveted boulder toward the end of the day, feeling slightly reluctant to try it all alone with just the pads I had with me. Days like this don't come along often enough, and I knew the season would come to a close later that week, so I gave it a go. I stuck the committing final move to the lip long enough to swing out, but as I swung back in my hand was ejected from the hold and I slammed onto my back at the base of the boulder… I had missed the pads in my calculated landing zone and I fought to take a breath as I pawed my way out of the hole I was in. After a moment, I was breathing normally again and realized I had somehow avoided serious injury. I huddled into my down jacket, sat there in front of the boulder, took a deep breath, and drifted away into my surroundings. The sound of the bubbling river calmed my shaky hands and a gentle breeze swept through and chilled me to the core. I enjoyed the silence that consumed me. The message was clear… this was a perfect moment in time. I shed my jacket and pulled my shoes back on. When I left the ground, my mind went blank… breathe… move… look… breathe… move… done. It was the perfect way to end the best day I had ever experienced in Leavenworth. I hadn't seen another soul all day. It felt as if each boulder I climbed on was enjoying the solitude as well and welcomed the energy and excitement I brought to share with it.

I have a deep love for this place, from the rock quality, to the setting, to the endless list of memories, and the moments I have shared with great friends in this arena… Leavenworth bouldering is the best!

Unnamed, oil pastel. Drew Schick (2014).

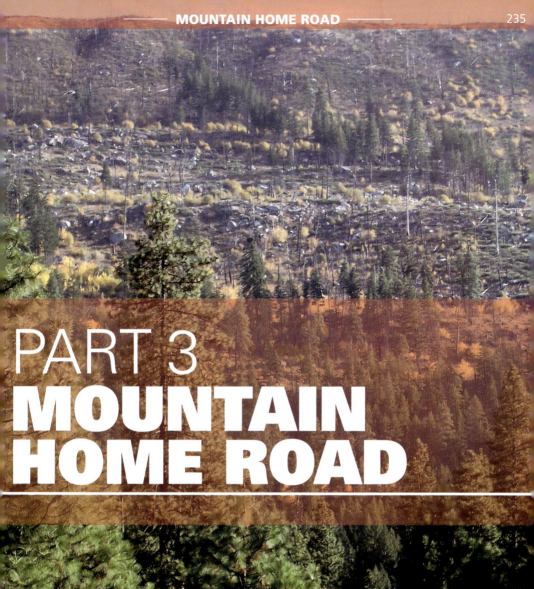

PART 3
MOUNTAIN HOME ROAD

MOUNTAIN HOME ROAD

Perched high on the hillside of Boundary Butte at the southern mouth of Icicle Canyon, the boulders of Mountain Home Road are Leavenworth's Druid Stones: a dense collection of quality stone set aside from the rest, the satellite area that is almost more enjoyable than the main thoroughfare. The white, compact granite and flat, grassy landings at Mountain Home are a pleasant addition to Leavenworth's wide array of rock types and landscapes. And unlike the Druid Stones, one is able to drive to the top of the steep hillside and actually walk down to go climbing. The setting at Mountain Home is comparable to Gold Bar's Clearcut area, both victims of the wide-scale logging operations which bring the northwest boulderer such mixed blessings. A wide variety of climbs can be found in the main Mountain Home areas of The Star Wars Boulder, The Pasture, and The South Seas, with something to satisfy everyone. There are also a number of newly-developed areas along the road like Geronimo, The Premonition, and Full Time Night Woman that offer a few difficult testpieces and are well worth their minimal approaches.

The open hillside of Mountain Home Road typically receives all-day sun and makes for a great evening spot. Mountain Home would also offer prime winter conditions for the gung-ho climber willing to snowshoe or ski up the unplowed road, but few boulderers feel the need to make the slog. During the rest of the year, the approach is mellow and the scenery fantastic. As at most Leavenworth areas, keep an eye out for rattlesnakes on warm summer days. Please help to keep this wonderful spot litter-free and access-friendly by picking up after yourself, sticking to trails, not drag-racing up the road, and refraining from camping here, as tempting as it may be. While the hilltop vista of Mountain Home may seem like the middle of nowhere, it gets many more visitors than one may think, including patrols by the Chelan County Sheriff, and local residents have voiced very legitimate concerns about the traffic, vegetation damage, and fire risk associated with camping in this fragile environment. Savor the view all day, but when it's time to start a campfire and settle in for the evening, drive down the hill and turn left onto East Leavenworth Road to zip up Icicle Canyon.

Getting to the Mountain Home Road bouldering spots is easy. All of the bouldering is accessed along the side of the road, which departs left off of East Leavenworth Road less than 0.1 miles from Highway 2, near the Safeway on the east side of town. The main Mountain Home Road areas are accessed from the small right-hand pullout 4.3 miles up the road, in the clearcut and across from a large white slab. See individual area sections for directions to the other areas.

MOUNTAIN HOME ROAD MILEAGE TABLE

MOUNTAIN HOME RD.	Mileage from E. Leavenworth Rd.	Mileage from Previous Area
Butter Boulders	3.40	
Geronimo	3.60	0.20
The Premonition	3.90	0.30
Full Time Night Woman	4.00	0.10
Star Wars Boulder	4.30	0.30
The Pasture	4.30	
South Seas	4.30	

THE BUTTER BOULDERS

The Butter Boulders are a smallish cluster of blocs in the woods next to Mountain Home Road roughly a mile before the parking for the main area. This cluster is still in development, so I haven't provided a map or any specific beta; only two or three problems have been established at time of writing. Check it out when you feel like exploring a little bit!

Park for the Butter Boulders 3.4 miles up Mountain Home Road in the large pullout near the "End of County Road" sign. The Butter Boulders are nestled along either side of the small rise about 50 yards to the right of the road. Please be sure to park such that you leave room for others, as this pullout is popular with mountain bikers, hikers, and other user groups. Please also minimize your impact when exploring and developing problems in this relatively pristine "new" area.

AREA

GERONIMO

Geronimo is a stand-alone boulder along Mountain Home Road that was developed after the publication of *Central Washington Bouldering*. Stop here on your way up the main Mountain Home area to check out Johnny Goicoechea's obvious arête *Geronimo* (V8) – you can't beat the approach!

Geronimo is located 3.6 miles up Mountain Home Road, about 0.2 miles past the white sign reading "End of County Road" that marks the Butter Boulders, roughly 0.7 miles before the pullout for the main Mountain Home bouldering area. Geronimo is visible 20 yards right of the road. Please park well off the roadway to avoid creating conflict with the many other users of this road.

❐ 1. **Geronimo V8** ★★★
Start standing on the roadside arête with a high left-hand sidepull and a head-high right-hand crimp. Slap to the sloping rail above and them compress and power your way to the jug on the lip. Beautiful! F.A. Johnny Goicoechea.
Variation (V8): Geronimo can be started with your right hand on the low left foot at the two foot level.

❐ 2. **Splash V8** ★★
Start as for Geronimo, but after you gain the sloping rail move left, set your feet up, and make a huge move to the lip. Impressive and scary! F.A. Joel Campbell.

❐ 3. **Project**
The face to the right of Geronimo has some intriguing holds…

❐ 4. **Project**
There may be a line up the tall, low-angle face right of the tree around the back of Geromino.

❐ 5. **Unknown V0** ★
The back side of the Geronimo boulder (facing south) has a nice but dirty climb that is also the boulder's downclimb. Climbing into the arête to the left makes for a fun V0.

❐ 6. **Shapeshifter V6** ★★
This climb is located on the wide, slabby boulder roughly 50 yards west of Gernonimo. Climb the center of the face from a prominent sloper… May need some cleaning.

AREA

Cortney Cusack sticks the crimpy first move of *Geronimo* (V8).

THE PREMONITION

Late in the summer of 2011, Leavenworth local Joe Treftz was driving up Mountain Home Road when a strange feeling swept over him. Pull over. Walk over the ridge. The result of Joe's compulsion is the Premonition Boulder, a lonely chunk of granite perched on the steep hillside below the road. The Premonition has a few quality problems on crisp salt-and-pepper granite, including the powerful and intimidating *Berserker* (V8), and stays shady in the summer months.

The Premonition is off of Mountain Home Road, 3.8 miles from East Leavenworth Road. Park in a faint pullout on the right just before the YARA boulder, a squat, white overhang above the road where the forest begins to open up. To find the Premonition Boulder, hike straight away from the road and follow the faint trail down the steep hill.

1. Yet Another Roadside Attraction V2 ★

Start with a head-high flat jug and squeeze and heel hook up the arête. A fun oddity.

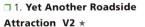

2. Kyle's Arete V8 ★
Start pinching the left arête of the steep face and climb to the lip. Top out via poor slopers as for Berserker. Grade unconfirmed.

3. Berserker V8 ★★★
Start on the sloping shelf in the center of the face and climb straight up using a high left-hand sloper and a sharp undercling crimp. Wide, powerful moves lead to a delicate, high top-out. F.A. Drew Schick.

4. The Premonition V4 ★★★
Start on the sloping shelf in the middle of the face as for Berserker, move right to sharp edges and an undercling flake, then top out to the right using the detached flake. Intricate.

5. The Omen V1
Layback and jam up the detached flake. Top out up and left.

6. Unkown V3
Climb up and left from crack holds in the small roof to a cramped top-out.

7. Project
Climb straight out the bulge on slopers.

8. Unkown V4
Climb edges up the right face. Grade unconfirmed.

AREA

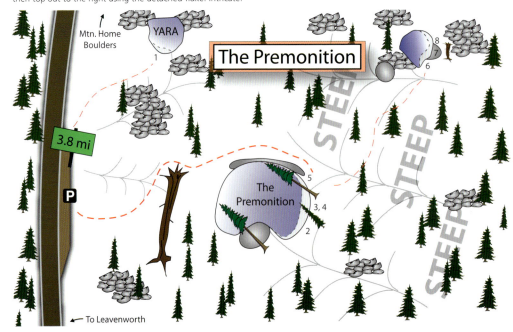

Joel Campbell eyes the tiny undercling on the second ascent of *Berserker* (V8).

FULL TIME NIGHT WOMAN

Full Time Night Woman is a solitary boulder in an open area shortly before the clearcut containing the main Mountain Home boulders. Park in a small pullout on the right 3.9 miles from East Leavenworth Road, roughly 0.1 miles past the squat white overhang of Yet Another Roadside Attraction (previous chapter). FTNW is on the downhill side of a large flat-topped boulder just downhill from the road. The pullout for FTNW is one pullout before the large pullout at the edge of the clearcut.

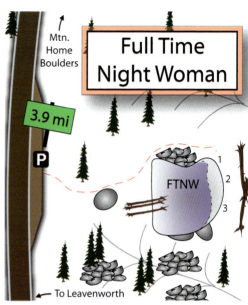

❐ 1. Jeremiah Johnson V4 ★

Climb the right arête of the steep face from a stand start with a flat left-hand edge and a right-hand flake crimp on the face. Grade unconfirmed.

❐ 2. Full Time Night Woman V9/10 ★★

Start in the center of the steep overhang with your left hand in the VCR slot and your right hand on a low sidepull crimp. Climb through an undercling to a big right-hand move to the "spike" jug, then punch up and right through jugs to top out. F.A. Johnny Goicoechea.

❐ 3. Project

Start on sloping shelf and climb to lip.

AREA

SCOTT MITCHELL

My wife Susan and I came to Leavenworth for the first time in June of 2004 for a week of bouldering. Six weeks later we arrived in a U-Haul filled with everything we owned, and we have been here ever since. We had spent the prior 9 years discovering and developing a multitude of granite eggs around the Tahoe region and wintering in the bouldering wonderland of Bishop. But as soon as we pulled into Leavenworth, we felt as if we'd stumbled across a forgotten gem. Beautiful, featured granite blocks in a pristine alpine setting, sitting on the edge of a quaint (albeit cheesy and somewhat obnoxious) little town. For the first few months, every trip out bouldering felt like we were "rediscovering" every boulder. No chalk… faint trails… no stumps at the base of problems. Those who had been there before had been careful to

hide their tracks and keep impact to a minimum. As little as 10 years ago, it was somewhat of a rarity to bump into another boulderer, even at Forestland, Mad Meadows, or Swiftwater.

Times have changed. Bouldering has continued to boom in popularity, and Leavenworth is now officially "on the map." One thing that hasn't changed, though, is the beauty of movement found on these incredible chunks of granite, and the massive potential for discovery. I can't help but feel that Leavenworth is on the cusp of its Golden Age – when boulderers are beginning to venture away from the roadside areas and unlock the secret stashes awaiting in the hills. I encourage you to get off the beaten track and go explore; become part of the unfolding story of Leavenworth's bouldering. Be safe, try hard, and be aware of your impact on the area. See ya out there!

THE PARKING BOULDERS

There are a few fun problems in the vicinity of the parking for the trail to the main Mountain Home Road bouldering area. While these boulders are not a destination in their own right, the easier climbs make for a nice pre-warm-up, and Ryan Paulsness' *Tron* (V6) and Drew Schick's *Brown Eye* (V10) are worthy testpieces that deserve more attention than they get.

The parking area for the main Mountain Home Road area is 4.3 miles up Mountain Home Road from East Leavenworth Road, 0.3 miles into the large clearing. Park on the right next to a head-high, slabby boulder, directly downhill from the large white Tron boulder roughly 50 yards above the road. Tron is at the top of a short, steep trail directly across from the parking, while the remainder of the Parking Boulders are scattered along the beginning of the trail to the Star Wars Boulder.

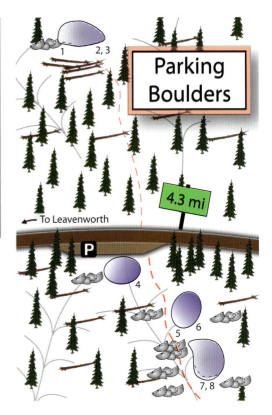

□ 1. Tron V6 ★★
Climb the short face on the left side of the large, low-angle boulder from incuts in the seam by the low adjacent boulder. Climb straight up the grainy face to the sloping rail, then top out straight up the slabby arête.

□ 2. Unknown V0 ★
Climb the right arête, cruising by the circular xenolith as you go. The current car-to-car slickfoot record for this one is under three minutes… how fast can you do it?

□ 3. #honnolding V0 ★
Start as above, but traverse left along the bottom of the slab and top out as for Tron. Scary!

□ 4. Unknown V0 ★
Climb the slabby arête around the back of the boulder next to the parking area.

□ 5. Project
Climb the blunt white arête next to the trail. Harder than it looks…

□ 6. Unknown V0 ★
Climb the slab on the downhill side of this flat-topped boulder.

□ 7. Brown Eye V10 ★★
This problem climbs the steepest part of the overhang on the downhill side of the next block down from the flat-topped boulder. Start on the sloper under the roof, move up and left to sharp crimps, then climb straight out the bulge over the adjacent boulder. Unrepeated at time of writing. F.A. Drew Schick.

□ 8. Unknown V5 ★
Start as for Brown Eye but move right to edges in the seam and top out up and right. Grade unconfirmed.

AREA

TRON

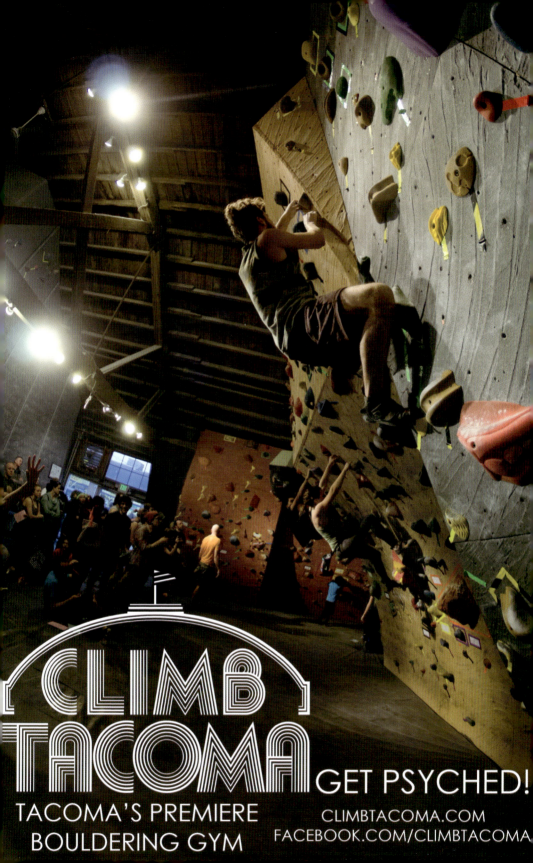

CLIMB TACOMA

GET PSYCHED!

TACOMA'S PREMIERE
BOULDERING GYM

CLIMBTACOMA.COM
FACEBOOK.COM/CLIMBTACOMA

THE STAR WARS BOULDER

The Star Wars Boulder is Mountain Home's premier block, home to some of Leavenworth's most striking problems. Discovered by Jeff Hashimoto and Damian Potts in the summer of 1999, the Star Wars has a grittier stone than other Mountain Home areas, often providing a week's worth of skin removal in just a few hours. The side-by-side classics *Yoda* (V9) and *Obi-Wan* (V9) are both uber-proud ticks, while the beautiful traverse of *Darth Maul* (V4) is a worthy testpiece in its own right. Along with the rest of the Mountain Home Road bouldering, the Star Wars boulder bakes in the sun during the better part of summer days. In winter, the road is not plowed; for the best sending temps try hitting the Star Wars on a cool spring or fall evening.

The parking for the Star Wars boulder is 4.3 miles up Mountain Home Road from East Leavenworth Road, 0.3 miles into the large clearing. Park on the right next to a head-high, slabby boulder, directly downhill from a large white Tron boulder roughly 50 yards above the road. Follow the well-worn trail downhill from the west side of the pullout for about three minutes, then head straight left for three more minutes to the obvious downhill-facing overhang. The Pasture and South Seas areas are another 5-7 minutes further downhill.

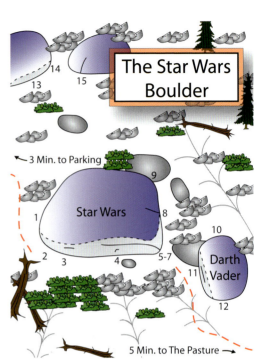

The Star Wars Boulder

← 3 Min. to Parking

Star Wars

Darth Vader

5 Min. to The Pasture →

❑ 1. Padmi Trainer V1 ★
Climb the left side of the first face reached on the approach. A nice but oft-overlooked option for warming up here.
Variation (V3): Start from crimps in the middle of the face, move right to a small crimp/pinch, and finish up and right.

❑ 2. Han Solo V3
On the left end of the overhang, jump start to opposing slopers on the lip of the bulge. Smear your feet high and pop to the lip.

❑ 3. Yoda V9 ★★
Start on the chest-high rounded crimp on the left side of the overhang. Pull on and dyno to the sharp, incut pocket on the lip, finishing up and right with friendlier holds. The force *must* be strong in you for this one.
Variation (V9): Finish up and left.

❑ 4. Obi-Wan V9 ★★★
Start sitting on a small boulder with a flat, angular crimp in the steepest part of the overhang. Slap up and right to a crapola sloper, then follow the seam left to the Darth Maul dyno and a tricky mantle. One of the few V9s that can truly be called a sandbag. F.A. Johnny Goicoechea.

❑ 5. Darth Maul V4 ★★★
Starting from a low jug on the right corner of the overhang, follow the obvious seam up and left 'till the crimps run out. Make a committing lunge for the lip and hold it together for the cruxy mantle. Classic!

AREA

"THERE IS NO TRY, ONLY DO."

- Yoda

❑ 6. Nice Men V2 ★
Start sitting on the arête as for Darth Maul, climbing straight up on jugs to a more delicate finish.

❑ 7. Emperor's Lightning V7 ★★
Start on the jug as for Darth Maul and Nice Men, but climb up and right through the lightning bolt seam to the lip and crack. Finish straight up with the left-facing flake on the lip. Any resemblance to the deep-south classic Skywalker is purely coincidental... F.A. Jeff Hashimoto.
Variation (V7): Do the first two moves of Emperor's Lightening, then finish straight up the shallow dihedral.

❑ 8. Wookie Crack V1
Climb the grainy hand crack on the right side of the face. The holds are good but the landing gets a bit hairier as you go.
Variation (V4): Start as for Wookie Crack but climb straight up.

❑ 9. Rich's Non-Star-Wars-Named Climb V3
On the uphill corner of the boulder, squeeze up the really low bulge on slopers. If you get tired, just sit down.

Kelly Sheridan tops out *Yoda* (V9).
[PHOTO] Cortney Cusack

Isaac Howard climbing a variation to *Wookie Crack* (V1).

10. Castle Run (In 12 Parsecs) V0
This somewhat cramped problem climbs the uphill side of the Darth Vader boulder. Start low in the small corner, avoiding the dab on your short journey to the summit.

11. Darth Vader V9 ★★★
Climb the overhanging face of the boulder adjacent to the Star Wars boulder from poor chest-high underclings in the seam. Slap to the sloping lip, throw a high foot to match, and grovel over using odd sideways compression and poor slopers. Very good. F.A. Joel Campbell.

12. Moon of Endor V2 ★
On the downhill side of the Darth Vader boulder, climb the left-leaning ramp from high crimps in the seam. Finish up and left.

13. Shapeshifter V7 ★
This boulder is roughly 30 yards uphill from the Star Wars boulder. Start on a high sloper in the middle of the tall, slabby face and mantle onto slopers to top out. Quite good, and not as easy as it looks.

14. Turdburgler V6 ★
Start in a cool dish-pocket on the right side of the boulder, then punch up the arête on sloping crimps. Not as easy as it looks…

15. Jabba the Slab V0 ★
Follow the seam up the center of the clean slab roughly 20 yards above the Star Wars boulder.

THE PASTURE

Along with the adjacent South Seas, The Pasture area at Mountain Home Road boasts some of the best rock quality in Leavenworth. Developed along with the Star Wars Boulder during the summer of 1999, these boulders scattered along the side of Boundary Butte appear to be glacially deposited chunks of granite from higher in the Alpine Lakes region. The stone is compact, well-textured 'salt and pepper' granite, and the lines are typically proud and independent. The clean arête of *The Barn Door* (V3) and the sandbagger's bulge on *Fairly Desperate* (V4) are not to be missed, nor is the striking classic *Cattleguard Arête* (V8). The open setting of the Pasture can be quite warm in the summer, but makes for a great evening spot even after hot sunny days.

The Pasture is located roughly five minutes downhill from the Star Wars boulder, just under ten minutes from Mountain Home Road. From the Star Wars, follow the trail downhill, then directly left, traversing roughly 150 yards along flat ground before eventually dropping through a small grove of trees to the obvious cluster of large boulders.

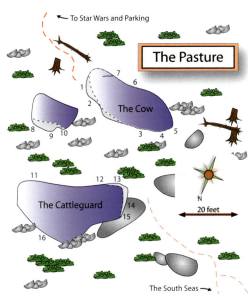

The Pasture

← To Star Wars and Parking

The Cow

The Cattleguard

The South Seas →

N
20 feet

⌐ 1. Feche la Vache V3 ★
Start sitting on the trailside corner of the Cow with a hidden undercling jug. Haul your butt off the ground and make a couple strenuous moves to finish on the right side of the arête. Cooler than it looks.

⌐ 2. Cattle Terrace V1 ★
Hop, skip, or jump to the good rounded ledge at the eight foot level, trusting slippery footholds as you finish up and left.

⌐ 3. Goodnight Moon V7 ★★
The tall downhill face of the Cow. Make a giant leap to the decent handhold in the center of the face, then finish up and right via some tricky crimpers. Height dependent. F.A. Joel Campbell.

⌐ 4. BSE V3 ★★
Climb the tall arête on the right side of the face, eventually moving slightly left into the finish of Goodnight Moon. Great fun.

⌐ 5. Hoofin' It V0 ★
Climb the tallish slabby face just right of BSE on nice edges. Definitely not a lowball; makes a rewarding beginner climb.

⌐ 6. Slab Cow V1
Climb the one-move slab on the uphill side of the Cow boulder. Subtract style points if you skip the tiny edges and just hop to the lip…

CATTLEGAURD

⌐ 7. Cud Crack V2
Start with a small incut crimp in the off-vertical seam. Awkwardly work your feet up and onto the slab, then bust to the lip. More engaging than it looks.

⌐ 8. Cow Pattie V3
Climb the bulge on the left arête of the short, steep overhang. WARNING: At time of writing, the giant block that comprises most of this climb appears to be loose. Climb at your own risk!!!

⌐ 9. Slaughterhouse V5 ★
Start sitting on the right side of the small bulge with an undercling flake. Climb up and left just under the lip of the boulder, finishing with a tough mantle on the left side of the bulge.

⌐ 10. Fairly Desperate V4 ★
Start sitting as for Slaughtehouse but climb straight up the dihedral on confusing features. A little harder than it looks, to say the least.

⌐ 11. Andy's Arête V4 ★★
Traverse up and left along the obvious lip of the Cattleguard boulder. Use delicate footwork to reach a decent hold a few feet short of the apex of the arête.
Variation (V4): If the start didn't tire you out, following the lip all the way to the top adds a grade and a bit of adventure.

12. Cattleguard Dyno V9 ★★
This tough dynamic problem starts five feet right of the blunt Cattleguard Arête. Grab a tiny lefthand sidepull and even smaller righthand edge, paste your feet on, and huck to the flat crimp three feet below the top. Not very finger-friendly!

13. The Cattleguard Arête V8 ★★★
The area classic. Start hugging the blunt arête with your right hand on a small chest-high sidepull and your left on a high triangular pinch. Reach high for the sloping crimp, match, and campus up to better holds to finish. You may need a couple of pads to reach the left-hand start hold… Fantastic!

14. Cow Jumped Over The Moon V1
Starting from the flat rock, hop to the juggy lip and press out the mantle. Why not?

15. The Barn Door V3 ★★
Start sitting on the left end of the small overhung corner. Fight the swing as you follow clean slopers up the striking lip to mantle on the flat ledge.

16. Air Is Air V0 ★★
Several variations climb the wide low-angle slab on the back of the Cattleguard, all of which are fantastic warm-ups.

Jessica Campbell climbs the *Cattleguard Arête* (V8)

THE SOUTH SEAS

This is it folks – the end of the line. Scattered downhill from the Pasture area, The South Seas is Mountain Home Road's most remote bouldering spot, possessing something of an otherworldly feel under the right conditions. The stone is immaculate and the view breathtaking, with climbing to match. The South Seas has a great circuit of easy to moderate climbs, as well as a few testpieces like *Palm Down* (V7) and *The Ground Below* (V10). Most people will be content to warm up and check out the quality intermediates like *Tall People Suck* (V4), *Double Vision* (V4), and the host of moderates on the Dandelion Foot boulder. Along with the rest of the Mountain Home bouldering, the South Seas gets plenty of sun, making for great evening sessions in the slow-dying light.

The South Seas area is a nebulous group of boulders down-hill and east of the Pasture. To find Tall People Suck and Palm Down, head straight downhill from the Cattleguard boulder to the obvious round boulders. To reach the Vision boulder and the most concentrated South Seas area, head downhill from the Cattleguard for a few yards, then fol-low the faint trail to the left through some dense bushes, reaching the Vision boulder in about two minutes. Skirt the downhill side of the cluster to reach the Ship, the South Seas Arête, and Punk Ass Kid.

❐ 1. Tall People Suck V4 ★★

Climb the blank face from a high start on a left-hand sidepull and unique right-hand pinch, heading left at the lip to top out. It's as height-dependent as the name would suggest. **Variation (V7):** Start down and left of the stand start with a tiny right-hand gaston and a small left-hand undercling on the bottom of the check-mark-shaped flake. Climb into Tall People Suck and top out.

❐ 2. Piano Trainer V2 ★

Mantle onto the low arête from a stand start with a small incut. Finish up the slab. Harder than it looks!

❐ 3. Polish Bob's Slab V0 ★

Climb the scooped slab on the uphill side of the boulder. Many eliminates (reportedly up to V14) can be done to increase the challenge…

❐ 4. Palm Down V7 ★★

Climb the steep, undercut slab from a stand start in the middle of the face. Palm down, press up, and work your feet onto the face. Bizarre. The original method, which begins on two palm smears on the left side of the face and uses the *left* arête, is several grades more difficult. F.A. Joel Campbell.

❐ 5. Probletunity V2

Climb the nice clean slab near the right arête over a some-what intimidating landing.

❐ 6. Dandelion Foot V4 ★★

Climb the left arête from a stand start splayed between a good hold on the right face and an incut crimp on the left face. Slap to a good edge and top out to the right with your feet in the notch.

❐ 7. Unknown V4 ★

Start in the notch and climb up and left to top out as for *Dandelion Foot*.

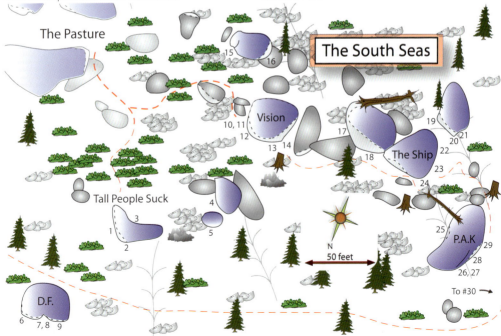

Adam Healey graniteering on *Tall People Suck* (**V4**).

❐ 8. **Unknown V6** ★★
Start in the notch and climb up and right on poor slopers.

❐ 9. **Unknown V4**
Jump start to the lip right of the notch and mantle straight over.

❐ 10. **Blurred Vision V4**
Start on a flat sloping ledge below the smallish dihedral and climb left along the low seam to finish up the arête.

❐ 11. **Neanderthal V1**
Climb the short, wide crack from the low, flat hold of *Blurred Vision*.

❐ 12. **Television V4**
Start on the corner just right of Blurred Vision with a low kneebar. Climb the arête.

❐ 13. **The Vision V2** ★
Mantle the low shelf on the downhill side of the boulder and reach high for the jug. This one is quite perplexing at first, but can be climbed in sneakers once you figure out the body position. Good fun.

❐ 14. **Double Vision V4** ★★
Start sitting matched on a low jug on the left side of the corridor. Climb up and left on tough crimps to top out straight up the blunt corner. Not the tallest climb around, but pretty darn good.

Drew Schick surfs across the fresh granite of *Punk Ass Kid* (V6)

15. Pair of Deuces V1
A few yards uphill from the Vision boulder, climb the wide crack from a sit-start. Swiftwater is definitely winning this crack climb poker game!

16. Full Metal Hairbrush V3 ★
Start crouched on the flat rock, hugging the low double arêtes. Climbing a few burly moves up the corner to top out slightly right.
Variation (V4): "*Full Metal Toothbrush*" Start matched on a crumbling crimp on the left face and climb rightwards to finish up the arête.

17. Abandon Ship (Project)
Climb the powerful moves on sloping edges up the overhanging face. The face moves are hard; the mantle harder. V14?

18. The Ground Below V9 ★★
Start matched on a high right-facing sidepull. Pull on and paste your right foot on a high flake under the roof, then make a huge move to the lip. Mantle straight over. Hard! F.A. Johnny Goicoechea.

19. Walk The Plank V2
Climb the short uphill arête from a stand start. Mind the tree, fear the talus.

20. South Seas Arête V0+ ★★★
Climb the tall downhill arête with big holds on beautiful stone. Classic.

21. Long John Silver V1 ★
Climb the face and arête just around the downhill corner of *South Seas Arête*.

22. Shiver Me Timbers V1 ★★
On the right side of the big slab, make a tricky mantle on small edges, finishing up the daunting face above. "…but it's a *real* 5.7 slab."

23. Ship of Fools V2 ★★
Start under the bulge in the middle of the face, slap up, and mantle, finishing as for Shiver Me Timbers.

24. Jolly Roger V2 ★★
Climb the left arête of the tall, clean slab to a long move for a crimp. Shuffle up and right on the big ledge to finish.

25. Shoeless Joe V0 ★
Great fun. Just downhill from The Ship, mantle the flat ledge on the uphill side of the big lumpy boulder, traversing left on the lip to finish. For full value, this one ought to be climbed in sneakers. "The first ascent was done in Airwalks, in the rain…"

26. Punk Ass Kid V6 ★★
Traverse right along the obvious seam from chest-high crimps near the left end. At the big sloping dish, mantle and shuffle right along the dirty shelf to top out. Pretty line.

27. Punk Ass Dyno project
Start as for Punk Ass Kid, but dyno up and right to the lip.

28. Thumper V3 ★★
Hop to the dish in the center of the face, mantle, and finish with the heady foot traverse of *Punk Ass Kid*.

29. The Desert of the Real V4 ★
Jump to a flat scoop on the right side of the tall slab. Top out on flat edges. This problem was listed as a project in *Central Washington Bouldering*, and doesn't see much traffic.

30. Unknown V0
This problem is located roughly 25 yards downhill and west of Punk Ass Kid. Climb the north-facing white arête, topping out with good feet on the left side of the boulder.

That rock we were camped against was a marvel. It was thirty feet high and thirty feet at base, a perfect square almost, and twisted trees arched over it and peeked down on us. From the base it went outward, forming a concave, so if rain came we'd be partially covered. "How did this immense sonumbitch ever get here?"

"It probably was left here by the retreating glacier. See over there that field of snow?"

"Yeah."

"That's the glacier what's left of it. Either that or this rock tumbled here from inconceivable prehistoric mountains we can't understand, or maybe it just landed here when the friggin mountain range itself burst out of the ground in the Jurassic upheaval. Ray when you're up here you're not sittin in a Berkeley tea room. This is the beginning and the end of the world right here. Look at all those patient Buddhas lookin at us sayin nothing."

"And you come out here by yourself…"

"For weeks on end, just like John Muir, climb around all by myself following quartzite veins or making posies of flowers for my camp, or just walking around naked singing, and cook my supper and laugh."

- Jack Kerouac, Dharma Bums

Adam Healey sticks the lip on *The Ground Below* (V9)

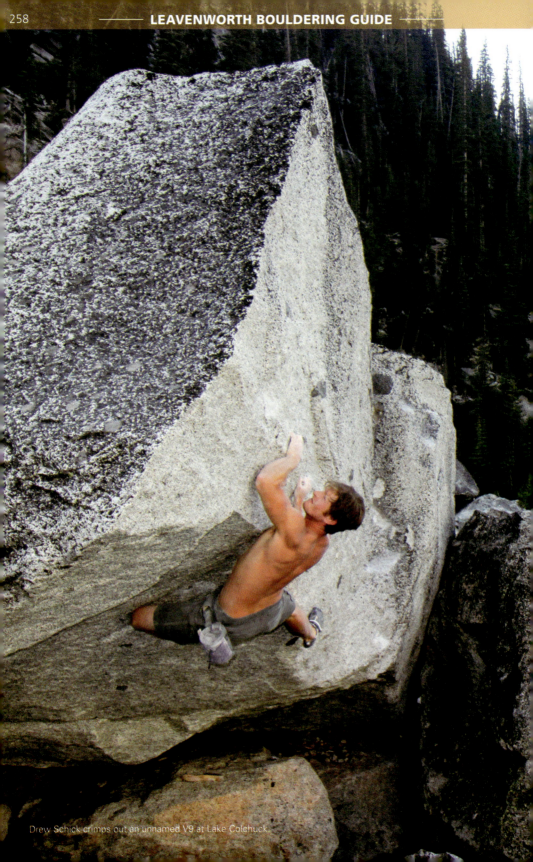

Drew Schick crimps out an unnamed V9 at Lake Colchuck.

PART 4
OTHER AREAS

OTHER AREAS

Though there are more problems in Leavenworth – between those established and those still waiting to be found – than most people could climb in a decade, the Central Washington region is home to a wide array of other areas that offer a variety of stone, movement, and settings (check out John Stordahl's eloquent description of the processes behind this diversity in the Geology section). Alpine and semi-alpine areas offer respite from the summer heat, while a handful of lower-lying areas offer a winter climbing fix when Leavenworth's nuggets are covered under a blanket of snow. Sometimes it's also just nice to get off the beaten path and have an adventure…

This section is not intended to be comprehensive, and the beta it provides is by no means a 'guide' to any of these outlying areas, but I've provided basic directions that should at least enable you to find some climbing. For more detailed directions, try asking around, looking on www.mountainproject.com, posting on one of the many social media groups that have propagated in the last several years (on Facebook, try "Washington Climbers Coalition," "Cascade Corridor Climbers," "Expouldering," or "Seattle Smack Down"), or shooting me an email (leavenworthbouldering@gmail.com). One final note: At the risk of nagging, and while it's always important to minimize your impact when visiting a bouldering area, many of the areas in this section have been only very lightly touched by the presence of climbers, and it is absolutely critical that you take care to avoid trail proliferation and vegetation damage, pack out everything you bring in, and be aware of the impact your presence has on other user groups when visiting them. Hikers, hunters, birdwatchers, and many other impact-sensitive user groups are present and have significantly more powerful lobbies than climbers, and our ability to visit and climb in these areas will be greatly compromised if boulderers come to be seen as the "bad guys" by the majority of other users. Please do your part to keep these areas pristine and accessible for future generations of pad people.

LEAVENWORTH AREA

ALPINE LAKES

For many climbers and non-climbers alike, Leavenworth's Icicle Canyon is one thing: the gateway to the beautiful Alpine Lakes Wilderness. Comparable in feel to the granite wonderland of California's High Sierras, the Alpine Lakes are home to a mind-boggling amount of beautiful white granite. Though many of the higher lakes and peaks are best reserved for backpackers or ambitious trad climbers, several of the lower lakes are worth hauling a crash pad to. Nada Lake, Lake Colchuck, and to a smaller extent, Lake Stuart are all surrounded by virgin, pristine granite boulders within a few hours and several thousand vertical feet of your vehicle. But be warned, this is "off the beaten path" bouldering (though the hordes of backpackers sort of betray this description). You'll be doing plenty of hiking for your climbing, and it's definitely not the Happy Boulders; the features are sparse and the emphasis lies more on the scenery and remote atmosphere. This is true alpine bouldering – talus landings, great big boulders, and perfect stone are all the norm.

For Nada Lake, park at the Snow Lakes trailhead 4.1 miles from Icicle Junction, fill out a Forest Service day pass, and hike roughly six miles up many switchbacks and pleasant straightaways to the lake. For Lakes Colchuck and Stewart, turn left off of Icicle Road onto Eightmile Road, 8.3 miles from Icicle Junction, and follow it to the Colchuck/Stewart trailhead at the end. After filling out your day pass, hike roughly two miles to a trail junction. Lake Stewart lies several mellow miles ahead, while the trail to Lake Colchuck departs to the left, climbing several steep miles to the gorgeous blue waters. If you're especially hardy, the 20-ish mile trek from Lake Colchuck over Aasgard Pass, down through the Upper and Lower Enchantment Lakes, and past Snow Lakes and Nada Lake to the Snow Lakes trailhead makes for an epic but memorable (and long) day. Stop by the Forest Service ranger station in Leavenworth or search on the internet or in hiking guides for maps and more information – my favorite resource is Vickie and Ira Spring and Harvey Manning's classic 100 Hikes in Washington's Alpine Lakes Wilderness for its confusing choose-your-own-adventure style directions and refreshing 1970s-era environmental rants ("Something wicked this way comes. The machine. The wheel."). A $5 day pass or Northwest Forest Pass (currently $75 annually) are required to park at the Snow Lakes and Colchuck/Stewart Lake trailheads.

PESHASTIN PINNACLES

The Peshastin Pinnacles are a group of sandstone towers 10 minutes east of Leavenworth on Highway 2, site of the state's first bolted climb, as well as a plethora of scary sandbagged sandstone slabs. From the Safeway at the east end of Leavenworth, drive 8.3 miles east on Highway 2 and turn north onto Dryden Road, following signs for Peshastin Pinnacles State Park. According to Wenatchi legend, the spirit Coyote placed the pinnacles, which resemble the breached heads of salmon swimming upstream, in order to remind the tribe to have annual feasts of offering and ask the Salmon People to return each fall. The pinnacles are now within a 34-acre state park that is open from mid-March through October, from dawn to dusk. Though the pinnacles are probably best visited for daydreaming and wandering, there are a handful of fun boulder problems on Orchard Rock, the first formation encountered from the parking area.

CHUMSTICK SANDSTONE

There is ample evidence of sandstone in the Chumstick Valley, which heads north out of Leavenworth from Dan's Market, from the lumpy boulder on the left a minute out of town, to the "lost" Chumstick Snag, to the white stone scattered around the steep hillside separating the Chumstick Valley from Plain. "Water, water everywhere, nor any drop to drink…" The Chumstick stone that's been explored is highly sandy and no good for climbing, but rumors persist of a hidden sandstone band, described to Scott Mitchell by a hotshot fire fighter as several hundred yards wide, 20 feet tall, and 45 degrees overhanging, persist today. It has never been found. Does it exist? Will you be the one to rediscover it?

STEVENS PASS

SMITHBROOK

There are a couple of small clusters of boulders off of USFS Road 6700, which leaves the north side of Highway 2 4.0 miles east of the Stevens Pass summit and is signed as "Smithbrook" in both directions. Turn north off Highway 2, cross the bridge, and follow the narrow dirt road for 1.3 miles to the obvious cluster of boulders straddling both sides of the road. There are several problems on the roadside boulders to the left, and a brutally-hard unrepeated Johnny Goicoechea testpiece through the narrow corridor on the right that is spray-painted "B#3" (no joke – someone will have to redo the graffiti once it gets repeated!). At 1.4 miles, near a second, less promising cluster on the right, there is a small pull-in campsite on the left; a nice cluster can be found roughly 50 yards in the woods behind this campsite. There is also a decent-sized cluster of boulders roughly one mile up the Smithbrook Trail, which leaves the road 2.7 miles from Highway 2. NF-6700 continues around the back of Rock Mountain and follows the Rainy Creek drainage to the western end of Lake Wenatchee; I've heard secondhand rumors of a mega-bounty of boulders hidden somewhere in the hills above Rainy Creek, but like Captain Ingalls' gold, it has never been found…

SKYLINE RIDGE

The steep mountainside across from the Stevens Pass summit is Skyline Ridge, home to a large talus field housing much bouldering potential. The arduous hike is a bit of a deterrent, however, and the area has not seen regular visits. To reach Skyline Ridge, follow the Ramone Rock trail from the north side of the summit, criss-crossing the old service road to the picturesque Skyline Lake. From the lake, traverse westward and uphill on a faint trail to the obvious cluster of white granite boulders some 10 minutes from the lake. Though most problems at Skyline Ridge have neither names nor grades, the area's crown jewel is Johnny Goicoechea's No More Time (V10), the striking arête protruding from the cluster's apex that is visible from Highway 2. There are also a handful of problems in the gentle basin of bluish boulders 500 feet below the main area, but the boulders shrink as you get closer… Don't get suckered in by the direct approach visible from Highway 2 – I've hiked to these boulders from the Old Cascade Highway, and I won't ever make that mistake again!

MIDDLE EARTH

There is a small cluster of boulders on the south side of Highway 2, 3.0 miles west of Skykomish, that was developed in the early 2000s and has mostly mossed over by now. Park on the north side of Highway 2 roughly 100 yards east of Milepost 51 (25 yards east of a gated private drive) and walk roughly 200 yards east until a few lumpy, mossy blocks become visible in the woods on the south side of the road. Because the passing lane makes this a high-speed portion of Highway 2, please park well off the road, walk outside the guardrail, and take extreme care when crossing the highway. The area was termed "Middle Earth" because a) some people really geek out on J. R. R. Tolkien, and b) the boulders sit in a patch of forest sandwiched in the middle of two open, swampy areas; the area's biggest boulder, a large boxcar-sized block, is just barely visible from Highway 2 at the edge of the eastern swamp. Directions and a crude topo can be found on RCNW.net.

MORPHEUS

Morpheus is a recently-developed area off of Highway 2 a few miles west of the town of Skykomish that has blossomed into a popular and bountiful area. The rock is a finely-textured granite that is closer to Gold Bar than Leavenworth, but the rock quality is varied and there is a good diversity of problems and styles. Turn north off of Highway 2 at the turn for Money Creek Campground (roughly 100 yards west of the only tunnel on Highway 2), making a forced right-hand turn onto Miller River Road after less than a mile. Roughly 3.5 miles up Miller River Road, there is an old green gate on the right. Park in the pullout just before the gate and hike up the old road grade for roughly 5 minutes until a cluster of low boulders on the right signals that you are at the start of the first cluster, which straddles the trail. After five more minutes, the trail crosses an open slide area just above a fun, whitish boulder, and another cluster lurks on either side of the trail a few minutes after you re-enter the woods. Morpheus will be included in a forthcoming guidebook from prolific Seattle developer Pablo Zuleta, which is worth looking forward to in the coming years.

INDEX

Equal parts artsy, outdoorsy, and sketchy, the town of Index is best known for its world-class trad cragging and multipitch routes, and has become an extremely popular destination among intermediate to advanced trad climbers in the last decade. In response to the threat of renewed quarrying, the Lower Town Wall was purchased by the Washington Climbers Coalition in 2011 with funding donated by the climbing community in a generous display of solidarity. At time of writing, the WCC is in the process of transferring Index to the state for establishment as a state park under the condition that climbing will always be permitted. For the pebble-wrestlers, there is a small cluster of boulders below the Lower Town Wall, a few scattered blocks in the woods below the Private Idaho crags (the remainder likely chopped up and carted away in the town's quarrying heyday), and a small but mind-bogglingly good cluster of boulders on the bank of the Skykomish. To reach Index, turn north off Highway 2 onto Index-Galena Road, then turn left and cross the bridge into the town of Index after roughly a mile. For the Midnite/Zelda Boulders area, park in town, walk south to the railroad tracks, then hike along the tracks for a few minutes until an overgrown but well-worn trail departs the tracks and crosses the ditch to the right. Midnite is five minutes up this trail; the Zelda Boulders are visible to the left of the trail about a minute before Midnite. To reach the Lower Town Wall, drive through town, turn left at the Bush House, and follow Avenue A across the tracks and south to the only right-hand pullout, roughly a mile from the Index store. Don't leave anything in the car, and leave your windows down – the freight trains passing between the parking lot and the cliff make for great cover, and break-ins happen on a weekly basis in the summer. For the River Boulders, continue another mile past the LTW and park on the left just after a gated road bearing a Gates of the Sky State Park sign. Walk down to the railroad tracks, then along

Dimitry Kalashnikov attempts to *Follow the White Rabbit* (V10) at Morpheus

the tracks for five minutes until the obvious riverside cluster becomes visible down the hill; the legendary Hagakure boulder is in the woods to the right of the approach roughly 50 yards before it reaches the tracks. The LTW boulders are covered in *Central Washington Bouldering*, while the Midnite and River Boulders areas are not.

LAKE SERENE

Across the Skykomish Valley from the town of Index, the clear blue waters of Lake Serene lie below the steep 1,000 foot east face of Mt. Index. This picturesque but popular lake boasts some fantastic bouldering on unique stone, which seems to be some metamorphosed blend of basalt. The hike is a total ass-kicker with a pad, but it's not as long as those to the lower Alpine Lakes, and the boulders offer a solid weekend's worth of steep, featured faces. As an added plus, camping is permitted outside of a quarter-mile radius of the lake, meaning the hike can be split between two days without the difficult-to-procure overnight permits required in the Alpine Lakes Wilderness. Reach Lake Serene from the Bridalveil Falls trailhead on Mt. Index Road. From Highway 2, turn north onto Mt. Index Rd. just west of the narrow Skykomish bridge, roughly a half mile west of the left turn to Index. Turn immediately right into the trailhead parking lot, where parking requires a $5 day pass or Northwest Forest Pass. The trail follows an old logging road for a mile or so before beginning the steep stair climbing past the falls to the lake, a trip of 3.6 miles one-way. Information for this popular hike can be found via the internet and in a plethora of hiking guidebooks.

GOLD BAR

Gold Bar… Covered in the "previous edition" of this book, the Gold Bar boulders are a truly fabulous, highly-concentrated area above the town of Gold Bar roughly one hour east of Seattle. Gold Bar has some of the best granite in the country, and is considered by some to be the finest bouldering in the northwest. The area's magic is almost impossible to describe, with an ever-appealing texture to the stone, features that seem like they were sculpted for climbing, and a gorgeous hillside setting split between a forest that provides cool shade in the summer and a (now-reforesting) clear-cut that offers sunny and dry stone in the winter. Formerly a no-holds-barred ORV area, the Washington Department of Natural Resources closed the Reiter Road area to off-road travel in 2009 under pressure from environmental groups, which had the unfortunate consequence of forcing boulderers to hike up the two-and-a-half mile logging road. Climbers-only vehicular access to Gold Bar was negotiated with the landowner timber company by the Washington Climbers' Coalition in 2011, but was revoked in 2012 under pressure from the state, and the WCC has decided for strategic reasons not to actively pursue vehicular access at this time to avoid any potential backslide to pedestrian access. Still, Gold Bar is always worth the hike, and it offers a whole lot more solitude these days… For those who are inclined to stay closer to the road, the Five Star Boulder, stacked with difficult climbs almost beyond belief, is just a 10-minute walk, and the roadside Camp Serene Boulder is well worth its two-minute approach. Check out an old copy of *Central Washington Bouldering* or ask around for beta!

HIGHWAY 97 / I-90

LIBERTY

The ghost town of Liberty is one of several abandoned mining camps along the southern side of Blewett Pass that were established after the discovery of gold in Swauk Creek in 1873. There is a very small cluster of solid sandstone boulders off a dirt road near Liberty that hint at more potential in the southern Blewett area (but which has never materialized). To find the Liberty boulders, drive roughly four miles east of Leavenworth on Highway 2, then turn south on US-97 and drive for 32.1 miles to the well-marked turn east (left) onto Liberty Road. Just before you reach the ghost town, turn left onto NF-9712, a.k.a. Cougar Gulch Road, then follow that road for roughly 3 miles to an unmarked left turn onto NF-9705. The boulders are a short way down this road on the left. A fun diversion if you're passing through…

ROSLYN

There are a number of scattered sandstone areas around the town of Roslyn off I-90 just west of Cle Elum. To find some of the more developed spots, take Exit 84 off I-90 and follow Route 903 into town. Turn right on Pennsylvania Road and park at the edge of town… And explore. There are also some boulders above Salmon La Sac, roughly 15.5 miles past Roslyn and a few hundred yards up NF-4315, below a cliff that is visible five minutes above the road.

EASTERN WASHINGTON AREAS

VANTAGE

To state the obvious, Vantage is an extremely popular beginner-to-moderate sport climbing area in a scenic desert coulee setting along the Columbia Gorge. And deservedly so, as the hundreds of columnar and face sport climbs on Frenchman Coulee's basalt are easily accessible, well-bolted, and reliably "sunny and seventy" during the dreariest months of the winter. Excluding the diminutive 25-foot clip-ups at the Feathers, there is almost no bouldering in Vantage due to the area's poor rock quality. There is one very notable exception: The Onidevadekim boulder, which is home to a handful of variations in a steep and blocky alcove near the bottom of the coulee. From I-90, take Exit 143 for Silica Road, turn left toward the river, then turn left on Old Vantage Highway after less than a mile. Drive 2.2 miles into the Coulee and park on the left where the road meets the coulee floor. Hike up the coulee along a faint old roadbed for roughly 10 minutes to find Onidevadekim lurking at the base of a cliff directly below

Cole Allen on *Ganja Roof* (V10) at Lake Serene.

the Feathers parking area. The direct approach by the Balls Wall is very loose and definitely not recommended. The Onidevadekim formation, which takes its name from portions of the names of the three or four people who established it, has reportedly been topped out (there is a single old bolt) but I would not recommend making a run at it...

Banks Lake

Banks Lake is a gorgeous lakeside area roughly two hours east of Leavenworth that is a coulee-country mini-Leavenworth, offering sport and trad climbing, bouldering, and even deep water soloing on rough-grained granite. The rock in Banks Lake tends to be slightly granier and more spread-out than Leavenworth, and the area lends itself to exploring. To get to Banks Lake, follow Highway 2 roughly 85 miles east of Leavenworth and turn north onto Route 155 in Coulee City, heading toward the Grand Coulee Dam for roughly 20 miles. Though there are many small areas scattered around Banks Lake. For starters turn right on Northrup Road in Steamboat Rock State Park and park at the obvious cluster below the broken dome on the left. The Golf Ball boulder, on the far side of the golf course is also well worth a visit – if you can find it!

Spokane Areas

There are a number of smaller areas in the Spokane area, including an impressive amount of real rock climbing within the city itself. Minnehaha, on the eastern side of the city, is probably the best, offering a lovely secluded feel and a handful of fun problems in a nice pine forest setting. There is a small basalt cave in Liberty Park, which is literally in the middle of the 'hood, as well as a handful of sport/toprope climbing spots in town like Dishman, Mirabeau, and Cliff Drive. Tum Tum is about 45 minutes north of town and offers hundreds of problems on a funky, chunky stone that appears to be an acquired taste to say the least...

> Two Tiny, Tricksy,
> Toad-Toed Thunder Trolls
> Travel Timely Through Treacherous Talus Towards
> Triceratops Tricia's Treasure Trove Tower.
> Thankfully, Tricia Transported the Treasure Today to
> Three Transparent Teepees to
> Thwart the Troll's Treasure Theft.
>
> - Adam Healy, *The Enchantments*, 2012

Johnny Goicoechea sticks a tough move on an unnamed V9 near Salmon le Sac.

Kelly Sheridan on Xibalba (V7) high above Snoqualmie Pass.
[PHOTO] Cortney Cusack

LEAVENWORTH GPS COORDINATES

AREA ICICLE CANYON	GPS	BOULDER (IF APPLICABLE)
The Fridge	N47.54712 W-120.69563	
The Bond Boulders	N47.54886 W-120.69614	
Upper Bond Boulders	N47.55140 W-120.69565	Against the Grain
	N47.55176 W-120.69488	Bury the Hatchet
Starfox	N47.54626 W-120.69857	
Y.F.A.W.	N47.54504 W-120.71361	
Fern Gully	N47.54582 W-120.71352	
The Moudra	N47.54431 W-120.71560	
Watercolors	N47.54154 W-120.72127	
The Sleeping Lady	N47.54172 W-120.72655	Sleeping Lady
	N47.54175 W-120.72747	La Hacienda
	N47.54119 W-120.72797	Dog Dome Boulders
Mad Meadows	N47.54253 W-120.72341	The Peephole
	N47.54286 W-120.72264	Hanta Man
	N47.54289 W-120.72104	Pimpsqueak
The Airfield	N47.54426 W-120.72144	Lower Boulders
	N47.54578 W-120.71968	The Croissant
	N47.54668 W-120.71841	The UFO
Mitchell Flats	N47.54482 W-120.72553	Mitchell Flats
	N47.54558 W-120.72602	Mega-Proj
The Fist / Rob's Corral	N47.54257 W-120.72795	The Fist
Clamshell Cave	N47.54492 W-120.72908	Clamshell Main
	N47.54498 W-120.73024	CCST
The Zapper	N47.54353 W-120.73063	
Chiefed Joseph Boulder	N47.54126 W-120.73492	
Barney's Rubble	N47.54338 W-120.73494	Barney's Rubble
	N47.54243 W-120.73481	The Fin
Forestland	N47.54367 W-120.73496	Parking
	N47.54462 W-120.73287	Lower Forestland
	N47.54545 W-120.73247	Ruminator
	N47.54567 W-120.73276	Practitioner
	N47.54563 W-120.73381	Teacup
The Locksmith	N47.54639 W-120.73226	Johnny's Prow
	N47.54680 W-120.73048	Second Cluster (hike)
	N47.54713 W-120.72927	Locksmith
	N47.54705 W-120.72881	Locksmith Dyno
The Domestic Boulders	N47.54441 W-120.73792	Parking
	N47.54602 W-120.73877	Bootin' Dookie
Muscle Beach	N47.54365 W-120.73883	
The Lonely Fish	N47.54459 W-120.74076	Lonely Fish
	N47.54349 W-120.74067	Millenium
Hook Creek Boulder	N47.54270 W-120.74440	

AREA	GPS	BOULDER (IF APPLICABLE)
Straightaway Boulders	N47.54501 W-120.74376	Forget Your Rubbers
	N47.54454 W-120.74504	Beautification
	N47.54515 W-120.74618	The Freezer
	N47.54539 W-120.74564	Icehouse
	N47.54597 W-120.74618	Answer Man
	N47.54590 W-120.74797	WAS
	N47.54640 W-120.74925	Cotton Pony
	N47.54655 W-120.75003	Turbulence
Icicle Buttress Boulders	N47.54742 W-120.75207	Batman
	N47.54689 W-120.75127	The Dock
Bulge Boulders	N47.54985 W-120.75688	Bulge Boulders
	N47.54936 W-120.75588	Ocho's Problem
	N47.54918 W-120.75715	Impossible Problem
Rat Creek Boulders	N47.54921 W-120.75989	Crossing
	N47.54853 W-120.75848	Bubble Boy
	N47.54576 W-120.75816	Lower Rat Creeks
	N47.54150 W-120.76157	Upper Rat Creeks
Blister Boulder	N47.55158 W-120.76036	
JY Boulders	N47.55235 W-120.76315	Green Lung
	N47.55303 W-120.76333	Mad Max
	N47.55418 W-120.76469	King Kong
	N47.55432 W-120.76470	Upper Boulder
The Washout	N47.55446 W-120.76647	
Carnival Boulders	N47.55552 W-120.76843	
Pretty Boulders	N47.55760 W-120.76918	
Jess Campbell Memorial	N47.55462 W-120.77034	
The Orange Wall	N47.56171 W-120.77698	
Twisted Tree	N47.56247 W-120.78000	
420 Boulder	N47.56302 W-120.77858	Mr. Yuk
	N47.56229 W-120.77633	420
	N47.56303 W-120.77643	Upper 420s
	N47.56347 W-120.77577	Reflection of Perfection
Little Bridge Creek Wall	N47.56709 W-120.78303	
Bridge Creek Free Site Boulders	N47.56023 W-120.78115	Bridge Creek Free Site Bould·
	N47.55992 W-120.78005	Best Day Ever
	N47.55838 W-120.77760	Tigerlily
Nurse Boulders	N47.55151 W-120.77609	Lower
	N47.55130 W-120.77675	Upper
The Saber	N47.55091 W-120.78532	Parking
	N47.55162 W-120.78617	The Saber
The Machine Gun	N47.56779 W-120.78512	

AREA	GPS	BOULDER (IF APPLICABLE)
The Sword	N47.56942 W-120.78759	Parking
	N47.56896 W-120.78699	Underwear Rock
	N47.56892 W-120.78614	Sword
Scat Boulders	N47.56973 W-120.78305	
Egg Rock	N47.57195 W-120.78952	
Fuzz Wall	N47.57397 W-120.79279	
Tin Man	N47.57650 W-120.79256	
Daydream	N47.57737 W-120.79772	
Mighty Mouse	N47.58652 W-120.80908	Mighty Mouse
	N47.58739 W-120.80977	The Sloping Lady
	N47.59013 W-120.80390	Grandview
Jack Creek Boulder	N47.60419 W-120.91813	

TUWATER CANYON

AREA	GPS	BOULDER (IF APPLICABLE)
The Last Unicorn	N47.58685 W-120.68049	Last Unicorn
	N47.58715 W-120.68156	Warmups
Exit Drop	N47.58753 W-120.68281	
The Canal Boulders	N47.58707 W-120.68363	
The Torture Chamber	N47.58744 W-120.68617	Torture Chamber
	N47.58822 W-120.68649	Pick Your Poison
The Labyrinth	N47.58762 W-120.68719	Squamish Problem
	N47.58850 W-120.68817	Warmup
	N47.58898 W-120.68715	Nine Iron
	N47.58879 W-120.68891	Grlfunk
	N47.58901 W-120.68889	Gracious Mama Africa
Test of Cole	N47.58660 W-120.69010	
The Range Boulders	N47.58422 W-120.69254	
Beach Parking / Trail	N47.58800 W-120.70729	Gaze of the Grasshopper
	N47.58648 W-120.70570	HSLT
	N47.58822 W-120.71020	River Boulder
Grandmother's House	N47.58206 W-120.70210	
The Beach	N47.59345 W-120.71271	U-Boat
	N47.59457 W-120.71422	Beach Forest
	N47.59911 W-120.71501	Beach Beach
The Pitless Avocado	N47.59614 W-120.71312	Pitless Avo
	N47.59724 W-120.71343	Hueco Crimper
Driftwood	N47.60502 W-120.71628	
Jenny Craig	N47.60841 W-120.71817	
Drip Wall Boulder	N47.61459 W-120.71885	Drip Wall Boulder
	N47.61394 W-120.71985	Hophenge
King Size	N47.62634 W-120.72281	
That Demon	N47.63964 W-120.72003	
Swiftwater	N47.65483 W120.73004	South
	N47.65608 W-120.72950	North

AREA	GPS	BOULDER (IF APPLICABLE)
The Marley Boulder	N47.66538 W-120.73890	

MOUNTAIN HOME ROAD

AREA	GPS	BOULDER (IF APPLICABLE)
Butter Boulders	N47.55261 W-120.65524	
Geronimo	N47.55069 W-120.65778	
The Premonition	N47.54886 W-120.66149	
Full Time Night Woman	N47.54775 W-120.66347	
Parking Boulders	N47.54496 W-120.66657	Parking
	N47.54462 W-120.66594	Tron
Star Wars Boulder	N47.54466 W-120.66831	
The Pasture	N47.54418 W-120.67136	Cattleguard
	N47.54429 W-120.67201	Tall People Suck
	N47.54484 W-120.67201	Dandelion Foot
South Seas	N47.54394 W-120.67213	Vision
	N47.54378 W-120.67238	Slab
	N47.54375 W-120.67271	Punk Ass Kid

LEAVENWORTH QR CODE MAPS & DIRECTIONS

The Fridge

AREA

Mad Meadows

PEEPHOLE HANTA MAN PIMPSQUEAK

The Bond Boulders

AREA

The Airfield

LOWER AIRFIELD CROISSANT U.F.O.

The Upper Bond Boulders

AGAINST THE GRAIN BURY THE HATCHET

Michell Flats

AREA MEGA PROJECT

Starfox

AREA

The Fist / Rob's Corral

AREA

Y.F.A.W.

AREA

Clamshell Cave

AREA C.C.S.T.

Fern Gully

AREA

The Zapper

AREA

The Moudra

AREA

Cheifed Joseph Boulder

AREA

Watercolors

AREA

Barney's Rubble

AREA THE FIN

The Sleeping Lady

SLEEPING LADY LA HACIENDA DOG DOME

Forestland

PARKING LOWER FORESTLAND PRACTIONER

Forestland Cont.

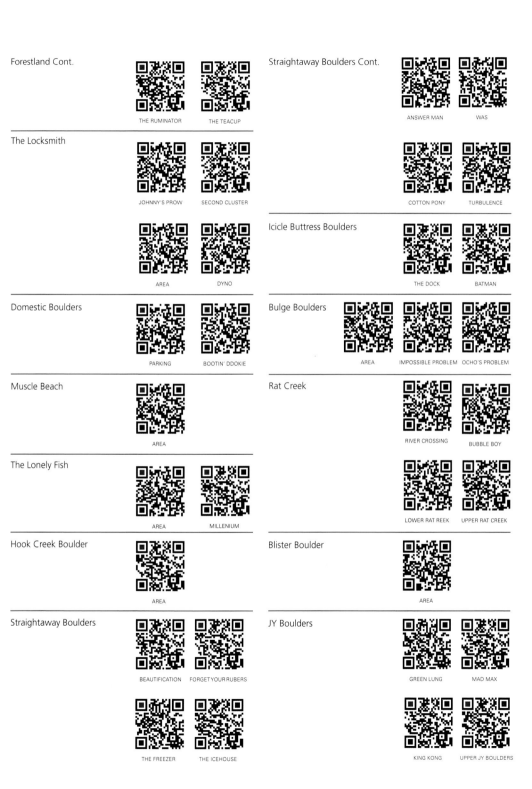

THE RUMINATOR

THE TEACUP

The Locksmith

JOHNNY'S PROW

SECOND CLUSTER

AREA

DYNO

Domestic Boulders

PARKING

BOOTIN' DDOKIE

Muscle Beach

AREA

The Lonely Fish

AREA

MILLENIUM

Hook Creek Boulder

AREA

Straightaway Boulders

BEAUTIFICATION

FORGET YOUR RUBERS

THE FREEZER

THE ICEHOUSE

Straightaway Boulders Cont.

ANSWER MAN

WAS

COTTON PONY

TURBULENCE

Icicle Buttress Boulders

THE DOCK

BATMAN

Bulge Boulders

AREA

IMPOSSIBLE PROBLEM

OCHO'S PROBLEM

Rat Creek

RIVER CROSSING

BUBBLE BOY

LOWER RAT REEK

UPPER RAT CREEK

Blister Boulder

AREA

JY Boulders

GREEN LUNG

MAD MAX

KING KONG

UPPER JY BOULDERS

LEAVENWORTH QR CODE MAPS & DIRECTIONS

The Washout

AREA

Bridge Creek Free Site

BCFS

Carnival Boulders

AREA

BEST DAY   TIGERLILY

Pretty Boulders

AREA

Nurse Boulders

LOWER   UPPER

Jess Campbell Memorial

AREA

The Saber

PARKING   THE SABER

The Orange Wall

AREA

The Machine Gun

AREA

Twisted Tree

AREA

The Sword

PARKING   UNDERWEAR ROCK   THE SWORD

420 Boulders

MR. YUK   AREA

UPPER 420   REFLECTION

Scat Boulders

AREA

Egg Rock

AREA

Little Bridge Creek Wall

AREA

Fuzz Wall

PARKING

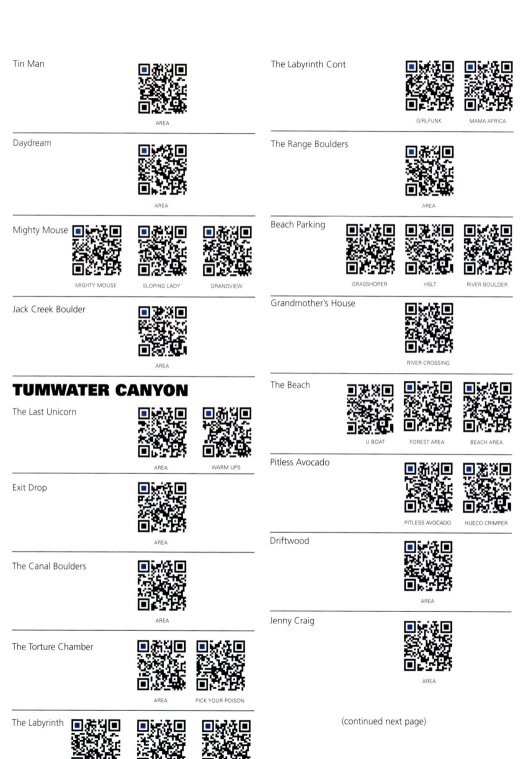

Tin Man

AREA

Daydream

AREA

Mighty Mouse

MIGHTY MOUSE   SLOPING LADY   GRANDVIEW

Jack Creek Boulder

AREA

TUMWATER CANYON

The Last Unicorn

AREA   WARM UPS

Exit Drop

AREA

The Canal Boulders

AREA

The Torture Chamber

AREA   PICK YOUR POISON

The Labyrinth

SQUAMISH PROBLEM   WARM UPS   NINE IRON

The Labyrinth Cont

GIRLFUNK   MAMA AFRICA

The Range Boulders

AREA

Beach Parking

GRASSHOPER   HSLT   RIVER BOULDER

Grandmother's House

RIVER CROSSING

The Beach

U BOAT   FOREST AREA   BEACH AREA

Pitless Avocado

PITLESS AVOCADO   HUECO CRIMPER

Driftwood

AREA

Jenny Craig

AREA

(continued next page)

LEAVENWORTH QR CODE MAPS & DIRECTIONS

Area	**QR Code/s**		

Drip Wall Boulder

DRIP WALL BOULDER   HOPHENGE

Star Wars Boulder

AREA

King Size

AREA

The Pasture

CATTLEGAURD   SLAB COW   DANDELION FOOT

Swiftwater

SOUTH   NORTH

South Seas

TALL PEOPLE SUCK   PUNK ASS KID   VISION

The Marley Boulder

AREA

MOUNTAIN HOME ROAD

Butler Boulders

AREA

Geronimo

AREA

The Premonition

AREA

Full Time Night Woman

AREA

Parking Boulders

AREA   TRON

LEAVENWORTH PROJECTS

In addition to the 1,200-plus established problems, there are still many projects in Leavenworth, a number of which are included in this guide. Some will be legendary problems in the future, others just haven't been tried yet because they're too low, too silly, or just too damn blank. The following is a list of projects included in this guide in the hope that they may inspire, challenge, or taunt folks into making their own additions to Leavenworth's bouldering. Good luck!

Bond Boulders #6	Cramped roof on Sean Connery boulder
Upper Bond Boulders #1	Left side of first face
Fern Gully #14	Hexxus project in center of main boulder
The Moudra #3	Steep face with crimps
Mad Meadows #9	Cramped horizontal roof behind Swordfish
Mad Meadows #40a	Hole-Flake linkup
The Airfield #11	Bottlecap-hold project in cave
The Airfield #14 sit	Pit start to slab on back of Bottlecap-hold project
The Airfield #26	Tall face on downhill boulder
The Airfield #35	Drive On Project
The Fist / Rob's Corral #2	Fist Right project
Clamshell Cave #21	Dyno project next to cliff
Clamshell Cave #22	Lip traverse on right side of cave
The Zapper #3	Straight up from Zapper start (dirty)
Barney's Rubble #4a	Slice of Cake direct, post-break
Forestland #8	Sloper project right of Backdoor Ass Attack
Forestland #52	Alcove project left of The Ruminator
Forestland # 78	Crimp project right of Dave's Problem
Forestland #86	Low roof past The Teacup
Locksmith #2	Huge triangle roof 2/3 way up trail
Locksmith #4	Sit to Locksmith
Locksmith #5	Huge prow right of The Locksmith
Locksmith #8	Steep crimp roof at far end of cluster
Domestics # 10	Downhill arête of Ginopapacino boulder
Domestics # 19	Domestic Violence Low
Domestics # 23	Right arête of Ear Hold Slab
Lonely Fish #2b	Dirty Dude Low Low
Lonely Fish #7	On back of highball calcium face
Lonely Fish #18	On back arête of Millennium Boulder
Straightaway Boulders #3	Rail to arête below Alphabet Wall
Straightaway Boulders #7	Ditch project near Icehouse
Straightaway Boulders #19	Short steep face above Icehouse
Straightaway Boulders #38	Icicle buttress boulder dyno
Straightaway Boulders #39	Steep compression arête
Straightaway Boulders #40	Cramped gaston problem
Bulge Boulders #5 variations	Low start to Johnny's Bulge
Bulge Boulders #7	Impossible Project
Bulge Boulders #12	Far left on Ocho's Boulder
JY Boulders #20	Problem on right as exit tunnel from Mad Max
JY Boulders #21	Tall jump start arête through Mad Max cave
JY Boulders #22	Wide compression arête
JY Boulders #27	Steep dihedral halfway b/t Nosebleed and King Kong

JY Boulders #32	Downhill arête/scoop of Upper JY boulder
Carnivals #30	Broken-key arête
Carnivals #31	Steep cave
Pretty Boulders #9	Pretty Hard arête
Pretty Boulders #10	Pretty Hard face
420 Boulder #9	Face right of drilled arête
420 Boulder #17	Tall crack left of Reflection of Perfection
Bridge Creek Free Site Boulders #6	Blank face right of Members Only
The Sword #28 variation	Resurrection Direct Low
The Sword #35	The Sword Toprope
Fuzz Wall #2	Steep wall left of Epoxy Flake
Fuzz Wall #3	Epoxy Flake low?
Daydream #3	Left arête
Exit Drop #2	Steep face
Torture Chamber #1	Lip traverse on first boulder
Torture Chamber #2	Thin face on first boulder
Torture Chamber #10	Inner arête
Labyrinth #1	Steep roof next to Squamish Problem
Labyrinth #5	Jump start on white face
Labyrinth #31	Face right of Green Tea
Labyrinth #33a	The Zebra low start?
Beach Parking #1	Steep downhill face of Grasshopper boulder
Beach Parking #6	Technical dihedral right of Gaze of the Grasshopper
Grandmother's House #2	Steep dihedral
Grandmother's House #4	Grandmother's House project
The Beach #34	Low start / right finish to Goicoechea
The Beach #35	Tall slabs on west side of Goicoechea boulder
The Beach #36	45 degree wall above Goicoechea
The Beach #2 (U-Boat)	U-Boat direct project
The Beach #3 (U-Boat)	U-Boat backside pedestal project
Driftwood Boulder #5	Straight up from jug. Extremely thin.
Driftwood Boulder #6	Traverse right from jug on sidepulls.
Jenny Craig #1	Kim & Randy project
Drip Wall Boulder #1	Huge and easily-accessible face
Drip Wall Boulder #2	Left side of face
King Size #1a	King Size low start
Swiftwater #6	Snake eyes project
Swiftwater #55	Downhill face of Footless Traverse boulder
Swiftwater #63	36 Chambers
Geronimo #3	Tiny crimps up face right of Geronimo
Geronimo #4	Slabby face away from road
The Premonition #7	Squeeze problem out bulge below Premonition
Full Time Night Woman #3	Sloping shelf in left side of face
Parking Boulders #5	Blunt arête next to trail (above Brown Eye)
The Pasture #17	Abandon Ship project

INDEX OF NAMED ROUTES

INDEX BY GRADE

V1 AND UNDER

V2

V10 AND ABOVE

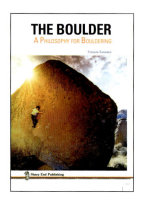

ABOUT THE AUTHOR

Originally a Rhode Island native, Kelly Sheridan moved directly to Leavenworth in 2005 after graduating from Dartmouth College, where he began climbing on the schist crags of Rumney and the myriad granite erratics hidden among the folds of New Hampshire's White Mountains. Kelly moved to Seattle following the publication of *Central Washington Bouldering* in 2007, where he worked at Stone Gardens in Ballard before attending the University of Washington School of Law. Kelly now lives in north Seattle with his wife, Cortney Cusack, N.D., and works in downtown Seattle, where his law practice focuses primarily on commercial litigation and products liability and medical malpractice defense. Kelly has climbed 5.13 and V11, but his true passion is discovering, cleaning, and establishing new boulder problems on Washington's abundant granite, with an emphasis on quality over quantity and the practice of sustainable, ethical development. You'll find Kelly climbing at the many beautiful areas in this guide, or developing new spots in and around the Cascades from his and Cortney's new cabin in the area.

GET A DIGITAL EDITION

Printed in South Korea